In a Defiant Stance

John Phillip Reid

**In a
Defiant Stance**

---

*THE CONDITIONS OF LAW
IN MASSACHUSETTS BAY,
THE IRISH COMPARISON,
AND THE COMING OF THE
AMERICAN REVOLUTION*

The Pennsylvania State University Press
University Park and London

Library of Congress Cataloging in Publication Data

Reid, John Phillip.
   In a defiant stance.
   Includes bibliographical references and index.
   1. Law—Massachusetts—History and criticism.
2. Law—Ireland—History and criticism. 3. United
States—History—Colonial period, ca. 1600–1775. 4. Ireland
—History—18th century. I. Title
KFM2478.R4   340′.09744   76–42453
ISBN 0–271–01240–4

For
William Desmond and Jane Gordon Walsh
of Holden Green

Contents

1

In the Very Face
of Government[1]

*THE AMERICAN
COMPARISON*

As the British Empire recedes toward its final days, its last gasps have a way of conjuring echoes from a grander past. "The British military," a recent newspaper dispatch relates, "seem to have concluded ruefully, after their disagreeable three-year experience of spasmodic conflict in Northern Ireland, that it is impossible to 'win' an irregular or guerrilla conflict while at the same time following all the rules of traditional common law."[2] This comment, dated from the town of Lisburn in the North of Ireland during July 1972, undoubtedly reflects the sentiments of many other British army officers who, during the first three decades following the Second World War, undertook the defense of empire against the rising tide of nationalism, whether in Asia, Africa, or Europe, in Cyprus or in the Malay Straits or in Palestine. Indeed, had there been foreign correspondents two hundred years ago, the dispatch could have been filed, almost verbatim, by anyone reporting to a London newspaper the situation in the American colonies. Often, in fact, were these very thoughts expressed by Major General Thomas Gage to his superiors at home during the years of crisis when the British army was assigned the task of maintaining law and order in those small, rebellious ports of Philadelphia, Charles Town, and Boston.

It is risky to compare revolutions, yet it is a temptation historians find hard to resist. Commonly, the American Revolution is compared to the French, either to demonstrate that the American Revolution was truly revolutionary[2] or that it was the opposite—conservative. The comparison is useful when the lesson to be drawn is limited and the point under investigation turns on semantics. Yet if we seek information about the American Revolution itself—not whether it was part of a world movement or how it reflected the intellectual currents of the eighteenth century but how and why it was

1

fought—there is another people, the Irish, who could tell us as much, if not more, about our Revolution than can the French. The American Revolution, after all, sprang from a constitutional history and a tradition of civil and political rights that the colonists inherited from England and were not shared with Bourbon France. To discover that the American Revolution was less violent than the French may show that it was "conservative" as some historians believe. However, it may better prove a point seldom noted and never explained: that the British authorities in North America during the 1770s possessed less coercive power than did royal officials in France during their revolution.

Historians of the American Revolution have often called attention to the relative absence of violence on the rebel side. They comment, for example, on the fact that no British official was lynched by an American mob and conclude that it reveals much about our Revolution. There is, however, a related perspective that deserves as much attention. Few have noted the other source of revolutionary violence—governmental violence or what is now occasionally termed police violence—violence on behalf of British imperial authority.

There was a fundamental difference in the governance of the two main English-speaking parts of George III's eighteenth-century empire, a difference that demands explanation. Officials of British imperialism could suppress sedition in eighteenth-century Ireland; in eighteenth-century North America they could not. It was law and the conditions of law that made the difference.

By the "conditions" of law is meant not merely substantive rules of law, but the certainty, the power, and the effectiveness of that law, and whether it was directed by a unicentric or multicentric authority. Knowledge that the imperial garrison maintained in Ireland was about five times the size of the British army that fought the battle of Waterloo may tell us much about the policing of the eighteenth-century Irish. To learn that the imperial army could not be constitutionally employed to control rioting crowds or to act against civilians in the North American colonies tells us even more about the policing of the eighteenth-century Americans. "Troops," General Thomas Gage observed of the conditions of law in Massachusetts Bay, "served more to embroil and create Disturbances than to strengthen the hands of Government, and preserve Tranquility." Gage, it is important to recall, was the commander-in-chief of that army. He understood the legal dilemma and so did his junior officers. It was an "absurdity," one of them agreed, to keep soldiers in Boston "for the purpose of preserving tranquillity & aiding the Civil Magistrate."[3] Both men were lamenting the conditions of law.

It is important to stress the words "conditions of law." Gage and his subordinate were lamenting the conditions, not the substance of American law. It was, as they well knew, the same common law whose writs ran in Wales and Ireland as well as in the former kingdom of England. They were lamenting the conditions controlling that law, not its rules, its maxims, or its principles. A glance at the judicial system reveals the imperial weakness. In Ireland all courts were controlled by the British government and what

London promulgated these courts enforced. In North America the fact that the courts were influenced by colonial interests tells but part of the story. A more striking lesson lies in what happened to a special court—the vice-admiralty jurisdiction—that the British government created to enforce certain imperial statutes. The vice admiralty was not a substitute but an alternative for the colonial judicial system, having cognizance only over a few areas of imperial law in which American judges had demonstrated marked and persistent hostility.[4] We learn something of the efficiency of imperial law when we discover that the special court did not operate as the British parliament had planned. We learn even more of the impotency of imperial control when we see that same specially created court immobilized and rendered ineffective by legal institutions controlled by the local colonial populations.

The reach of law and legal institutions was greater than historians of the prerevolutionary era have thought. Even so important a factor as the refusal of colonial courts to enforce imperial statutes or to protect imperial interests has been ignored or has been treated more lightly than it deserves. Control of the judiciary in a political struggle may well determine which side is punished and which is protected.

There is a question that has never been asked, and the time has come to ask it. Name a prosecution of an American whig, a prosecution in which a colonist was put in the dock and made to stand trial for sedition or for treason. If none can be recalled, consider how striking that fact is when compared to history in other parts of the British Empire. The history of the American Revolution lacks chapters of drama and tales of sacrifice that Americans have not missed, but the Irish might. Indeed, if we consider the history of Ireland after the American Revolution was fought and won—after the British might have learned a lesson from their failure in the transatlantic colonies—we find a story that can be told in large part by recounting great trials and dramatic speeches from the dock. Recall the Rising of 1798, an Irish rebellion inspired to no small degree by the success of the American whigs, and memorable prosecutions come to mind—Patrick Finney, Henry Sheares and his brother John, Oliver Bond, and Wolfe Tone. Five years later occurred the trials and executions of Thomas Russell, Owen Kirwan, and the pathetic Robert Emmet. In British North America there is only Nathan Hale and he, after all, was a spy.

British imperial law gave to the American cause no martyrs to mourn, no heroes to quote, no victims to inspire the young or embolden the hesitant. As that law made no need for an Easter Monday with its futile gallantry, so there could be no executions to bring glory to the unknown or exultation to a lost cause. Where are the Americans who accomplished nothing yet are remembered for everything: Padraic Pearse, Thomas MacDonagh, Joseph Plunkett, Eammon Ceannt, Thomas Clarke, James Connolly, and Sean MacDermott? Where is there an image of American nationalism to equal that of Cathleen ni Houlihan standing before the bar of British judgment in the person of a young Robert Emmet or an even younger Kevin Barry? The law that could exact so marvelous a scene was a law unenforceable in eighteenth-century America.

A law impotent in Boston had the dint in Dublin to make a hero of Emmet by furnishing him the forum for his one claim to immortality—his speech from the dock, "every line of which," it could be said during the nineteenth century, "is known and dear to the hearts of the Irish race":

> Let no man write my epitaph; for as no man who knows my motives dare now vindicate them, let not prejudice or ignorance asperse them. Let them and me rest in obscurity and peace; and my tomb remain uninscribed, and my memory in oblivion, until other times and other men can do justice to my character. When my country takes her place among the nations of the earth, *then* and *not till then*, let my epitaph be written.[5]

The British courtroom in Ireland provided the rebels of that land with a platform to prepare their people for battle. It was a forum no American ever shared. "I mean," Thomas Russell said as he was about to be sentenced to death, "to make my trial, and the last of my life, if it is to close now, as serviceable to the cause of liberty as I can."[6] No Virginian, no Bostonian ever had Russell's opportunity.

American whigs often put British law on trial, but they did so in newspapers, a medium that lacked the impact of another available to their Irish counterparts. Instead of standing content with judgment by British law, the condemned of Ireland asked their nation to remember that those were British judges presiding over Irish courts. "To lift this island up," Thomas Francis Meagher announced from the dock,

> to make her a benefactor to humanity, instead of being, as she is now, the meanest beggar in the world—to restore to her her native powers and her ancient constitution—this has been my ambition, and this ambition has been my crime. Judged by the law of England, I know this crime entails upon me the penalty of death; but the history of Ireland explains that crime and justifies it.[7]

If the literature of the American Revolution seems barren next to that of the Irish risings, one reason is to be found in the conditions of law. It was law, not choice, that kept British officials in the American colonies from executing Irish policies. As a result of law there are no American Robert Emmets for schoolchildren to memorize, no American Kevin Barrys about whom to sing, no American poems such as *Wake of William Orr* to keep alive the rebel flame.

> Why cut off in palmy youth?
> Truth he spoke, and acted truth.
> "Countrymen unite!" he cried,
> And died for what his Saviour died.[8]

The conditions of law in prerevolutionary British North America have left us no legends of houses being broken into during the dead of night for none were ever entered, no accounts of secret arrests because no American whig was ever arrested, and no records of internments without trial because no one could be interned on this side of the Atlantic. No local leader was ever dragged off to Kilmainham or the Provost's prisons for there were no such institutions in the colonies. No American whig held the attention of the world—through August, September, October, and November—as would Terence MacSwiney, lord mayor of Cork, with a 74-day hunger strike terminating with his death in a London jail. There were those in eighteenth-century North America who had the courage to write a similar story, but no colonist could be a martyr to a law unable to touch him.

The American Revolution has not even left us a famous acquittal or a dramatic defense attorney such as Ireland's John Philpot Curran. None of the Stamp Act rioters was put on trial; no member was indicted of the mobs that tarred and feathered tories in Boston or forced every stamp agent in America to resign his commission during 1765. No prosecution grew out of the Boston Tea Party or any of the other conspiracies aimed against the Tea Act in 1773. None of the men who invaded Fort William and Mary in Portsmouth harbor and tore down the royal ensign was arrested. Instead, when we recall the trials of the American Revolution, we think of the Boston Massacre, where the British, not the Americans, stood in the dock. Compared to Ireland, the records of British law in the colonies stand in impotency. There is irony here, an irony we must bear in mind if we are to understand the American Revolution and why so many foreign writers have called it either conservative or relatively nonviolent.

A vital dimension has been missing from the histories of the American Revolution. To write a history while ignoring local law and the conditions under which imperial law operated is to tell a truncated tale.[9] Even when not ignored, law and the conditions of law have all too often been taken for granted, leaving conclusions to be assumed. Thoughts about law are, after all, formed by words and impressions and are conditioned by expectations associated with those words. We encounter the term "imperialism" and know that in its colonies imperial power is represented by a governor. Thinking of imperialism as a manifestation of power we expect imperial governors to be authorized to govern with a firm hand backed by force. What do we make of the word "imperial" in eighteenth-century North America when we find that it was not British officials but the colonists who governed? The imperial governor was sent out from London, true enough, but he was sent to warm a powerless seat. A lieutenant governor of Ireland could order the military to arrest civilians or to destroy whole villages. He might not be loved by the Irish but his voice was one that was heard with respect. Due to the conditions of law the governor of a North American colony was more a voice of adynamia than an imperial voice.

We must not attempt to ask more of our sources than our sources can provide. It is not revolutions or the causes of revolutions that can be compared, it is law when law is the same. The nationalistic yearnings that convulsed twentieth-century Africa or the Asian subcontinent bear little resemblance to the constitutional yearnings that gave birth to rebellion in eighteenth-century America. Certainly the misrule and exploitation that produced the bloody history of modern Ireland was never practiced in the colonies across the Atlantic. The grievances of the Irish were not the grievances of the Americans. There are important contrasts between the sole revolution in America and the many risings in Ireland, and that dispatch from Lisburn pointed up one when it referred to the frustration felt by military officers restrained by the rules of common law. Their counterparts in eighteenth-century North America were also restrained, and by the same common law, yet they would not have sympathized with their brother officers in Ireland—neither then nor now. For those stationed in eighteenth-century America, the common law was not, as it was in Ireland, a set of procedural rules that had to be followed before a rebel could be incarcerated, but that always could be suspended by special legislation. Far from being an annoyance occasionally hindering direct military action, law was a weapon possessed and manipulated by their enemies in a manner and to a degree that no rebel movement in British-ruled Ireland ever approached.

When General Gage and his colleagues complained about the common law they had better cause than did the soldiers garrisoned in the Irelands of 1798, 1918, or 1976. They had been left in America after the defeat of France in 1763 to support the law, and from the Shawnee frontier to the port of Boston they were to learn that the law did not support them.

2

It Signifies Little
Who Is Governor[1]

THE LOCUS
OF LAW

It is institutions we should compare, yet we must never forget that men administered those institutions. An imperial official in eighteenth-century North America served the same king and reported to the same ministry whom an imperial official in contemporary Ireland served and to whom he reported. A casual observer commenting on the governance of the two realms of George III might note beneath the similarity of regimental flags, executive proclamations, judicial titles, and ceremonial tunes but one contrast—the official stationed in Ireland would more likely be English, or perhaps Scots, than would his counterpart in America. This difference tells us more than we might think. The writs, the summonses, the juries seem alike, but due to men the common denominator is not there. The law flows from the same source, it takes the same form, yet it serves a different goal. The fate of Ireland in 1798 is not to be the fate of Massachusetts Bay in 1776.

The common law as applied in Boston and Massachusetts Bay may not have been typical of all British North America, but it was that common law, the glory of the English and the envy of their neighbors, that would prove the undoing of an empire so recently made safe from the French. It deserves our attention for it was the common law—civil as well as criminal—that gave the agents of imperial authority their greatest challenge, the common law by which they were told to govern the most ungovernable of King George's subjects.

"The town of Boston," a Massachusetts governor during 1771 complained to his predecessor, "is the source from whence all the other parts of the Province derive more or less troubled water."[2] The British honored Boston's leadership, in a backhanded fashion, by calling all American rebels "Bostonians." During 1775, Guy Johnson spoke the sentiment of many a tory when,

7

using the symbolism of Indian oratory, he invited the Six Nations of the Iroquois League "to feast on a Bostonian and drink his Blood."[3]

We must avoid exaggeration, yet when stressing the role of Boston in the coming of the American Revolution exaggeration is not an easy feat. It was the people of that seaport who, when other whigs were hesitant and fearful, prepared themselves both psychologically and physically for confrontation with the mother country and for the risks of violence. Among the ways that they began to prepare was to bend the law to their political purposes, mold the courts to serve their cause, and harass the executive power into near impotence.

Perhaps "power" is not the word to describe the Massachusetts executive. The Irish comparison with the American colonies is nowhere more striking than in the contrast of executive authority. The essence of British government in Ireland was that it was centralized and narrowly based. The essence of British government in North America was local control and popular consent, and what the Americans could not control they soon learned to negate.[4]

There are many reasons why the administration of Ireland should be different from that of the North American provinces. A larger population is one factor, religion another, Ireland's location in Europe near to Great Britain yet not far from the French enemy a third. Not to be overlooked, however, was history, a long history of warfare, rebellion, and mutual hatred. Also there was the fact that Ireland was peopled by Irishmen while America was peopled largely by the English. England had ruled or tried to rule Ireland for centuries before there was a Great Britain, and the laws that the English imposed upon the Irish were not always the same as the laws the English made for themselves.

The most important figures in Irish government were the lord lieutenant, the chief secretary, and the lord chancellor, traditionally Englishmen tied to the British interest. The lord lieutenant was a member of the British administration,[5] and his task "was to prevent Ireland from adding to the problems and difficulties of the British Prime Minister; Burke had truly said that the desire of all British Governments was to hear as little of Ireland and its concerns as possible."[6] Representing the king, the lord lieutenant "was responsible for the peace and security of the kingdom; he possessed wide statutory powers; he exercised the prerogative of mercy and he appointed to numerous offices."[7]

When compared to Ireland's lord lieutenant, the governor of Massachusetts was almost powerless. He was the king's representative but he could not cut a kingly figure. "It was not easy," Thomas Hutchinson, who served as lieutenant governor, acting governor, and governor, asserted, "to devise a system of subordinate government less controlled by the supreme, than the governments in the colonies." Hutchinson's predecessor agreed. "Whoever he is," Francis Bernard wrote of the governorship while still in that office, "he must either live in perpetual Contention in vainly endeavouring to support the royal Rights, or he must purchase Peace by a prudential Sacrifice of them."[8]

The lord lieutenant of Ireland had to answer to the British cabinet; the governor of Massachusetts had to answer to the local council. "I labour under many difficulties," Governor Bernard complained at the height of the Stamp Act crisis, "and none more than that the Council, which I have to advise with, is composed almost wholly of gentlemen whose connections and properties are in Boston. . . . By these means nothing can pass the Council that is like to be displeasing to Boston; expedients are thereby rendered very few and spirited measures are quite impracticable."[9] The council was not appointed by the governor as it was in Quebec and some other colonies, and as it undoubtedly would have been in Ireland had there been an Irish council. Rather it was elected each year by the lower house of the assembly which in turn was elected by the people. "In the Province of *Massachuset's Bay*" Governor Bernard explained, " . . . the appointment of the Council is left to the people, to be made by annual election; and yet the Royal Governor, in all Acts of prerogative, is subject to the controul of the Democratical Council. This solecism in policy has been as hurtful in practice as it is absurd in theory, and it is the true cause of the extreme imbecillity of the power of the crown in this government, at times when the exertion of it is most wanted."[10] After the controversy began with the mother country, the Massachusetts house stopped electing king's men to the council, providing the whigs with an effective veto on the executive power.[11] "I would give it as my Opinion," Bernard concluded, "that if He [the king] cannot secure to himself the Appointment of the Council, it is not worth while to keep that of the Governor. For it would be better that Mass Bay should be a complete Republic like Connecticut than to remain with so few Ingredients of royalty in it as shall be insufficient to maintain the real royal Character."[12]

Just as the royal governor of Massachusetts did not possess the authority of an Irish lord lieutenant, so the Irish parliament did not enjoy the power of a Massachusetts assembly. In both theory and practice the assembly or general court stood about halfway between an Irish and a British parliament. Through election of the council it exercised much control over the executive while the Irish parliament had none, but like an Irish parliament and unlike the one at Westminster it could not make or unmake governments; on that point, the comparison ends. Massachusetts assemblies were elected yearly, while until after the American Revolution Irish parliaments were subject to no septennial act. Only the demise of the sovereign could force a dissolution. One eighteenth-century parliament lasted through the entire reign of George I, another the reign of George II, which meant that it sat for 33 years.

A more vital difference was representation. The Massachusetts lower house was elected by the people in town meeting, although just how democratic the electorate was is a matter of dispute. Some historians say that the franchise was widely distributed in prerevolutionary America, and others point to such matters as the type of laws passed and the fact that balloting was not secret to show, by twentieth-century standards, that the lower houses were not "democratic." The debate is irrelevant to the question of the locus of law in the colonies. The important point is that the members of the assemblies were selected by those in power on a local level and represented local political interests. In Ireland, the members of parliament represented a different constituency which by comparison should make their American counterparts seem "democratic" even to today's new left.

The members of the Irish house of commons, Arthur O'Connor said, were "a set of self-constituted individuals . . . at liberty to sell themselves to the corrupt controul of the British Ministry."[13] Even for a government official of the energy and caliber of those generally sent to protect Britain's interests in eighteenth-century Ireland, the purchase of votes was hardly a difficult feat in parliament where two-thirds of the membership was returned by individuals and even a majority of the borough representatives were elected by less than a hundred persons. It was accepted—indeed it was expected constitutional practice—that a member should vote as directed by his patron or resign. Less wealthy borough owners either served themselves or sold their seats to others who were free to deal on their own.[14]

Private gain was the object of many members of Ireland's parliament. While the representatives in the lower houses of American assemblies sat as spokesmen of local interests, intent on decreasing the prerogatives of royal authority and slowly bringing power into the hands of the popular element of government, Irish members were concerned with selling their votes. "While I was a member of the House of Commons," O'Connor stated, "the frequent conversations amongst the Members was—how much has such an one given for his seat? From whom did he purchase? Has not such an one sold his borough? Has not such a Lord bought? Has not such a Peer so many Members in this House? Was not such Members with the Lord Lieutenant's Secretary to insist on some greater place or pension? Did not the Secretary refuse it? Has he not gone into the Opposition?"[15]

To carry the "election" that was held during the American Revolution, the Irish government created seventeen new peers in a single day; seven barons became viscounts and five viscounts became earls in payment for returning safe men to seats that they owned. The chief secretary is said to have drawn up a list of new pensions amounting to £10,000 a year, that would have to be granted to insure a favorable result. Public offices were invented during 1784 just to have places with salaries attached that could be used as bribes to keep the great peers loyal. By 1790, over one-third of the 300 members of the commons were in receipt of salaries or pensions from the treasury.[16]

"The keynote of the government system," says H.M. Hyde, "was therefore corruption, which increased in direct proportion to the embarrassments of the Crown."[17] "No man," the lord lieutenant apologized in 1780, "can see the inconveniences of increasing the number of peers more forcibly than myself; but the recommendation of many of the persons submitted to his majesty for that honor arose from engagements taken up at the press of the moment, to secure questions on which the English Government was very particularly anxious. I feel the same about Privy Council and pensions, and I had not contracted any absolute agreement of recommendations either to peerage or pension till difficulties arose that occasioned so much anxiety in his majesty's

Cabinet, that I must have been culpable in neglecting any possible means of securing a majority in the House of Commons."[18]

Thus the governance of British Ireland was in radical contrast to the governance of British America. With local control of much of the power of authority at the heart of the Massachusetts system, the locus of law was different than in Ireland where all writs flowed from Dublin castle. The common law of England might run in both colonies, but the forces that controlled that law were not the same.

The constitutional argument also had to be different. Irish reformers were primarily intent on changing parliament, making it both representative and responsible to the people, Catholics as well as Protestants. The Americans sought to retain what they already had, local control and a responsive legislature. The entire thrust of American discontent was based on constitutional theory. "No representation, no taxation," was the whig slogan Thomas Hutchinson wrote.[19] Unconstitutional taxes, the invasion of placemen, the dependence on the crown by the judiciary, plural officeholding, and standing armies were the chief complaints of the colonists. Even British military men recognized that the causes of dissension were constitutional. "The Question," General Thomas Gage admitted in 1765 during the Stamp Act crisis, "is not the inexpediency of the Stamp Act, or of the inability of the Colony to pay the Tax, but that it is unconstitutional, and contrary to their Rights, Supporting the Independency of the Provinces, and not Subject to the Legislative Power of Great Britain."[20] In Ireland, on the other hand, the rate of taxation was a grievance, especially tithes which bore heavily on the Catholic tenants, while providing nothing in return.

Yet for all these differences, there remain many legal points in common between eighteenth-century Ireland and North America. After all, both the Irish and the Americans had the same British constitution to which to appeal. Wolfe Tone could be inspired by the Saxon past, just as could Thomas Jefferson.[21] Irish reformers made constitutional claims that could as easily have come from Boston as from Dublin, and even resolutions passed by Catholics occasionally had a ring that echoed American whiggery.[22] Irish dissidents knew that if the British parliament could make law for America, it could make law for Ireland, and the American Revolution had profound effects upon the Irish constitutional argument.[23]

On both sides of the Atlantic the complaint was made that the rights and privileges won by the British people in the Revolution of 1688 had not been extended beyond the home island. The crown had lost the prerogative of removing judges in England but retained it in America. The hereditary pension lists in England and Scotland had been abolished but remained in Ireland absorbing two-thirds of the annual revenue and doled out by the British cabinet to favorites, pensioners, and placemen.[24] In the end both the Americans of 1776 and the Irish of 1798 could appeal to the same legal argument to justify rebellion. The British parliament, they would say, had violated the old constitution, usurping powers and trampling on the rights of the people. "We could not," argued Arthur O'Connor, who was a lawyer as well as a former member of parliament and high sheriff of county Cork, "have an intention of destroying a constitution, of which we did not believe there was one particle in existence." Formally parliament may have spoken for the nation but now that it represented only itself and was controlled by the crown, "the vital principle which created the Constitution, and which alone could preserve it from bankruptcy and ruin, was at an end."[25]

Although a history filled with conquests and military occupations gave the Irish less justification than Americans for appealing to the British constitution, the lesson of Ireland was not irrelevant to the American constitutional argument. After all, if the legal doctrine of "right of conquest" gave conquerors the constitutional authority to impose laws upon the conquered, that doctrine applied in Ireland only to the Catholics, not to the Protestants. The Protestants of Ireland, Presbyterians as well as Anglicans, were not a conquered people. They were "settlers," with whose legal condition the Americans could equate themselves as they too claimed to be settlers. The theory was that settlers carried with them the rights and privileges of English subjects and were entitled to those rights and privileges to the same extent as if they had remained in the mother country until changed by local legislation enacted by their representatives. The Indians were the conquered people of America for whom the king could declare law. True, Blackstone denied this theory, insisting that both Ireland and the American plantations were conquered lands. But Blackstone's word did not settle the issue, and the status of the British constitution in both Ireland and North America was one of the many points of controversy on which even crown lawyers did not agree.

The lessons of Ireland were important to prerevolutionary America for the colonial whigs, perhaps more than any other American generation, were attuned to reading danger signals from current history. They feared that what had occurred to other people could occur to them unless they manned the barricades of freedom and fought for every threatened right. Otherwise they could end as "slaves" of the British parliament. Recent history furnished them with a long checklist—Turkey, France, Sweden, Poland, and Denmark—of how tyranny had crushed the ancient liberties of entire nations. Surely from their perspective, the history of English and British rule in Ireland was the most dangerous signal of all.

If the American whigs were determined to make a constitutional stand against the right of the British parliament to impose the Townshend duties, the history of Ireland gave them an incentive. Even after the American Revolution ended, parliament would be restricting "Irish trade as a sop to English manufacturers."[26] As early as 1663, Ireland, which had recently developed a prosperous trade, was excluded from benefits of the navigation acts, and two decades later the export of Irish manufactured wool was prohibited. Writing of the period of the American Revolution, a nineteenth-century historian favorable to imperial rule in Ireland concludes that Great Britain "had cut Ireland off from the sea by her Navigation Laws, and had forced her into a contraband trade which enlisted half her population in organized resistance to the law."[27]

Where the American whigs, claiming to be the heirs of English constitutional traditions, could turn to history—to Coke, Pym, Hampden, and the Glorious Revolution—to justify their rebellion against Great Britain, the rebels of Ireland turned to a different history to explain theirs. They turned to the history of British rule in Ireland; a history that colonial whigs also bore in mind.

The history of Ireland was the history of an occupied country, sprouting a wretched tenantry and a stratified society of class wealth and abject poverty. One of the results of the American Revolution would be to end the possibility that the colonies would suffer the same fate.[28] "England," one historian summarizes, "for her own purposes condemned the country to barrenness, and its inhabitants to misery and want. She rejected them when they petitioned to be incorporated in the Empire. She extinguished their manufactures and their shipping, and discouraged them long even from cultivating their estates, lest the value of her own lands should suffer from the rivalry. The settlers were essentially an army of occupation, of which the gentry were the officers; yet half of them were allowed unlimited leave of absence, deserting their special charge, and handing over the people committed to them to be plundered and ground to wretchedness."[29]

Those settlers and their descendants formed the Irish aristocracy, a breed, Henry Grattan once said, fit only to carry claret to a chamber pot.[30] Almost exclusively Protestant, they rested comfortably on the secure foundation of enforced Catholic labor. By the end of the eighteenth century the Catholics, who comprised three-fourths of the population, possessed one-fifteenth of the land. "It is England," Wolfe Tone charged, "who supports that rotten aristocratic faction, among which not the tenth part of your population has arrogated to itself five-sixths of the property and power of your nation."[31] So divided were the classes that Tone himself did not know a single Catholic until he took up their cause in 1791.[32]

While Ireland was bled by her landlords, her industry stripped for the benefit of Great Britain, the American colonies prospered. They were ruled by the same empire that ruled Ireland, but not in the same way. Even the imperial law was applied with a more detached fist. The argument has been persuasively made that the burdens imposed by the British on North America were light, that in the plantations there was no tyranny, no oppression, but if anything a weakness of British rule. The American people enjoyed a higher standard of living than any other in the world—with a lower class of poor laborers amounting to perhaps 20 percent of the white population, a middle class of substantial farmers and artisan property owners totaling 60 percent, and at the top the merchants, large landowners, lawyers, and other professionals of about 20 percent.[33]

Writers of the left find fault with historians who emphasize the 80 percent at the top to prove that eighteenth-century America was a social and economic democracy. Rather, it is said, concentrate attention on the "inarticulate" at the bottom of the social ladder to discover the causes of the Revolution. Granted they will find poverty in small towns and people in the cities with economic grievances. But the perspective should be eighteenth century, not twentieth century; when seeking symptoms of discontent, a comparison with the Ireland of then is more valid than with the world of today.

In eighteenth-century Ireland the typical holding was a potato patch and a thatched hovel shared with the family pig—a pig known in rural areas as "the gentleman that pays the rent."[34] In contemporary Massachusetts even the very poor could boast of more wealth than that. It may be revealing to learn that by 1771 perhaps 29 percent of the adult males of Boston were of a propertyless proletariat.[35] A question, however, is whether these men considered themselves trapped by an immobile class structure or belonging to a society in which "the progression from class to class on the scale of wealth . . . was a continuous and even flow."[36] They could not compare their condition to standards that did not yet exist, but they could to their fellows in Europe or in Ireland. At that very time, Lord Nuneham said, half the inhabitants of Dublin were "in absolute rags, and one-third of them without shoes and stockings, and almost naked."[37] There was no mobility in Irish society. The poverty into which a person was born was the poverty in which he or she remained. The Irish and the Americans might rebel against the same rule. But the type of rebellion that they waged and its causes were bound to be different.

The constitutional arguments that led the Americans to take up arms did not carry so deep a hatred as did the social and economic grievances of the Irish. Call American local government what we will—"a democracy of the aristocracy" as in Virginia or a "democracy without democrats" as in Massachusetts[38] —it was in essence a government controlled by local forces and was threatened by rulers in London who had been taught by their experience in Ireland to think of colonies from an imperial perspective.

Some American whigs such as Samuel Adams had difficulty understanding the insensitivity of British whigs to Parliament's encroachments on American rights. When Adams learned that the appointed governor of Massachusetts was to be paid a royal salary, an innovation that threatened to make him independent of the local assembly and the popular will, Adams professed shock at the silence of British whiggery. "Is not this perfect Despotism?," he asked. "What can the people of Britain mean, by suffering their great men to enslave their fellow Subjects? Can they think the plan is confined to America? They will surely find themselves mistaken."[39]

Adams missed the historical lesson. When British whigs saw laws being imposed on the American colonies, they did not automatically draw analogies to Charles I and James II. Far more likely, they were conditioned to think of Ireland, where parliament had for a century been imposing a policy far more harsh than anything likely to be imposed on the Americans. Tyranny in Ireland, as a whig would define "tyranny," had not led to tyranny at home. When parliamentary legislation was extended to North America, British whigs had slight cause to be alarmed for their own liberties.

If the British whigs could see little danger to their liberty by what occurred in America, the American whigs could see danger to theirs in the history of Ireland. They drew wonderful propaganda from the sufferings of the Irish, though they had little need to exploit the theme. The exiles flowing into the colonies from Ulster during the 1770s performed the task better since they were living reminders of the argument that what the British had done "there" they might yet do "here." [40]

The Americans were attentive, and most were sympathetic to Ireland's ordeal, yet we may doubt if many were alarmed. There was slight chance the British ministry would turn Massachusetts or Virginia into another Ireland. Even the most confirmed British tory would have recognized the risk and backed away. But there was always the question, a faint suspicion at the very least, and had the American whigs obtained some of the letters of Governor Francis Bernard, that suspicion could have grown into a general concern. [41] During the Stamp Act crisis of 1765—the first of the prerevolutionary controversies destined to divide the thirteen colonies from the mother country—Bernard urged a member of the British cabinet to consider the necessity of reforming the governments of Massachusetts Bay and other North American colonies. It was a long letter written by a frustrated man, yet if we seek to find the locus of law in an eighteenth-century American colony, it is well to linger on it. It tells us much of British imperial rule in Ireland, even more of British imperial rule in America.

Bernard wanted the government of Massachusetts Bay reformed and his model for reform was the government of contemporary Ireland. It was, he wrote, a "perfect" model.

> Ireland affords an Example of the Usefulness of this Work & the Manner of doing it. It was owing to the wise Administration of S[ir] Edward Poynings in the Henry the 7[th's] Time, that the Form of Government of that Island, which is as perfect for a dependent, as that of Great Britain for a supreme Power, has lasted now for 270 Years, without wanting the least Amendment of Fundamentals. Haply America has not had a Poynings to regulate her Policy & prevent the Mischeifs, which the Uncertainty of the Relative Powers of civil Government, imperial & subordinate, is now bringing on like Torrent. The Civil Policy of America is composed of temporary Expedients all derived from the Crown only; not one of the American Governments has that Sanction which none of them ought to be without, a parliamentary Establishment. And untill the parliament shall establish the American Governments upon a constitutional bottom, & ascertain the Limitation's & extension's of their Legislatures, It must be expected that the Governments will be continually subject to disturbance whenever the Americans think fit to complain of innovations upon & infringements of their Rights; that is whenever any thing is required of them which they don't like.
>
> Ireland also affords Instances of every Kind of Regulation which America wants; which may be brought under these Heads. . . . There should be one Form of Government as like as possible to that of Great Britain, that is the same as Ireland, with a true Middle Legislative Power, appointed by the King for Life & separate from

the privy Council.* 3. There should be a certain & sufficient civil List laid upon perpetual Funds for the Support of all his Majestys Officers, so that they may not be too much dependent upon the People. 4. The Several American Governments should Maintain such standing Forces as shall be thought necessary to be kept up in America as their quota of the general Armament of the Empire, by raising the Sums requisite therefor & paying the same into the Kings Treasury in America; the Numbers of Men, & proportions of the several Governments to be settled by the Parliament of Great Britain. 5. There should be a solemn Recognition of the Supremacy of the Parliament of Great Britain over the American Governments, which should be the first act of each Legislature after its new Establishment & be The condition of its Activity. 6. There should be a general Revisal of the Laws of America, that they may be reduced as near as possible to the Standard of England & the Administration of Government & Law may be rendered as similar thereto as well may be.[42]

We must pause for reflection or we may too hastily draw a superficial conclusion. Governor Bernard was outlining the differences between the governments of Ireland and of Massachusetts Bay, true enough, and he was doing much more. He was marking the locus of law in eighteenth-century colonial America. From the imperial perspective there is fault to be found and he is willing to find it. The complaint is not that there is too much federalism, it is that there is not enough. There must be a balance between federal units, yet from his seat of power Bernard finds no balance for as governor he is sitting in a powerless seat. The law with which he is expected to govern is located with constitutional and local institutions administered by officials neither appointed by nor responsible to the king. To acknowledge that the governments of America were deficient one need not accept Ireland as the "perfect model." England too is a model, but it is a matter of shading and Ireland is the litmus. From the imperial point of view the measure of the deficiency is the extent to which government and law in North America fell short of the Irish ideal.

---

*The councils of most American councils were also the upper houses of the assembly.

3

Source from Whence
the Clamors Flow[1]

THE CONDITIONS
OF LAW

We must be cautious of broad generalities, for they seldom stand the test of particular proof. Yet there is one generality that, while very broad, seems safe to assert: British officials in eighteenth-century Ireland were there to rule; British officials in eighteenth-century Massachusetts were mainly there. True they had functions to perform and decisions to make, but they were not in control. They might influence events, but they could not shape them. A century and a half of detached indifference on the imperial side and need for protection from the French on the colonial side gave them an illusion of governing a cisatlantic Ireland. Surely Governor Francis Bernard had thought he was going to a new-world version of Dublin when he first sailed for North America, or his disappointment would not have been so great and his plea for reform so anguished. If the reality did not match the dream it was because the vision had been shaded by an emerald hue.

It would not do to assert that American governors expected or even wanted to emulate their colleague in Dublin castle. Bernard, for example, was a grasping man who went to America to make his fortune as much as to serve his king. But even a public servant with no dedication to public service expects to receive the amenities of office. A chief executive hopes to act as a chief executive should, to give orders, not receive them. The truths of American constitutional law were a rude awakening for the profligate official as well as for the unselfish patriot.

When Governor Bernard and his tory supporters asked what had gone wrong for imperial rule in Massachusetts Bay, they could not blame the organization of the courts. Unlike the Irish bench that was modeled on the English system of six superior courts, with exchequer chamber receiving appeals from four of them and further appeal lying in London, the Massachusetts judicial system was free of the expense and delays inherent in English law with its rival, competing jurisdictions. There was no king's bench fighting with common pleas for business, no chancery enjoining actions at common law, adding costs for the litigants and unpredictability to the legal process. A party beginning an action in a Massachusetts court completed it in the same court.

Nor could the British blame the judges for the breakdown of imperial law in the colony. Like the Massachusetts bar, the judiciary of Massachusetts Bay during the 1760s and 1770s was politically sophisticated and professionally competent. While there were more laymen than lawyers on all levels of the system—from the superior court of judicature at the top through the inferior courts of common pleas to the justices of the peace on the local level—most were educated men of social standing and there are no records of citizens complaining about the quality of justice, at least not in cases that lacked political overtones.

That Massachusetts judges were generally competent, respected leaders in their local communities may help explain why judicial tenure was not so troublesome an issue in Massachusetts as in some colonies to the south, although they are not the only reasons. More significant was the fact that while Massachusetts judges, like those elsewhere in North America, were appointed at the king's pleasure rather than for good behavior as in England, in practice the crown could not remove them at will. The governor of the province might nominate the officers of the court system—the judges, sheriffs, and justices of the peace—but his nominations were not the same as apppointments. They had to be confirmed by the popularly oriented council, and in that requirement we find more than an imperial weakness, we find a source of antiimperial strength. It gives the council more than a veto over the power of London to crowd the bench with royal placemen; it allows the council to demand not only local men but men who do not take office to serve the interests of imperial rule. The form of the British constitution seems to be reproduced; the Massachusetts chief executive has the appearance of an Irish lord lieutenant, but it is only the form and only the appearance.

Thomas Hutchinson, who was the chief spokesman for imperial rule in prerevolutionary Massachusetts, relied on this provision of the colonial charter to hush whig suspicions that local justice could be made subservient to the British cabinet. "The Commissions of the Judges of this Court," he told the Suffolk county grand jury while he was chief justice of the superior court, "are, it is true, during Pleasure;—but when we consider by whom our Judicatories are appointed, we shall find that we approach very near the Priviledge enjoyed by our Brethren in England: At least, we are in a Middle between them, and some of our Brethren in America, whose Judicatories are erected at Home, their Judges appointed from thence, and are removable at Pleasure."[2]

Hutchinson's last point, that Massachusetts judges even though they did not enjoy tenure for good behavior were not removable at pleasure, reveals the most significant aspect of the Massachusetts judiciary during the prerevolutionary era. Just as the governor could not appoint without council confirmation, so he could not remove without the consent of the council any judge or justice of the peace even for neglect of duty.[3] "This," Hutchinson claimed, "amounts to near the Priviledge of People in England:—*There*, the Judges hold *quamdiu*, &c.; and *here*, they are displaced by the Governour, *with the Consent of Council* ... this People are as secure, and as firmly established in their *Liberties*, as they are in Great Britain. I know of no Difference."[4]

Not only were the people secure in that liberty but, Hutchinson might have added, they were secure in the possession of one of their most effective weapons for undermining royal authority through the conditions of law. It was this constitutional fact-of-life—the lack of royal power to remove judges, especially the justices of the peace—which, more than anything else, would shape the political role of the judiciary of Massachusetts Bay during the two decades before the Declaration of Independence.

Probably because of the need to select competent men financially able to devote time to public service, the members of the Massachusetts council confirmed the appointments of some tories as judges of the superior court, even after 1766 when the whigs were in command. The elevation of tory Peter Oliver to the chief justiceship and the appointment of Edmund Trowbridge are two examples. The council, however, appears to have kept the lower courts safely whiggish, especially the magistrates, or the justices of the peace. Thus, while the judges of the superior court might be tory, the justices of the peace were, in the main, whigs, and there was nothing either the governor or the colonial secretary back in London could do to alter the situation.

There is still another explanation why the Massachusetts judiciary was less controversial than courts in some other colonies—at least until 1773 when the crown sought to bypass the local assembly and pay directly the judges' salaries. The province did not receive any of the English, Scottish, or occasional Irish placemen sent over to staff American courts. Ireland also suffered from this abuse and some of the southern colonies were badly treated by British appointments.[5] The judges, the magistrates, the attorney general, the advocate general, and most other law officers in colonial Massachusetts were native sons, they were not imported placemen.

Massachusetts was not, however, completely free of some of the other aspects of contemporary British political theory which the colonists regarded as defects in good government and were among the causes for growing whig opposition to British rule. One was the practice of plural office holding. In Massachusetts, plural office holding was symbolized by Thomas Hutchinson. While chief justice of the superior court and giving most of his official time to performing duties connected with that post, he was also lieutenant governor, a member of the executive council, and held several other minor government positions as well.

The practice of plural office holding was for the British a necessity if reliable and competent individuals were to be entrusted with public service and maintained on the relatively low salaries available. For Americans of the whig persuasion it was an abuse and their hostility could have serious political repercussions when men of local prominence were denied offices filled by plural holders.[6]

A second defect or abuse from the whig perspective was the current British tradition that a government office was a sinecure owned by the occupant to be held for personal profit, not public service. Again, this was a grievance not as serious in Massachusetts as in some other colonies since Massachusetts judicial salaries were low—too low to be bargained for. Judges were paid by the local assembly, not by the imperial government, and there was simply not enough money available to allow a judge to hire a deputy to do the work while he remained at home enjoying part of the income. All of the Massachusetts common-law judgeships and legal offices were filled by the men appointed to them.

Imperial positions, independent of the Massachusetts charter, however, were sometimes subject to private bargains, a situation that could weaken their efficiency and prestige. Should that happen the damage could have consequences in Massachusetts when the court involved was created by the home government either to correct or to supplement shortcomings in the enforcement of imperial law by the Massachusetts judicial system.

A case in point would be the vice-admiralty court, the most important imperial tribunal on the continent. It had been created to avoid hostile juries in the old colonies and located in Halifax, Nova Scotia, a garrison and naval town, to be free of political pressure. The judgeship was "one of the fattest political jobs open to the legal fraternity in America," paying a permanent salary of £600 a year in return for duties that did not interfere with the incumbent's private law practice. In 1769 the appointment went to Jonathan Sewall, who, at that time, was both attorney general of Massachusetts and advocate general of the vice-admiralty court sitting at Boston. Sewall surrendered the advocate generalship, but stayed on as attorney general as well he might. He did not have to go to Halifax, as he could farm out the office, conducting his judicial business through a deputy while retaining as much of the salary as he could contract for with that deputy, a privilege American whigs equated with corruption. In fact, if not in legal theory, the judgeship belonged to him and he was free to take out of it whatever profits he could, consistent with parliamentary statutes.[7]

The situation is best illustrated by a letter Sewall received from Thomas Hutchinson during 1771. Francis Bernard had written from London, informing Hutchinson that the British government, hoping to make the attorney general independent of the assembly, had decided to bestow a permanent salary of £150 on that office. The result, Bernard suggested, might have to be some complicated office juggling to satisfy Sewall. "In the first place, Mr. Sewall can't hold the Attorney General's place and the place of the Judge of the Admiralty also." It was hoped, Hutchinson reported, that he would surrender his judgeship. To persuade him to do so, treasury officials in London had found two candidates for the Halifax post willing to sweeten the prospect by making up part of his loss. John Robinson, who had fled the Boston mob and preferred to live in the safer town of Halifax, offered to exchange jobs. Sewall could have his Boston-based position as a commissioner of the customs paying £500 a year, if Robinson got the judgeship.[7] Governor William Franklin, of New Jersey, experiencing financial difficulties at the time, was so anxious to find new income that he proposed paying one-third of the salary he expected to receive if Sewall resigned.[8]

Neither proposal bore fruit, for Sewall retained both offices, not relinquishing the attorney generalship until 1775, when as a tory he could no longer function in it. He remained on as judge of the vice-admiralty for over twenty years, never living in Nova Scotia, but collecting the salary, perhaps as a pension or reward for his loyalty to the crown.[9]

Surely this private-privilege attitude toward public office affected performances and diminished usefulness. First-rate lawyers might be appointed but when they farmed out their duties they must have had to settle on lesser figures who would be satisfied with the diminished salary. At the very least, the sense of public obligation, traditional in the English judicial system, was lacking. The consequences may have been minimal with some other farmed-out law offices which were understood to be sinecures, but an active admiralty judge at Halifax might have made a contribution toward enforcement of the Trade Acts, the Navigation Acts, and the customs laws—the most important and frustrating challenge faced by British authority in North America after 1763. Considering all the problems encountered by those who had the responsibility for making these laws work, it surely did not help to have the vice-admiralty judge in Halifax devoting his time to a different office at Boston. The point that must be borne in mind is that in Massachusetts this practice weakened the enforcement of imperial law, and only of imperial law. It was unknown among that part of the judiciary enforcing local common law.

The Massachusetts bar, from which many of the judges came and which provided the lawyers who practiced before them, had few members educated at the Inns of Court, but it was well trained and professionally competent. By 1775 there were seventy-one lawyers in the province, of which twenty-nine would become loyalist exiles. Those figures do not indicate the full strength of tory legal feelings for they do not include such men as Edmund Trowbridge, attorney general and later superior court judge, whose leanings were toward the loyalist side of the political controversy. By withdrawing from politics before the battle of Lexington, Trowbridge was able to remain in Massachusetts, practicing law and training a new generation of law students in the conservative tradition.[10]

The law that prerevolutionary Massachusetts attorneys practiced was a law inherited from England, but it was not an imperial law. It was a Massachusetts version of English common law, locally controlled and locally administered. "If any one fact about the legal system of pre-Revolutionary Massachusetts stands out," writes William E. Nelson, who has studied the conditions of eighteenth-century law in that colony more extensively than any other scholar,

> that fact is the closeness of the law to the Bay Colony's local communities and to its people. Colonial law was not the instrument of

some distant sovereign legislator used or even capable of use by that sovereign in order to promote a well articulated, coherently defined social policy. Legal and social institutions and the substantive and procedural rules of law were simply too haphazard for any one institution to dominate the entire legal system. The most powerful institution within the system was the jury, however the jury was not one but many bodies, each of which possessed its own separate existence only for a very brief period of time during which it had virtually no opportunity to alter the direction of the entire system. No single man or group of men, in fact, possessed such power.[11]

Law in Ireland was almost the exact opposite. It was both centrally controlled and centrally administered—controlled for the benefit of British imperial rule and administered for the benefit of the Protestant ascendancy. The lawyers lived in Dublin whence the judges were sent out on circuit to apply a uniform judgment upon a people who had nothing to say about the substance of the law. "During the last decade of the eighteenth century," one legal historian has observed, "a judge's work on circuit must have been sometimes almost past endurance." The number of criminal cases he tried would have staggered an American lawyer.[12] An Irish judge could hear during a single assize more capital trials than a Massachusetts judge would witness in a lifetime at the bar and on the bench. The selection of grand jurors prone to indict was one factor, the severity of the law another. "Is not Ireland," Robert Emmet would ask, "already traceable in the statute book as a wounded man in a crowd is traced by his wounds?"[13] Arthur O'Connor posed a similar question: "If internal tranquility and a willing obedience to the laws, be the best criterion to judge of the justice or wisdom with which they have been made, or of the moderation with which they have been administered, in what period of our history, in what quarter of our country, shall the Government and Legislature of Ireland find their justification?"[14] O'Connor was a lawyer, supposedly trained in the same legal traditions and well-grounded in the same law as the attorneys of Massachusetts Bay. But no Massachusetts lawyer would have asked the question O'Connor asked. They praised their law; they did not doubt it; and their praise was not the familiar chauvinism of insular common lawyers. Although they knew that Massachusetts law might not be perfect, they knew it served society; it did not demand that society serve it.

Law in prerevolutionary Massachusetts was responsive to a community consensus rather than a sovereign's will, reflecting a concern for individual liberty as well as local ethical standards. To put the matter differently, it was a democratic law as the word "democratic" is properly defined, not as it is often used. Twentieth-century Americans might not think so, but that would be because their consensus is not an eighteenth-century consensus. In the Massachusetts of Samuel Adams, liberty could mean freedom from corrupting temptations as well as from arbitrary rule. And the ethical standards, the social values, that law reflected may not be those we would endorse—"that men be punished for their sins, that they keep the agreements into which they had entered and the trust which others had reposed in them, and that they pay for whatever benefits others had conferred on them"[15]—but they were the standards of Boston, not the standards of London, the standards of Worcester, not the standards of York, and the standards of Salem, not the standards of Bristol. In the realization that they were Massachusetts standards lies the key to understanding the thrust of the Massachusetts legal system and the source of Massachusetts law. Should we be willing to draw an even bolder conclusion it could be plausibly asserted that the same fact explains much of the difference between eighteenth-century Massachusetts law and eighteenth-century Irish law.

In Ireland the law did not reflect social values, rather society reflected the law. People were not punished for their sins in the Massachusetts sense, they were punished for violating the law. Irish law did not mirror a society of contract and agreement, rather society mirrored a law of status and suppression. One status was that of landlord, another that of tenant, and as far as a tenant was concerned the law enforced by Dublin castle permitted a landlord to be a law unto himself. He was Ireland's version of the Massachusetts legal system for he was, in fact, the local law of Ireland. We may be familiar with the arrogance of class yet the Irish landlord defies belief. Arthur Young, an impartial observer who was traveling through Ireland as an agent for Lord Kingsborough during 1775–76, the very years when Americans were turning their constitutional argument into a war against British rule, has supplied a valuable description. Young left a vivid picture of the conditions of local Irish or landlord law, a law no Massachusetts magnate would have dared emulate. Even on the high seas, stern as they may have been, Massachusetts merchant captains could not be such tyrants or expect such submission.

> A landlord in Ireland can scarcely invent an order which a servant, labourer or cottar dares to refuse to execute. Nothing satisfies him but an unlimited submission. Disrespect or anything tending towards sauciness he may punish with his cane or his horse-whip with the most perfect security; a poor man would have his bones broke if he offered to lift his hand in his own defence. Knocking down is spoken of in the country in a manner that makes an Englishman stare. . . . It must strike the most careless traveller to see whole strings of cars whipped into a ditch by a gentleman's footman to make way for his carriage; if they are overturned or broken in pieces, no matter, it is taken in patience.[16]

Young was speaking of districts where the tenantry was Catholic. Where the tenantry was Protestant the treatment was more gentle. That was another status—religion—that the law fostered in Irish society. Catholics, William Sampson later wrote from his exile in New York, were "ground into dust" by the "penal" code. "They had no part in the framing or execution of the laws, being excluded from the parliament and the bench, and from juries and from the bar. Their only *duty* was to *bear* with patience the penalties inflicted on them, and be spectators of the ludicrous, though interested, quarrels of their oppressors. When any question under the penal laws was tried *against* them, it was by a Protestant judge, a Protestant jury; and as they had a Protestant prosecutor, so they must have a Protestant advocate."[17]

"It is," John Mitchel has been quoted as saying, "an irksome and painful task to pursue the details of that penal code; but the penal code is the history of Ireland."[18] The theory that lay behind the penal code was summed up by a resolution passed by the Dublin corporation during the early 1790s: "A Protestant King of Ireland; a Protestant Parliament; a Protestant hierarchy; Protestant electors and Government; the Benches of Justice, the Army and the Revenue, through all their branches and details, Protestant; and this system supported by a connexion with the Protestant realm of England."[19]

The penal code of Ireland, a series of laws beginning in 1695, need not be detailed. It was not, as the name suggests, a criminal code, but a set of statutes placing civil disabilities on Catholics, forbidding such incidents of citizenship as education, land owning, and the practice of medicine or law. For Irish attorneys, all of whom were Protestant and many of whom were English, the penal laws furnished much of their practice. "The lawyer found that they diminished the competition while they increased the business of his profession."[20] A Catholic, one former chief secretary who later became a British imperial governor explained in 1773, "cannot be a lawyer, for the law is not his friend."[21]

The penal code not only alienated a large section of the population against law and government, it had destructive economic results. A Catholic could lease property for only thirty-one years, at the end of which time he had to bid against others for a new lease and face eviction if someone offered the Protestant owner of the fee a higher rent. Not only did a Catholic tenant farmer lack all incentive to make improvements, it was not unusual, when the termination date approached, for him to waste the farm, rendering it less attractive to potential competitors. In New England, where the belief existed that landowners held by the only form of freehold tenure known to the common-law world—allodial—the law furnished a different incentive. In all of the colonies, as a matter of fact, the civil side of English common law—still essentially a law of land tenures at home—had undergone a remarkable change. Formulated for an aristocracy of owners and based on incidents of service, it had not only been transplanted to a wilderness but made to serve a society in which there were no lords, stripped of its feudal characteristics except in those districts where quitrent remained (rendered almost meaningless through annual suspension acts passed by the local assembly), or among the tenant farmers of New York (where tenantry was based more on contract than on tenure).[22]

The extent of the penal code of Ireland may best be summarized by considering its repeal. It was only at the time of the first stirrings of whiggery in America that the rulers of Ireland began to relax its harsher aspects. The initial concession, in 1760, was to allow Catholics into the army and navy—in the noncommissioned ranks, of course. During 1771, Catholics willing to expend money and labor to reclaim useless bogland or marshes were granted leases for 61 years. The great change occurred in 1778, after the American Revolution had begun, when the Catholic relief act authorized leases up to 999 years on all land. "Moreover, they [i.e., Catholics] were given the ordinary rights of disposition and inheritance; hitherto they could not dispose of any estate in land by will—there had to be an equal division among their sons, unless one chose to cheat his breathren by conforming to Protestantism, in which case he inherited the whole."[23] In 1782, Catholics were allowed to become schoolmasters and private tutors, to own horses exceeding the value of £5, and to acquire land in socage tenure. Finally, the relief bills of 1792 and 1793 permitted them to enter the lower ranks of the bar, to serve on juries, to take university degrees, to hold military commissions, to become magistrates, and to be elected to municipal corporations. When they sought membership in parliament, however, the Irish Protestants and the British government drew the line.

The judges who enforced the laws of British-ruled Ireland must have been a hardy breed. They not only did their duty; they sometimes rejoiced in it. Sentencing Owen Kirwan to death for rebellion in 1803, Baron George wondered aloud why some Irish people were discontented living under "our unequalled Constitution." It was, he remarked, "truly astonishing how any man, or body of men, could be found meditating attempting the destruction of so beautiful a system!"[24]

Surely the whigs of North America two generations earlier would not have recognized beauty in that Irish system. Theirs was a different law and a different complaint, for they had reason to be satisfied with their domestic law while rebelling against imperial law. "One of the most pervasive concerns of men in prerevolutionary Massachusetts was the preservation of liberty and the containment of arbitrary power," Nelson writes,[25] and local Massachusetts law reflected that concern. In contemporary Ireland, by contrast, law was the embodiment of arbitrary power. "Law in Ireland," said Aubrey de Vere, "was the friend neither of the people nor of justice, but the impartial persecutor of both."[26]

The whigs of Boston, Salem, and Worcester had every reason to think of their local law, if they thought of it at all, as more a friend than an enemy. Granted there were groups that did not share its full benefits—the merchant seamen, for example—but even they found more fault with imperial law than local law.[27] "A legal system," Nelson concludes, "which so gave effect to community values seemed eminently satisfactory to all elements of prerevolutionary Massachusetts society, except perhaps the immediate representatives of the crown, who sometimes found that the system frustrated their exercise of power. There is no evidence that any of the men who led Massachusetts into Revolution or any of those who followed acted for the purpose of bringing about fundamental changes in the rules and institutions of which Massachusetts' legal system was comprised."[28]

Eighteenth-century Irish rebels had fundamental changes in mind, for in their country the common law of England did not give effect to community values satisfactory to all elements of society. In fact, it was not even satisfactory to all lawyers. Arthur O'Connor wrote an indictment of transplanted British law in Ireland with which not a few attorneys agreed.

> Instead of a clear, digested and uniform code; customs, traditions, precedents, laws, written and unwritten, heaped together, have been consecrated; and their contradictions and confusion have been celebrated as a glorious *uncertainty* by its professors. No wonder, that, in this barbarous mass of complexity, chicane, and fraud, it were vain for those who seek justice to consult the professors to tell them the law. No wonder, that precedents equally strong should be found on one side as well as on the other. The whole is enveloped in form and fiction; and, in the slightest omission of either, substantial justice is lost. Trial after trial may be had in the same cause; and whilst innumerable forms enable the agents to increase the expenses, and to prolong the duration, it is their interest to extend both as far as they can. In vain shall the upright Judge hold the balance of justice wih equal hand, if it is placed scarcely within the attainment of the rich, and out of the reach of the poor. It cannot be justice, unless it is common; it cannot be common unless it is cheap.[29]

Again we must be certain that we understand precisely what was said. O'Connor's complaint was not the familiar list of procedural defects that critics of the common law will one day make the rallying call for reform. It was substantive law that earned his wrath: its unpredictability in which the only certainty was expense; its incredible professionalism making a mystery of everyday affairs; and its class favoritism that always gave the appearance and usually had the reality of judging a litigant by religion and deciding a cause by rules rather than by justice.

A foreign lawyer, one from France, or Spain, or Prussia, might tell us that the law of which O'Connor wrote was the same as the law of New England. This would be partially true, yet there was a substantive difference between the two laws which reveals much about the eighteenth-century revolutions the two realms would fight against British rule. In America the complaint was about constitutional law, in Ireland it was also over positive law. The Irish reformers had a law to fight against; the whigs of Boston had a law for which to fight.

4

Democracy Is Too Prevalent in America[1]

THE CIVIL TRAVERSE JURY

We have drawn contrasts and we must draw others, and as we do it is important to realize that differences were not always a matter of degree. The lord lieutenant of Ireland had more power, the governor of Massachusetts Bay less, between them there was a constitutional scission putting performance by one beyond the capacity of the other. The difference was not in function or in goals, it was in the degree of decision-making authority each possessed. But what was true for executive prerogative was not true for all conditions of law in the two areas of empire. With some the difference was more than of degree, it was a difference in kind.

A judicial institution in Ireland could serve ends the opposite of those served by the same institution in North America. What upheld imperial law in eighteenth-century Ireland often diminished it in eighteenth-century Massachusetts Bay. What Arthur O'Connor would have praised in American law, an Irish tory would have found the very antithesis of law itself.

A British tory lawyer visiting prerevolutionary Boston might have taken O'Connor's indictment of Irish law and applied it to Massachusetts law. His complaint would have been procedural rather than substantive and his scorn directed not at the bench or bar but at the grand and traverse juries. It would have been a complaint we must not overlook, despite historians of the Revolution who tend to overlook it. Even those who argue that the debate culminating in the American Revolution was to a large extent a debate on constitutional issues have missed a closely related point: when tories and whigs confronted one another during the decade before Lexington, one of the weapons that they employed was law.

In their arsenal of legal warfare, perhaps the most unrenowned instrument the whigs possessed was the civil traverse jury, especially in Massachusetts

27

where the conditions of local law made the jury a remarkably effective device for "punishing" those placemen bold enough to enforce imperial law. "Hampering activities of the customs officials by suits at common law," the historian of vice admiralty has written, "had long been a defensive weapon at the disposal of aggrieved merchants."[2] During the 1760s the civil jury became an offensive weapon as well.

Common-law judgments in civil (not criminal) cases were used not only to harass but to drive customs agents out of both Charles Town, South Carolina, and Albany, New York. Naval officers who seized vessels for violating the trade or navigation statutes faced the prospect of being sued for large sums and having both their assets and their careers tied up for years in litigation. George Talbot, commander of a British man-of-war enforcing the revenue laws along the Delaware river, seems to have thought that American merchantmen welcomed inspection for then they had a pretense to sue. "When an Action is laid, Justice is out of the question," Talbot claimed. "We are sure it will be against us, no one will be our Bail, not a Lawyer in the Province that has a Salary from the Crown, and any we employ will seem to Act for us, but Secretly Act against us."[3]

Failure of bail was depressing enough; the hostility of the bar was even more menacing, yet worst of all was the certainty of a plaintiff's verdict. It might be thought that Talbot was exaggerating a bit, giving a typical layman's view of the law: a trap in which the innocent are ensnared; a maze through which only the unjust can find their way. But what he says was not untrue; it was not an exaggeration. When recalling the judicial institutions of prerevolutionary America we must not color our understanding of yesterday by our knowledge of today. Eighteenth-century courts were not the same as twentieth-century courts and one reason was that eighteenth-century juries enjoyed far more prerogatives than do twentieth-century juries.

It was apprehension of whig jurors, not of substantive law, that made naval captains cautious when seizing a vessel or condemning a cargo. The presiding judges might instruct the jury that the defendants' conduct had been lawful or was not answerable to a writ of trespass, but such would be the court's law. The jurors could adopt a different law and the law they applied became the "law," at least for the case at bar.

There are three simple and related points about the conditions of law in prerevolutionary Massachusetts that have sometimes been misunderstood: a political majority could control Massachusetts juries; juries were the judges of law as well as of fact; and courts had little power to control and no power to overrule jury verdicts.

The whigs could, if they wished, control the civil traverse juries, because they controlled the town meetings. As one contemporary Bostonian wrote to the English radical John Wilkes, "By a Law of this Province the Jurors are return'd by the Selectmen, after the choice has been made by the Town."[4] True, to obtain unanimous verdicts the whigs would have to control the meetings of every town in the county, not an easy task as Boston's dislike of customs officials was not always shared with the same intensity by the inland farm communities of Suffolk county. Yet there was enough unity of purpose for tories to believe that a Bostonian could boast that the whigs "would always be sure of Eleven jury men in Twelve."[5]

After 1765, a tory juror would probably have to come from a town outside Boston. The chances of getting one diminished as the political controversy intensified, or so it appears from Chief Justice Thomas Hutchinson's charge to the jury at the March 1769 term of the Suffolk superior court. He confessed "*some Reason* to fear" that town meetings were sending jurors willing to convict ordinary criminals, but who "connive at and pass over in Silence and entirely smother other Crimes of an alarming Nature." Hutchinson had to be referring to riots and political crimes, though he also asserted that some Suffolk county towns had a history of returning jurors who were interested in prospective litigation.[6] Happily for a customs-official defendant, if a tory was returned, the whig plaintiff could not remove him by challenge as no challenges were allowed in civil cases. While we cannot guess what the chances were that a tory could be on a Suffolk jury, it must be stressed that even the certainty of one or more militant-tory jurors would not have deterred a political plaintiff from using the courts to harass crown officials. Although he might know he would not win damages, a hung jury would serve his political objective: of striking back at the customs official, putting him to personal expense in both money and time, warning him to be more cautious in the future, and gaining the esteem of the Boston mob by demonstrating the plaintiff's whiggery. Besides, as the Richardson murder conviction was to demonstrate, eleven jurors were sometimes all that the whigs needed.[7]

Secondly, control of the jury meant everything in Massachusetts at that time. Perhaps straining contemporary English law to suit their own predilections, lawyers interpreted *Bushell's Case* as holding "that the jury should always decide the law as well as the fact."[8] John Adams spoke for most members of the bar, including some tories, when he insisted that it was the duty as well as the right of a juror "to find the Verdict according to his own best Understanding, Judgment and Conscience, tho in Direct opposition to the Direction of the Court."[9] The legal theory has been summed up as follows: "In each case, a jury is free, if justice requires, to reach the same result reached by other juries in analogous cases in the past; if, on the other hand, justice requires departure from past verdicts, the jury is free so to depart."[10] So, too, when politics required, the jury was free to depart, and as often as not it did.

There is a still deeper dimension to jury autonomy that deserves our attention. Had jurors been required to follow court instructions it is doubtful they could have done so in some of the more controversial litigations, as they might not have known what the instructions were.

When instructions were given, and they were not often given, they were rendered *seriatim*, and since all cases were tried before at least three judges and sometimes more, jurors were often left to determine which judge's interpretation of the law was "correct."[11] If the court agreed on one charge, the jurors might still be confused. Judges were not the only ones to explain law to them. Throughout the prerevolutionary period, advocates in Massachusetts jury trials were permitted to argue law as well as fact. Lawyers in their summations spent as much time quoting from law books and expounding rules or principles as they did clarifying their evidence or attacking testimony presented by the other side. If their rules or principles were whiggish, a Boston jury might well conclude that they better knew law than did the tory judges and would take "instructions" from them. Advocates were free to score political points as they were permitted to say just about anything they pleased. "Customs house officers," John Adams argued in one case for the plaintiff, "[are] vested with very important power and if deviated from may become fire brands in the hands of Fools." It may or may not be significant that in this instance the jury returned a verdict for Adams's client of £2,700 on goods worth £1,041.[12] Certainly significant is the practical result: that jurors more than judges or lawyers made the law of prerevolutionary Massachusetts; and in political cases, whig juries made whig law.

Erving v. *Cradock* is a case in point. The plaintiff, John Erving, was a member of the governor's council and the defendant, George Cradock, was temporary collector of the port of Boston. Here is a tory's view of that litigation, explained by Governor Francis Bernard to the lords of trade:

> Mr. *Cradock* . . . as Collector, seized a Vessel of Mr. *Erving's* charged with contraband trade & libelled her in the Court of Admiralty. Mr. *Erving* appeared personally in Court & prayed leave to compound [i.e., to settle][13] which being agreed to by the Governor & Collector as well as the King's Advocate, was allowed by the Court at one half of the value, which upon appraisement was ascertained at above £500 sterling. This sum Mr. *Erving* paid into Court; & it was equally divided between the King, the Governor & the Collector. . . . And now Mr. *Erving* has brought this action against Mr. *Cradock* for damages accrued to him by means of this seizure.[14]

In other words, after compounding the seizure in open admiralty court and paying the compromise sum, Councillor Erving turned to the common-law courts to recoup his loss and, perhaps, to punish Collector Cradock for his official zeal. The writ was trespass, and as Bernard put it, "The pretence for this action is, that the seizure was illegal and a trespass, and that the payment of Mr. *Erving* was not voluntary, but extorted by violence and *duress*."[15] The governor, who had already received his one-third share of the settlement, was alarmed. The common-law suit was, he asserted, a plot to destroy both the admiralty jurisdiction and the customs service. True it was a personal action, "But," he warned the lords of trade, "it is generally understood that Mr. *Erving's* is only a leading action to a great many others; and that if he meets with success, every one that has had goods condemned, or been allowed to compound for them at their own request, will bring actions against the officer who seized them. Your Lordships will perceive that these actions have an immediate tendency to destroy the Court of Admiralty and with it the Custom house, which cannot subsist without that Court."[16]

As far as Bernard was concerned, the suspicion of a conspiracy was confirmed by the conduct of counsel and judges when the case came on for trial at the inferior court of common pleas before a Suffolk county jury. There, if we believe the governor, and it seems reasonable to do so, "the chief subject of the harangues of the council for the plaintiff (and some of the judges too) were on the expediency of discouraging a Court immediately subject to the King and independent of the Province and which determined property without a jury; and on a necessity of putting a stop to the practice of the Custom house officers, for that the people would no longer bear having their trade kept under restrictions, which their neighbors (meaning Rhode Island) were entirely free from."[17] Two of the judges,[18] according to Bernard, "directed the jury to find a verdict for the plaintiff, and give him for damages every farthing he was out of pocket; and said they must put a stop to those proceedings of the Customs house officers; if they did not there would be tumults and bloodshed; for the people would bear with them no longer."[19] Thus *Erving* v. *Cradock* contained three elements that boded ill for the enforcement of imperial law in Massachusetts over the next decade and a half: whig political theory was offered to the jury as controlling law; the jury was invited to use civil tort damages as a criminal-law-type sanction to punish a revenue-agent defendant for enforcing an unpopular statute; and the vice-admiralty jurisdiction was put on trial. The vice admiralty was "convicted" and in a real sense so was Collector Cradock. The jury returned a verdict "near 600 sterling damages," about £100 above the sum for which Erving had compounded.

Cradock appealed to the superior court of judicature, which meant a trial *de novo* with each party allowed to enter further pleas and offer new evidence. More important, it meant trial before judges more of the tory persuasion. Had they been partisan they would not have to bring in politics as had the inferior-court judges. They could and did instruct the jury according to precedent and precedent was clear: whether Cradock had been guilty of a trespass (a fact not proved, the court pointed out), he was purged of that trespass by the composition confirmed in the vice-admiralty court, the decrees of which were of equal force with a judgment at common law.[20] Chief Justice Thomas Hutchinson was emphatic. There were no exceptions to the rule, he charged, "that the decree of the Court of Admiralty, where it had jurisdiction, could not be traversed and annulled in a court of common law."[21] Notwithstanding the jury found for the plaintiff, voting him damages of £740 lawful Massachusetts money or £555 sterling.

Cradock was now in a serious position. He had been performing his duty and the upper court had ruled he was not liable, but the jury held otherwise and he faced the prospect of paying for more than his share of the "compounding" or going to debtors' prison. The court could not enter judgment for him, no matter how valid the judges thought his defense.[22] He might move for a new trial, a motion not without precedent in the superior court of judicature,[23] but not applicable in this case. The law was emphatic: a motion for a new trial could not be granted on the ground that the jury had disregarded the court's instruction.[24] In Massachusetts the civil jury's verdict was truly final. All that Collector Cradock could do was take an appeal outside the province, to the king in council, while trusting that the governor would somehow delay execution of judgment or keep him out of jail until orders came from London.

Cradock took his appeal and Erving withdrew, confessing in superior court that the second judgment had been satisfied.[25] His decision should not surprise us. In a similar situation John Hancock did the same. One of his ships had been seized and condemned at the Boston admiralty court for importing more goods than had been entered at the customs house of the Scottish port where they had been loaded. Hancock sued the officers of customs for the value of the ship and cargo. Again Chief Justice Hutchinson gave the jury instructions that an admiralty decree could not be traversed at common law and again the jury ignored him. When the customsmen appealed to the king in council, Hancock, like Erving, withdrew. Thomas Hutchinson believed that Hancock did not dare to pursue the appeal because trial in London would have exposed his smuggling operations and hurt his reputation.[26] This explanation is doubtful. Hancock did not defend the appeal because he knew that he had no more chance of winning before the king in council than the customs officials had had of defending themselves before a Boston jury. Besides, if his purpose was to harass the revenue service, both he and Erving had done well enough. As these were personal actions the defendants had been put to expense out of their own pockets as well as to a good deal of trouble, being forced to take time from their duties to consult with their lawyers and attend the trials. Moreover, a civil suit in Massachusetts could be a very real annoyance as the plaintiff had the option of attaching all of the defendant's property. All in all, just to lose in superior court, even without paying the judgment, could be costly. A few actions of this type, and Hancock and his fellow merchants could expect the customsmen to proceed more cautiously in the future—even if appeal to London meant certain reversal. If the appeal were defended and the facts of harassment brought officially to the notice of the British government, the crown might be obliged to indemnify the customs officers. Without an appeal, the whigs could hope that the revenue men would be left to bear the costs themselves.[27]

There is one further case to consider, for it sheds light on whether whig litigants sought to win money damages or were as interested in using the traverse jury to harass the revenue service. It is the case of James Otis against John Robinson, an especially unpopular customs commissioner, and it was the *cause célébre* of the day. Otis and Robinson staged a cane-swinging brawl in a tory coffee house, and Otis, having received the worst of it, sued Robinson alleging damages in the amount of £3,000. The traverse jury for the inferior court of common pleas brought in a plaintiff's verdict, setting damages at "the astounding amount of £2,000, higher than any contemporary tort award and, in terms of twentieth century purchasing power, an exceptionally substantial recovery."[28] Not satisfied, Otis appealed to the superior court of judicature. He must have thought it likely that a second jury would vote an even higher sum. So, too, did Robinson. Through his attorney he confessed his liability and gave Otis the apology he had demanded.[29] Otis thereupon remitted all but £112, 10s. and 8d., an amount covering the costs, the medical bills, and his attorney fees. The revealing fact is that Otis could have easily gotten more money and not run the risk of an appeal to the king in council. His lawyer, John Adams, could have asked the jury for damages in the amount of £299, and there seems to have been no rule to stop him from informing the jurors that such a sum was one pound less than the statutory amount required for an appeal to London. The jury verdict would have been final (save for Robinson's useless right to appeal to a superior-court jury) and Otis would have been richer. Instead, Adams pressed for an unrealistic verdict and the unpopular revenue agent, to avoid the expense of appeal, was forced to humble himself before the whigs. It cannot be doubted that Adams could have persuaded the jury to bring in the lesser amount.[30] "From the best account I can get of the trial," Hutchinson wrote, "had Mr. Otis assaulted Mr. Robinson, in the same manner after receiving the like insult and abuse, the jury would not have given him a shilling."[31]

"They now begin to talk," Governor Bernard wrote of the whig merchants, "of bringing more actions against Custom house officers who have made seizures and have had them condemned or compounded in Court for them. A Custom house officer has no chance with a jury, let his cause be what it will. And it will depend upon the vigorous measures that shall be taken at home for the defence of the officers, whether there be any Custom house here at all."[32]

Bernard does not say what the British government should do, but surely he knew when he wrote in 1761 that London was not ready to interfere with Massachusetts juries. That day would not come until 1774.[33] Perhaps he thought the vice-admiralty court could be given exclusive jurisdiction over personal actions involving customs officials. But this solution too would have been a drastic innovation. The best he could hope for was the power to suspend execution of judgment until appeals could be heard by the king in council, for speedier and less expensive methods of appeals, and finally for a fund from which to reimburse government-employed defendants forced to pay damages resulting from politically inspired jury verdicts. The ministry did nothing, leaving the "custom house officials" with little choice but to consider their own interests and to proceed with greater caution when enforcing the trade laws.

Their need for caution was even greater when they examined the statutes they were expected to enforce. If the conditions of Massachusetts law made them amenable to legal harassment, the conditions of imperial law compounded the possibility. The statutes under which they operated were so detailed that a reading could raise more questions than answers, at least for minor officials caught between hostile American merchants and unsympathetic superiors in London. Some passages were so vague or contradictory that the law officers in London did not agree on their meaning.[34] A customs man relying on such authority to make a seizure surely knew that a whig lawyer could persuade a whig jury that his interpretation had been too broad.

For royal officials serving in prerevolutionary Massachusetts, the conditions of imperial law as they existed in these statutes posed a dilemma. If they did not do their duty they might lose their source of livelihood. If they did their duty they might end up facing debtors' prison. It was truly a dilemma, a problem for which even the best legal advice could offer no sage solution. Nowhere was this fact better demonstrated than in Boston during the Stamp Act crisis, when Benjamin Hallowell was comptroller of the port and William Sheaffe was collector. As the time drew near when documents would have to be stamped, both men were in a quandary. The stamp agent, Andrew Oliver, had not only resigned his office but when they approached him for stamps he replied that he had no commission to distribute stamps and would not distribute them if he had. They then turned to the crown attorneys for advice, and one of the issues that they raised has been summarized by Edmund S. and Helen M. Morgan:

> Suppose they should refuse to grant clearances on the ground that they had no stamped paper. To grant clearances was their job and no one else could do it. If they refused would they not be liable to suits for damages from every individual who applied for a clearance and was refused? On the other hand, suppose they granted a clearance on unstamped paper, and suppose further that the ship proceeding under this clearance were seized by the British Navy and condemned for proceeding under improper clearance papers. Would they not be liable in such a case to a suit for the value of the ship? Whatever they did were they not thus liable to innumerable suits? And were not the New England merchants notoriously quick to sue customs officials whenever they could?[35]

These are apparently the questions that Hallowell and Sheaffe put to Edmund Trowbridge, then the attorney general of the province, and to Robert Auchmuty, the advocate general of the admiralty court. From one or both they received an answer that the Morgans characterized as "a reluctant opinion": that "the Comptroller and Collector would not be liable for damages if they cleared ships on unstamped paper, provided they certified that no stamped paper was available." For historians the opinion may be "reluctant." Considering that these were tory attorneys who rendered it, a lawyer might call it bold. While it said nothing about the constitutionality of the Stamp Act, it did give the whigs as much as they could have hoped for and was hardly calculated to please their superiors in London. Yet it satisfied neither the comptroller nor the collector, who seem to have wanted more of a guarantee of immunity than mere legal advice. They pressed the lawyers for more explicit assurances only to discover that Trowbridge had gotten "cold feet," for he replied that their dilemma was "a matter rather of prudence than of law." He could, he concluded, advise them no further.[36]

It may be, as the Morgans suggested, that the attorney general got "cold feet," but it is doubtful. Rather it seems that he was being asked a question no lawyer could have answered, and, on being pressed too far, he threw up his hands in disgust. Trowbridge was the most respected lawyer in Massachusetts Bay and it is true that he had a reputation to protect. Moreover, as attorney general he was caught between the passions of the whig population, some of whom were his private clients, and the governments, both in Boston and London, from whom he sought official favor. Had he been asked to rule on the constitutionality of the Stamp Act or to have given advice on whether it was legal to issue clearances without stamps, he might well have gotten "cold feet" and shied away from an answer. No matter what he ruled he would have been damned on one side without winning marks from the other. But from what the Morgans say, it seems that he was not being asked for an opinion on either of these questions. It was not the constitutionality of the Stamp Act that troubled Comptroller Hallowell and Collector Sheaffe, but their own personal liability. They did not ask whether London would fine them or remove them from office for using unstamped paper, but whether Boston merchants could and would successfully sue them if they refused to do so. They were asking Trowbridge an unanswerable question, and the explanation lies with Massachusetts Bay jurisprudence and especially with the rules of special pleading, not with a lawyer's cold feet.

As the verdict in *Erving* v. *Cradock* demonstrates, it was not difficult for a Massachusetts lawyer to frame a case that the court had to submit to a jury. There the superior court clearly did not have jurisdiction, for the matter had been settled in vice admiralty and the judgment of the court could not be traversed at common law. Yet the judges of the superior court had not only been unable to overturn the jury's verdict after it was rendered, they had not dismissed the action earlier. They did not because they could not do so since Erving's case was not patently bad on the surface, probably because the writ of trespass drawn by his lawyer said nothing about the fact that the seizure (or trespass) had been compounded in admiralty. Had the writ set forth the admiralty decree, the defendant, Cradock, might have demurred and the superior court would have dismissed the action. But if the writ omitted reference to the admiralty settlement, the defendant could not demur without confessing the allegation of trespass, and judgment would have been entered against him.

Unable to demur, the defendant's first alternative was to plea the general issue: answer "not guilty" to the charge of trespass. If he did so, however, he would not be able to bring forward his defense of law until the jury was seated and then it was for the whig jury, not the tory court to render the verdict. A second alternative for Cradock was to plead specially, that is, to raise the defense in his answer by citing the fact of the previous binding admiralty decree. If the plaintiff replied by admitting the decrees (and perhaps citing further special matter by way of avoidance) the court would have the legal issue before it and the judges could have dismissed the writ. No whig lawyer would have done so (nor would he have demurred to the answer as that also would have led to dismissal). He would have denied the fact alleged in the answer (i.e., the admiralty decree), and thus created an issue of fact that the court had to submit to jury. Once the jury was sworn and he began to offer evidence, the plaintiff's lawyer would no longer deny the admiralty decree. He would have gotten his argument before a jury despite the fact that it was bad at law, and, because it was a customs case, he could expect the jury to ignore the law and find for his client.

These rules of special pleading made it possible for a whig lawyer to get any case before a jury and made it impossible for the attorney general to advise the comptroller and collector how to make themselves judgment proof. As long as Boston juries were likely to ignore the "law" and vote their politics, no one could have advised them.

But what of the advice that Trowbridge did give them? The Morgans say that at first he (and perhaps also Auchmuty) told the two men that they "would not be liable to damages if they cleared ships on unstamped paper, provided they certified that no stamped paper was available."[37] If Trowbridge did say this, he was going just about as far as any lawyer would have dared to go. Perhaps all he was saying was that if the officials did make the certification of unavailability, it was unlikely they would ever be sued.[38]

It should be noted that Trowbridge was answering the second question that had been put to him by Hallowell and Sheaffe: whether the two officials would be liable for the value of a ship cleared on unstamped paper and later seized by the royal navy for sailing without proper clearance. Trowbridge's supposition had to be that if the unstamped clearance was accompanied by a certification that stamps were not available in Boston, the navy would not seize the ship sailing under such paper, or, if it did, the admiralty court would dismiss the seizure. There was a risk here, for no one knew what orders might come from London, but even if the supposition proved false and the ship was both seized and condemned, it was more than likely that the owner of the vessel would not sue Hallowell and Sheaffe; he would sue the captain of the naval ship. From a political point of view, to sue the captain might be more effective for it would cause the government greater annoyance, call to account a man who profited personally from the seizure, and perhaps tie up a naval vessel. From a legal point of view it would be preferable, for the writ of trespass could be used and the only fact that the plaintiff would have to prove would be the seizure. Even a tory judge would tell the jury that the burden was on the captain to justify his actions.

Trowbridge could reasonably render advice based on such suppositions— that was a lawyer's job. What he could not do was give Hallowell and Sheaffe a guarantee that they would not be sued at all. Consider the first hypothetical question that they put to him: what if they refused to grant clearance for a ship because the ship's papers were not stamped. This appears an easy case because unstamped papers are illegal; the comptroller and collector were obeying the law when they refused to sign them; therefore they are not liable for loss resulting from a failure to grant clearance. But, as Trowbridge well knew, the prospective plaintiff could avoid that legal defense. The writ would say nothing about stamps or the Stamp Act. All it would allege was that the defendants had harmed the plaintiff to his damage of such and such an amount. What the shipowner needed to sue the officials was a proper writ. To draft a proper writ his lawyer's problem was to frame the harm in the disguise of an actionable wrong without revealing that the harm was related to stamps.

The whig shipowner—whether he really wanted to collect money damages or was only doing his share to harass British customs officials—would have to frame his allegation of liability within an action on the case,[39] alleging that the defendant by failing to perform his duty (i.e., issue clearance papers) had done irreparable damage to the plaintiff in a stated amount of money. Although the count would be in nonfeasance rather than misfeasance the defendant would not demur to the writ. Massachusetts Bay courts during the prerevolutionary era permitted relief, by way of a common-law action, against a public official who had committed a breach of duty, even when the wrong was in the nature of nonfeasance.[40]

On one point there was no dispute, certainly not in the minds of crown officials. They were as liable in common-law actions as were colonial officials. Considering the political attitudes of Boston juries, they may have felt that the mere liability to answer the writ made judgment against them certain. Moreover, they undoubtedly suspected that damages were not the primary objective of some potential whig litigants. The whig shipowner-turned-plaintiff might be seeking nothing more than to establish with the "mob" his credentials as "a friend of liberty." Money certainly could be made by suing these two potential defendants, but better still was the opportunity to embarrass London.[41] The Stamp Act itself could be put on trial and a Boston jury could be asked to rule on its constitutionality. The verdict might be meaningless at Westminster Hall, but it would have marvelous propaganda value in the colonies.

Let us suppose that the Stamp Act had not been repealed and the collector of the port of Boston refused to issue clearance papers permitting the ship of a merchant to sail from the harbor. The merchant brings our writ of case alleging that the collector has neglected to perform his duty, as a result of which the plaintiff's ship was not able to sail, and that anticipated profits in a stated amount were thereby lost. Before he dare demur to the writ, the collector's lawyer would have to have absolute confidence not merely in the tory leanings of a majority of the court, but also that those judges would permit themselves to be guided by their political predilections and dismiss the case. They would be hard pressed to do so, for the writ will allege only that the defendant neglected his duty to the plaintiff's loss, not why he neglected it. Nothing will be said about the Stamp Act or unstamped paper. On its face, the writ should go to further pleading, and it is for the defendant to bring forth the defense that due to the action of the Boston mob, stamps were not available and without them clearance papers could not be issued.

But how does the defendant's lawyer, once he decides against the risk of filing a demurrer, establish these defences? The most obvious answer is to plead specially, not a common practice in colonial Massachusetts. In answer to the plaintiff's writ, the defendant would plead that it was unlawful for him to pass clearance papers without affixing stamps to them, and either that the plaintiff refused to purchase the stamps or that stamps were unavailable due to no fault of the defendant's.

In a nonpolitical case, a plaintiff might well demur to this answer thus framing a legal issue for the court. In our action of the Boston merchant against the collector of the port, however, the plaintiff will not demur and the defendant's attorney knows it. Rather the plaintiff would plead over by denying generally the facts stated in the answer, thus bringing the pleadings to a close and moving for trial by jury. Once the jury is impaneled, and arguments can be offered, all options are within the election of the plaintiff's attorney. He may either deny that his client refused to purchase stamps* or claim that stamps were unavailable (playing on whig suspicions that imperial officials had received the stamps and were hiding them until the controversy abated), thus creating issues of fact for the jury, or he may argue that the collector neglected his duty when he refused to issue papers without stamps because the stamp act was unconstitutional and he was not bound to obey it. Quite likely with a good whig jury the defense might choose the latter argument adding to the discomfort of British officials. Today the argument that the collector neglected his duty when he obeyed the Stamp Act would create a question of law for the court, but not during 1765. A Suffolk county jury could express popular dislike for the Stamp Act by returning a verdict of "guilty" and, in theory at least, would be holding that, as a matter of law, the Stamp Act was unconstitutional.

Because of the political implications of a holding on the issue of constitutionality, the defendant's lawyer (who quite possibly would be the solicitor general or another crown official) might not plead specially. Rather than answer the writ with a specific defense, he would plead the general issue, that is, "not guilty." The legal question and the evidence would not change; the trial would be much the same. But at least the whigs would not have the satisfaction of having the constitutional issue exposed by the specific pleadings. It would be hidden by the general issue, depriving the trial of some propaganda value.

Remarkably, the same rules of pleadings would have led to opposite

---

* Such denials did not involve perjury. The burden of proof to sustain his answer is on the defendant, and the plaintiff's lawyer would be arguing or denying that the defendant sustained that burden. Besides, at that time neither the defendant nor the plaintiff was competent to testify and there might be no direct evidence on the question. To be certain, a writ might be drawn alleging a date when no other witnesses were present. If witnesses had been present on other occasions when the plaintiff requested unstamped clearance and they testified to that fact, the plaintiff's attorney might still argue that the defendant had the burden of proving there had been no change of mind. If witnesses were testifying to the plaintiff's intention at the exact time the clearance was passed, they probably would not be whigs but persons easily discredited (e.g., other customhouse employees) by an effective lawyer. Yet it does seem that perjury was a factor in customs litigations. Thomas Hutchinson stressed it strongly in 1769, warning that witnesses who swore falsely in vice admiralty were guilty of an indictable crime even if they believed the court to be unconstitutional.[42]

strategies in that second hypothetical case posed by Hallowell and Sheaffe: a ship cleared without stamped paper and then seized by the royal navy for sailing without proper documents. There the defendant could have turned the tables on the plaintiff by pleading specially. Again the action would be case, not trespass, for although the defendant had acted and did pass the clearance papers, the damages were consequential, not direct.[43] To be actionable, the plaintiff would have to allege some fault on the part of the defendant, perhaps carelessness: his neglect to fix stamps to his documents as a result of which the ship's papers were not in order, the ship was seized and condemned, to the loss of the plaintiff in such-and-such amount. The defendant cannot demur, as the writ is good on its face. If he pleaded the general issue he could, at trial, establish all his defenses: the knowledge of the risk on the part of the plaintiff, the unavailability of stamps, the fact that there was no alternative to unstamped paper, his fear of mob violence, and the advice of the attorney general. But the merchant then could have put the Stamp Act on trial before a whig jury with the inevitable result. Rather the defendant would plead specially, denying that the loss was the consequence of his carelessness: that knowing stamps were unavailable the plaintiff had nonetheless demanded clearance and thus had assumed the risk of loss. Had the plaintiff demurred to this answer, Chief Justice Hutchinson would have dismissed the writ on the grounds that the answer was a good plea in abatement. True there was a factual element here—whether the plaintiff, by demanding clearance, had intended to exonerate the defendant from liability for the consequences—and the plaintiff might argue that the question should go to the jury. Chances are, however, that Hutchinson would have disagreed. But what else could the plaintiff do except demur to the answer? If he filed a replication he would have to support his allegation of carelessness by specifying the fact that the defendant failed to use stamps. In other words, he would be saying that the Stamp Act was constitutional. No whig seeking to embarrass the British government or to harass the customs officials would take that position. Even if his only purpose was to collect damages he would not want to proceed before a Boston jury, for he would be asking it to hold, as a matter of law, that parliament had auhority to impose an internal tax on Massachusetts. True, the decision would be implicit under the general issue, but it would not be on the record and a competent lawyer could persuade the jurors that it was not a serious consideration. It would be on record if the defendant pleaded specially and no whig would want to touch it. This consideration may be another reason why Trowbridge advised Hallowell and Sheaffe that if they certified the unavailability of stamps they would not be sued.

Of course, none of these writs was ever filed. The Stamp Act was repealed and, as ships that had sailed without stamps were never seized, the crisis passed away. But the idea was there and, as Hallowell and Sheaffe proved, customsmen were nervous. They felt harassed and had good reason to examine the law before they acted. For almost a century the grand and traverse juries of America had been reluctant to support their work with either indictments or convictions. That problem had been solved when Great

Britain introduced the vice admiralty. Now, in the 1760s, the juries added a new dimension to London's political difficulties in America, showing that they could be offensive as well as defensive instruments for keeping British officialdom off balance. Although parliament was aware of the challenge, there was little it could do short of destroying the American jury system.[44] True, private-law suits used as a criminal-law type sanction to harass imperial officials were more irritating than fatal and their use against revenue agents was not likely to destroy either the empire or the customs service. Still, a lesson had been taught, and as the constitutional controversy intensified and spread, the whigs found that there were other ways that the legal institutions which they controlled could be used to protect friends and punish enemies.[45]

5

Juries Lie Open
to Management[1]

THE USES OF
THE GRAND JURY

Lawyers of today would make much of the conditions of prerevolutionary law that gave the whigs control of the civil traverse jury, even more of those that rendered the bench impotent. It is nonlawyers, especially historians of the era, who have missed the tale that lies behind the conditions of law existing in colonial Massachusetts and how those conditions made the civil traverse jury an effective weapon in the hands of militant whigs.

For lawyers the contrast is with today. Had Thomas Hutchinson and his colleagues the power of our judges to grant new trials, to enter judgments notwithstanding the verdict, or to entertain motions to dismiss actions as contrary to law or based on insufficient evidence, the civil traverse jury in colonial America could not have been employed as a criminal-law type sanction. For nonlawyers, on the other hand, the Irish comparison may tell more. In eighteenth-century Ireland once again we find the opposite of eighteenth-century Massachusetts Bay.

If we can say, and it seems fair to say it, that Massachusetts jurors were returned by the whig or popular party, then it is as fair to say that Irish jurors were selected by the tory or government party. The lord lieutenant appointed the sheriffs and the sheriffs chose the jurors. While Boston town meetings kept a sharp eye on potential veniremen, returning generally safe whigs, the sheriffs of Ireland maintained an even sharper eye, returning not only safe men but men of the very safest type. With control of the criminal jury, Irish government left its opponents no room to control the civil. A whig weapon in Boston had no antiimperial role to play in the politics of British-ruled Dublin.

If the juries of Ireland were friends of government, so were the judges. It was they who brought partisan considerations into the halls of justice. A number were impartial and must have their due, but it is surprising how many were not. Their bias mattered more on the Irish assizes than it would have on a Massachusetts circuit, for Irish juries were told to take their law from the court and Irish juries were prone to listen to Irish judges. If a jury were stubborn and its law wrong the court did not have to accept the verdict. In Ireland there were grounds for overturning judgments and civil courts had some authority to grant new trials.[2]

Legal institutions should not be taken for granted. It does not do to think of judges and of juries and to limit their impact to what occurs in courthouses or at individual trials. In considering the Irish comparison we must be certain that we realize the full scope of the Massachusetts difference. The whigs of New England had more leverage than might be thought. They were not confined to employing the civil traverse jury as harassment against officials responsible for the enforcement of imperial statutes. It was also a means to discourage people who otherwise might obey those laws or aid in their execution. The whig civil jury could be a sanction not only to punish the active but make them passive and multiply the neutral. We need not dwell upon examples; one or two illustrate the point.

When British troops first landed in Boston their officers applied to the local justices of the peace to implement the Quartering Act. That statute, enacted by the imperial parliament, directed the province to furnish the enlisted men with "fire, candles, vinegar," and other items, including rum, which local magistrates were to procure. It was an extremely unpopular law and the justices of Boston refused to enforce it. General Thomas Gage thought they were afraid of the whig crowd. We may think they were following their whig predilections. Yet it is possible that we as well as Gage could be wrong. The magistrates may have been afraid, not of the whig mob but of the whig jury. It is unlikely that even a militant tory justice would have dared requisition candles or firewood without first being certain he was immune from an action of conversion or trover. An appropriate statute by the Massachusetts assembly, not by parliament, might have reassured him, and that was precisely what he would never get. Of course a tory justice knew that if he confiscated property and the legislature refused to pay the army would. The magistrate did not worry that the owner would not be reimbursed. He worried that the owner would sue him for the seizure even if reimbursed. The payment by the military might be a good defense at law, but the plaintiff could always avoid a ruling on the issue by denying the fact, thus bringing the question before a whig jury. The imperial government might enforce its quartering statutes in Ireland, but in America even its friends could be frozen into political inactivity by the thought of a Massachusetts jury.[3]

So too could a British army officer. There are many recorded instances of military officers hesitating or failing to act when they considered the American jury. One extreme but memorable incident may give us a hint of the apprehension that they felt. It offers only indirect evidence as the officer does not state his fear, yet we may make a reasonable guess.

Following the Boston Massacre, when Captain Thomas Preston of his majesty's armed forces lay in a Boston cell awaiting trial on the charge of murdering unarmed civilians, a rumor began to circulate among local tories and army officers that the whigs were likely to lynch him. The fear was groundless, but one concerned tory was James Murray, a justice of the peace. He wrote to Lieutenant Colonel William Dalrymple, the commander of the British troops stationed in Boston, offering "as a Civil Magistrate, to escorte two hundred men of your Regiment from the Castle to Town when the Trial is to come or sooner when ever there is notice of danger to him from the Mob."[4]

Dalrymple was an outspoken critic of civilian authorities in Boston, accusing even Lieutenant Governor Thomas Hutchinson of being indecisive, fearful of whig threats, and fearful of their law. Now, invited to act on his own authority, it was Dalrymple's turn to become a legalist and raise issues about authority that he implied were cowardly when raised by Hutchinson. "I do not," he explained, "suppose that the Lieut Governor will call the aid of the military, and I think without his interposition, the proposal of the single Justice would not be a sufficient authority to act upon." Dalrymple told Murray that he could lawfully act only "when called on by the Civil power"; it was not for a military officer to ask the magistrate for help. Murray accused him of quibbling. "What greater Violences in any state, tollerably civilized, can be committed than what have lately been committed in Boston?," Murray asked, "which violences I do in my Conscience believe will be crowned with the Murder of Captain Preston, if there is no military force to support a Magistrate and the Laws for his protection."[5]

James Murray was a loyalist whose support of the military and defense of the imperial laws made life somewhat unpleasant for him at that moment. It was he who had rented barracks to the army when the council refused to furnish public housing, a fact Samuel Adams did not let the people forget. He had, therefore, good cause to be annoyed. There is reason to suspect that Dalrymple hesitated to accept his offer not because he was concerned about overstepping constitutional bounds, but because he feared for his personal liability. The lieutenant colonel knew he would not be reprimanded should he act to save Preston as necessity required, even if the rescue touched off a rebellion. Far more likely to have worried him was the possibility that some civilian would be hurt. Then he might be sued in trespass with whig jurors deciding whether or not he had proceeded with legal justification. James Murray could have shared his fate, for magistrates who employed force were not immune from criminal charges. They had to act within law and could even be indicted for willful murder if a death resulted not justified under the circumstances.

Of course there was another consideration. Had death or even an assault occurred, Lieutenant Colonel Dalrymple might have found himself in the same cell with Captain Preston. Suffolk county grand juries were quick to indict British officers, even for telling their men to defend themselves when attacked by a mob.[6] The very fact Preston was in jail points up the legal dilemma faced by British soldiers in prerevolutionary North America when they took action unpopular with the whig majority. His military colleagues garrisoned in Ireland must have been astonished when they heard the news.

Preston had been acting lawfully when the soldiers under his command, frightened by a menacing mob, discharged their muskets in the direction of the whig crowd, killing six rioters.[7] We may be certain that in Ireland he would never have been put on trial, quite likely he would not have been indicted or even delivered to civilian authority. British troops in Ireland during the eighteenth century fired on people with far less provocation than did those involved in Boston's "massacre." One of Boston's martyrs was an Irishman named Patrick Carr. Before he died he told the attending physician that "he was a native of *Ireland*, that he had frequently seen mobs, and soldiers called upon to quell them; . . . that he had seen soldiers often fire on the people in *Ireland*, but had never seen them bear half so much before they fired in his life."[8] When troops fired in Ireland it was usually the victims and their relatives who alone regretted it. Even during the twentieth century trial before civilian jurors was not likely. Dublin's Bachelor's Walk Massacre occurred on 26 July 1914. As in Boston no one is sure if the order to fire was given by an army officer, but the troops did fire, killing three and wounding thirty-two others. An inquiry led to the dismissal of the police officer who had asked for military assistance, not to a common-law criminal trial as in Boston.[9]

In England, the law would have appeared much like that of prerevolutionary Massachusetts, but the outcome would have been closer to that of Ireland. Less than two years before the Boston Massacre, London's massacre of Saint George's Fields had occurred. Troops guarding the prison in which John Wilkes was lodged were confronted by a huge crowd. A magistrate may or may not have read the riot act, but he does seem to have started the shooting. Six persons were killed—one, not part of the mob, was ruthlessly hunted down and shot by soldiers under the command of an officer—and many were wounded. A coroner's inquest found that the officer and two of his men had committed murder. The grand jury indicted only one of the soldiers, who was acquitted on trial. Another grand jury returned a bill of willful murder against the magistrate who gave the order to fire. He too was acquitted. More significant was the attitude of responsible government officials. "His Majesty highly approves of the conduct of both the officers and the men," Lord Barrington, the secretary at war, announced in a message to the army after the massacre. In the event "any disagreeable circumstances" should arise, he wanted the soldiers to know, "they shall have every defence and protection that the law can authorize and this office can give."[10]

It may be as has been claimed that law made Barrington's assurances necessary: the soldiers could have been hanged had they not been obeying orders and Barrington was telling them they had been acting lawfully.[11] Yet no one thought a similar proclamation necessary after the Boston Massacre, and it can be doubted if any official would have dared issue one. That Barrington in London had published such a letter to the troops was noticed by the whigs of America. The massacre of Saint George's Fields became a sensation in the colonies, "the more so," as Bernard Bailyn observes, "when it appeared that convictions of the guilty soldiers by normal processes of the law courts were being quashed by the government."[12]

Whig orators and pamphleteers could be bold condemning Barrington for they knew when a similar event occurred in North America he would remain silent, he would not mock them with another letter. Their control of the grand and criminal traverse juries would mute his confidence and make his army squirm. If grand jurors wished to indict a tory it did not matter that the attorney general of Massachusetts would not cooperate. They either drafted the bills themselves or employed a whig lawyer to advise them. The courts had to accept their presentments. True, the attorney general often nullified their actions by entering a *nolle prosequi*, but when the whigs were insistent he could not do so and innocent men were forced to languish in a Boston jail until they could be heard in a tribunal that entertained defenses.[13]

Of the three juries, the grand and the criminal and civil traverse, it is the grand jury that marks the contrast in the conditions of law for most non-lawyers, as it is with the functions of that body they are most familiar, but it may be asked how much they understand. We must not think in twentieth-century terms; we must think of eighteenth-century institutions. Then grand juries performed a wider task than they do for us; they were entrusted with powers of supervision now vested with either the police or other local regulatory agencies. It was they, for example, who dealt with health regulations and similar matters, a fact giving the popular party remarkable control over local affairs, especially when we note that there was little or no appellate machinery for questioning grand-jury decisions.

One illustration should be sufficient to demonstrate the grand jury's potential usefulness in the struggle against imperial rule. The town of Albany, New York, sought land occupied by army barracks. General Gage was willing to negotiate a sale or exchange, but the bargaining moved too slowly for the provincials. At the next sitting of the grand jury the barracks were declared a public nuisance. A whig crowd then sallied forth and tore the barracks down. We might agree with the British military and think that a lawless mob had been raised. Local New York law put the event in another context. Thanks to the grand jury's action the crowd was a *posse comitatus*, the people had been assisting authorities to remove a legally designated nuisance, they had not been rioters.[14]

We need not rely upon uses that might surprise us to demonstrate the effectiveness of grand juries. The expected was much more common in pre-revolutionary America. Whig control of the Massachusetts grand juries, especially the grand jury of Suffolk county, which included the town of Boston, meant that it was impossible for the king's officials to obtain indictments against persons accused either of political offenses such as rioting or of violating imperial statutes such as the revenue laws. It was refusal to indict that gave the whigs a veto over the enforcement of criminal law. That veto in turn rendered imperial criminal law virtually impotent. New England whigs did not fear arrest even for serious offenses of the type that would have left their Irish counterparts rotting in dungeons or swinging from gallows.

If Thomas Hutchinson was disturbed by grand-jury political indictments, and he was—"I am sure," he once exclaimed, "the most innocent are the least secure"[15] —he was more alarmed when there were no indictments at all. As chief justice he felt the sting of grand-jury contempt, a rebuke that caused him, for one of the few times in his life, to lose his composure in public.

There were many frustrations but they need not all be considered. Again we may note one example to measure the depths of a tory's despair. It involved the law of seditious libel and Hutchinson's inability to enforce his interpretation of that law.

The story of the whig press in prerevolutionary America has been told often—the articles it printed and the role it played. Historians have noted that no newspaper editor went to jail, yet few have asked why. It must be evident that there were laws being violated. The *Boston Gazette* (which tories called the "Weekly Dung Barge") would have been suppressed dozens of times had it been printed in Dublin. There was a will in Boston, however, and there were tories who dearly wished for prosecution. Thomas Hutchinson was their spokesman, and on no other issue of positive law did a major official in eighteenth-century North America try so hard to enforce imperial rule than did Hutchinson through his efforts to punish seditious libel.

Hutchinson failed utterly; he did not even have the satisfaction of making whig editors feel uneasy. There were two legal impediments that stood in his path and there was no way he could avoid them. First, there was the substantive law. Neither he nor any other official, imperial or local, had authority to censure whig newspapers or to confiscate editions containing offensive material. The current British doctrine of freedom of the press consisted "in laying no *previous* restraints upon publication."[16] Under the law Hutchinson had to prosecute after the offense was committed, he could not act to prevent it, and that fact presented him with his second handicap, the grand jury. American whigs were incapable of recognizing anything offensive in a political statement or newspaper article supporting their side of the controversy with the mother country. Try as he might, the chief justice simply could not obtain an indictment.

Hutchinson did try. No one could gainsay his stubbornness. In term after term he warned of the dangers of seditious libel and in term after term the grand jurors could find no seditious libel to present. Without the jurors' support there was nothing imperial officials could do to silence the whig press, even though the law seemed very clear from their perspective and they were certain that if whig newspapers could be at least curbed, colonial opposition to British policy would have been less unified and less violent.

When we recall that nothing made life in North America so uncomfortable for the "friends of government" and gave more encouragement to the "friends of liberty" than the uncensored press, we better understand the frustration of Thomas Hutchinson when he last addressed a grand jury on the topic of seditious libel. Knowing he was defeated, the chief justice abandoned his usual reserve and wrung his hands in public. "I do not mention the matter of Libels to you, Gentlemen," Hutchinson told the March 1769 term of the Suffolk county superior court. "I am discouraged!—My repeated Charges to Grand Juries, on this Head, both in this and other Counties, being so entirely neglected. How these juries have got over their Oath, I tremble to think,—but I have discharged my own Conscience. In short, I have no Hope of the ceasing of this atrocious Crime, but from finding that they multiply so fast, are become so common, so scandalous, so entirely false and incredible, that no Body will mind them; and that all Ranks among us will treat them with Neglect."[17]

It was a lame performance and a lame hope; the spectacle of a strong man in a powerless office. No contemporary Irish judge would have shared Hutchinson's helplessness. On one occasion, a chief justice of Ireland summoned a prospective publisher to his house and told him, "if you print or publish what may inflame the mob, it behoves the judges of the land to notice it; and I tell you, by the Eternal, if you publish and misstate my expressions, I will lay you *by the heels*."[18] We may imagine what the next edition of the *Boston Gazette* would have said had a Massachusetts judge threatened it—even in private.

In Ireland, the *Gazette* would not have printed another edition. At the time of the American Revolution, the Irish press, though not free of private libel, was free of seditious and criminal libel. The government could and did suppress it. If it did not care to be troubled by judicial proceedings, either house of parliament might take direct measures to protect itself against seditious commentary. During 1783 when the lord mayor of Dublin reluctantly acted to arrest certain publishers for sedition, the commons sent its sergeant-at-arms with a guard of soldiers to take charge of the prisoners. Ten years later opponents of a bill for Catholic relief sought to prevent passage by claiming that Catholic leaders as well as the United Irishmen were responsible for a recent series of outrages. A secret committee of the house of lords was created to examine the evidence. The Dublin branch of the United Irishmen published resolutions asserting that the powers assumed by the secret committee were unconstitutional. By vote of the house, the chairman and the secretary of the Dublin branch were fined £500 each and sentenced to six months in Newgate prison for breach of parliamentary privilege.[19]

The courts of eighteenth-century Ireland seem to have been especially well protected from unfriendly comment. Shortly before the Rising of '98, Peter Finerty was indicted and tried for being the printer and publisher of a false, scandalous, and libelous letter addressed to the lord lieutenant. The letter had criticized the conviction and execution of William Orr, found guilty of administering the United Irish oath. During the trial the point was made that Finerty's newspaper, *The Press*, was the only one in Dublin not in the pay of the government, and his defense attorney, John Philpot Curran, told the jury that "the only Printer in Ireland, who dares to speak for the People, is now in the dock." The attorney general, on the other hand, explained "that he had been directed by the Executive, to prosecute the traverser for printing a most malicious, false, and scandalous libel on the government of the country; . . . a libel that rendered the Judges in the administration of justice odious and contemptible in the eyes of the people." Thus both sides, the prosecution as well as the defense, implied that the government, by putting Finerty on trial, was employing the judicial process to silence the one independent newspaper in Ireland. The jury found Finerty guilty of criminal libel. He was imprisoned for two years, ordered to stand in the peltory for one hour, fined £20, and required, on release, to give security, "yourself in 500 £ and two sureties in 250 £ each for your good behaviour for seven years."[20]

More effective than even the criminal sentence was enforcement of an act of parliament providing that "a Printer convicted of a libel shall be deprived of his property in the paper in which it had been inserted."[21] As a result Finerty lost *The Press*. In eighteenth-century Ireland, it would seem, the government could not only punish sedition, it might become the owner of any newspaper that dared question its policies.

An additional point is that Finerty's offensive comments were about the prosecution of William Orr, one of the most notorious in the long history of notorious Irish trials, "one of the blackest of judicial murders."[22] Even the friendly biographer of Ireland's judges called it "proverbial for injustice."[23] When the judges of Ireland employed seditious libel laws to protect their reputation they did not always have much to protect.

The comparative lesson goes further than realizing that the trials and convictions of William Orr and Patrick Finerty could not have occurred in Massachusetts Bay. The important contrast was not in the certainty of Irish indictment or the severity of penalty, but in the composition of grand juries and the role they played in the criminal process. Even more than in Massachusetts they were the organ of county and local administration, controlling the police and the prisons, for example. Though in theory similar to American grand juries, in practice they differed considerably for they were drawn primarily from the ranks of the great landowners and, besides representing a special constituency, were remarkably corrupt, even for Ireland. Irish judges willing to speak for official policy knew that when they addressed grand juries their words were heard with more sympathy than were those of Thomas Hutchinson when he pleaded with Suffolk county grand juries to uphold imperial law. During 1792 when Catholics were petitioning for representation in parliament, the government employed grand-jury addresses to revive religious animosity and recreate political opposition to the movement for Catholic emancipation. Little wonder that three years later, when Protestant Orangemen were driving Catholics from county Armagh, grand juries refused to return indictments.[24]

It might be thought that so reliable a prop beneath imperial rule would satisfy Dublin castle. Grand juries were, of course, employed by the government and were certainly dependable, but that is not our story. It was not how Irish grand juries were employed but how often they were not even utilized that would have made a Massachusetts tory weep. The contrast is more startling than most lawyers could imagine.

THE USES OF THE GRAND JURY

The grand jury in Massachusetts Bay might be whig controlled and antiimperial yet for the enforcement of criminal law it was constitutionally necessary. It had to be utilized or there could be no prosecutions at common law. The same institution in Ireland was reliable and imperial but these attributes were apparently not enough for the British rulers. They wanted it to be constitutionally unnecessary as well, and that is precisely what they made it. They could and they did ignore the grand jury when it suited them for there were means of prosecuting individuals without indictments, means not available to the attorney general of Massachusetts.

The Irish government, if it wished to bypass the grand jury, could obtain bills of attainder from parliament as in the case of James N. Tandy, charged with high treason. It would not do to think of this process as an arbitrary abuse of legislative power. Long after American jurisdictions made attainder unconstitutional, Irish judges not only upheld its validity, they recommended its use. When seventy or more political prisoners led by Arthur O'Connor offered during 1798 to make a confession if the lives of Miles Byrne and Oliver Bond, both convicted of treason, were spared, Lord Lieutenant Cornwallis consulted with the chief justice and the attorney and solicitor generals. The lawyers were unanimously opposed to a compromise. "When the Viceroy objected that under no circumstances was there a hope of a verdict against O'Connor and his companions, he was answered that more than one might perhaps be convicted, and that others could be proceeded against in Parliament. An attainder had much to recommend it."[25]

It was a remarkable argument and a revealing scene. We need not ask the politics of the judges to understand what had happened. There in some room of Dublin castle the leaders of Ireland's bench were called to a conference by the chief executive of the kingdom and asked to advise the government on how to deal with prisoners who might yet appear before their courts. They urged Cornwallis to prosecute, not be lenient, and if he had doubts about obtaining convictions, to ignore their tribunals and proceed by a method that made a mockery of the common law's role as constitutional guardian of the citizen's liberty. More remarkable still was the lord lieutenant's decision. On this occasion the notorious corruption of parliament worked against the government. Had the prisoners been prosecuted by attainder, public opinion in Great Britain would have assumed that the verdict was purchased and convictions might have done more harm than good. For that reason Cornwallis decided to accept O'Connor's offer.

Parliament had other functions besides attainder. Secret committees of the lords or commons could summon suspects to testify before them and if the answers were not satisfactory, order them sent to prison without indictment or trial. Before the government had the evidence to convict him of treason, Oliver Bond was dealt with by this process, committed to Newgate and fined £500 for breach of parliamentary privilege.

Perhaps the Irish power that would have most impressed a Massachusetts prosecutor was the government's practice of detaining suspects without preferring charges, holding them for indefinite periods, and releasing them only on bond. It was this technique that destroyed the leadership of the United Irishmen. Thomas Russell, one of their military commanders, was arrested in September 1796 and not freed until 1802, yet he was not brought to trial. John Keogh in Dublin and Charles Teeling from the north were charged with treason, but "they were never tried, as the informer who gave their names could not be induced to appear in court, and they were merely kept under lock and key."[26] Some men were imprisoned so long, Arthur O'Connor asserted, they lost both their health and their fortunes. Indeed, imperial law as enforced in eighteenth-century Ireland vested even greater discretion in its agents; suspects could be held after they had been tried and acquitted. O'Connor's brother is an example. When finally released, his affairs were ruined.[27]

Arthur O'Connor himself was arrested at least three times. On the first occasion, February 1797, he spent six months in Dublin castle on charges of seditious libel. One trial that he did face illustrates yet another technique of British justice in Ireland. He was tried not in Dublin but in England. Unhappily for his prosecutors a long list of English and Irish admirers appeared as character witnesses, testifying that they disliked the Irish government as much as did O'Connor. The jury, following the judge's instructions, found O'Connor not guilty. "He was leaving the court in triumph, but the Government knew their man too well to let him go so easily. He was at once re-arrested on another charge, and was restored to his quarters in Dublin Castle."[28] Confined for the third time during 1798, O'Connor was not tried and not released until June 1803.

If the circumstances were desperate, and in Ireland they often were, there might be no arrests at all. A military officer or sheriff who executed a suspected rebel could expect to be protected by special act of parliament. Then too, there was the power of court-martial, for the army might not surrender a prisoner to the grand jury but try him itself. Wolfe Tone, taken at sea wearing a French uniform and expecting to be treated as a prisoner of war, was charged with treason and condemned to death by a military court. The proceedings seemed irregular even to Ireland's judges.[29]

Had British officials in prerevolutionary Massachusetts just one of these means for bypassing the grand jury they might not have stemmed whig sedition, but they could have disrupted it. Surely several whig leaders would have seen the inside of a jail. Yet we may wonder if they would have remained there long. On the one occasion when the British found a device for prosecuting without an indictment, the whigs demonstrated that their control of local institutions allowed them to nullify even the strongest of imperial statutes. Ironically, the tool they employed to quash the proceedings was the very grand jury the British were seeking to circumvent.

Long before they arrived in Boston during 1768, the commissioners of the customs, a new board created by London to enforce the trade laws in America, were told that they could not obtain presentments from the Suffolk county grand jury. Faced with an institutional dilemma, they first sought to persuade the Massachusetts attorney general to proceed by information. That was a criminal process, often employed by the crown in Ireland, permitting prosecution at common law without grand-jury indictment. They selected what they surely thought was a perfect test case. John Hancock, the leading whig merchant, had ejected from the steerage of his brigantine *Lydia* a tidesman assigned to supervise the discharge of cargo. Customs agents could inspect topside, Hancock insisted, but not below deck. The controlling statute gave customs officials a right "freely to go and remain on Board until the Vessel is discharged of the Lading." Attorney General Jonathan Sewall not only refused to file an information, doubting its propriety in such a case despite the impossibility of obtaining an indictment, but ruled that the statutory words "on Board" meant "on the Deck." Customs officials going into "the hold" without a warrant were acting unlawfully.[30]

Sewall's interpretation of the statute was a common lawyer's opinion, justified by common-law rules of strict criminal construction, and it may be doubted if an admiralty court, following civil law, would have been so narrow.[31] The commissioners of the customs asked London to overrule Sewall's opinion and order him to proceed by way of information. When their request was rejected, the last hope was gone that Massachusetts common-law courts could be used to enforce the Revenue and Trade Acts.

Just why the commissioners wanted Sewall to proceed at common law is not clear. If they could not obtain a favorable grand jury, they stood little chance of obtaining a sympathetic hearing from a criminal traverse jury. Violations of laws that did not lead to indictments were even less likely to produce convictions.

It is possible that the commissioners preferred common law because of the alternative. They were newly arrived in Boston, visible symbols of the recently enacted and thoroughly detested Townshend revenue duties, and to begin prosecutions in vice admiralty might have made them more unpopular than they were. The stubbornness of the grand jury and Sewall's ruling left them no choice. Deciding to prosecute in the civil-law court, the commissioners were to learn by the first case that while the vice-admiralty jurisdiction might be free of the common-law traverse jury, it was not free of the common-law grand jury.

John Hancock was again the libelee. This time the ship involved was his sloop *Liberty*, seized by the commissioners for landing Madeira wines without paying the duties required by imperial law.

After the sloop was condemned in an *in rem* proceeding conducted at vice admiralty and "adjudged forfeit for breach of the Acts of Trade," the commissioners of the customs seem to have decided on a further test of legal strength. If so, John Hancock was a logical target. He had led the opposition ever since the commissioners landed at Boston, "both with his political attacks and with the example of his own violation [of the customs statutes]. If the law could be applied strictly to him, others would fall into line."[32]

The procedure that the commissioners selected was harsh and surely to a whig seemed to be high toryism at its most arbitrary extreme. They brought an *in personam* proceeding against Hancock, based on evidence supplied by one of their tidesmen. Their authority was the American act of 1764 permitting informations to be filed on the criminal side of vice admiralty against persons "assisting or otherwise concerned" in landing without the payment of duties. On this occasion there was no difficulty persuading Jonathan Sewall to draft the information. He was acting as advocate general in admiralty rather than attorney general and by naming himself "informer" became entitled to one-third of the judgment. The other two-thirds were divided equally between the crown and the governor of Massachusetts Bay.

When the matter came to trial it resulted in one of the splendid fiascoes of eighteenth-century British imperial law. The jurisdiction of vice admiralty had been invoked and was performing the precise task for which it had been created. But it would never render judgment; the whigs were to demonstrate again that a local institution could check the course of an imperial institution. When the prosecution's key witness offered his testimony, John Adams for the defense attempted to impeach him. Joseph Maysel could not testify, Adams argued, because he was a fugitive from justice, guilty of a "heinous crime," a fact that at civil law could be proven by oral evidence. The admiralty judge ruled against Adams, relying on the common-law rule that a witness could not be impeached for such cause unless the moving side produced a written record of his conviction.[33] Unimpeached, Maysel was competent to testify, and conceivably his evidence might have been enough to justify Hancock's conviction. It was at this point that the whigs displayed their resourcefulness and the admiralty procedure, with its long delays, came to their aid. Before Maysel's evidence could be taken down, the Suffolk county grand jury indicted him for perjury, and he fled the province. The case against Hancock was then dropped. It is not certain just why Sewall felt he could not proceed, but a good reason seems to be the failure of evidence, especially the departure of Maysel.[34] If so, and it is likely, the whigs had engineered a splendid little coup, demonstrating that when necessary they had one technique that could be used to frustrate tory judicial proceedings even at vice admiralty.

Though we may marvel at the difference we must not misinterpret it. The salient point is not that in Ireland a grand jury would have failed to come to Hancock's aid. It is that in Ireland the government would not have cared. The testimony of a witness was unnecessary. If Hancock needed a lesson there were ways to teach it without adhering to traditional forms of law.

But if we seek the depths of the imperial dilemma we should return to Thomas Hutchinson and the law of seditious libel. After he became governor of the province, an article appeared in the *Massachusetts Spy* calling him "a monster in government . . . a USURPER," and arguing that "any act of assembly consented to by him, in his pretended capacity of governor, is *ipso facto*, null and void and consequently, not binding upon us."[35] The accusation was more than a libel, it was a seditious repudiation of the imperial government's authority over the colony.[36] Hutchinson was certain the offensive words were indictable: "the attorney general thought it so plain a case that no grand jury could, upon their oaths, refuse to find a bill," he explained.[37] The attorney general was wrong. The grand jury, packed with men whom Hutchinson described as the "most active persons in encouraging the opposition to government," refused to indict.[38]

Once more the lesson had been taught that seditious libel against the imperial regime was not a crime in Massachusetts.[39] Indeed, the affair proved more than embarrassing for Thomas Hutchinson. The failure of imperial law gave the whigs new incentive to mock him and his office. "It is stupid," a correspondent wrote Boston's *Evening-Post*, "to insinuate that the dignity of the post a man sustains, entitles him to that awful reverence which would suffer him to destroy the commonwealth, without a murmur."[40] The words were directed against Thomas Hutchinson but the idea was applicable to any imperial official, even George III. Thanks to the veto of the grand jury, the whig press during the prerevolutionary era had the time and the freedom to prepare Americans to think new thoughts.

Although Thomas Hutchinson was not about to concede the struggle, he did take the lesson to heart. Later that same year he acknowledged it was useless to ask a Massachusetts grand jury to indict a newspaper editor for sedition. The *Spy* printed a second article, so scandalous that the governor became suspicious. The piece, he concluded, had been written in hopes of exacerbating him: if he would react in anger, perhaps attempt prosecutions, the whigs would have an excuse to "raise fresh riots and other disorders."[41] Political judgment and knowledge that indictments could not be obtained warned him to ignore the matter, but the offensive article had been addressed directly to King George, an insult Hutchinson could not overlook.[42] The problem was how to deal with it yet avoid the humiliation of going to the grand jury. Not knowing the answer, the governor wrote London for advice.[43]

While Hutchinson awaited the cabinet's reply, the *Spy* and other whig newspapers kept the matter before the public primarily by pressing the argument that calumnies such as the one it had printed went unpunished when published in the British press.[44] In one issue, for example, the *Spy* copied an intemperate address to George III that had originally appeared in the *Middlesex Journal*, observing that "*No notice was taken of it, either by the king, his privy council, Lord Mansfield, or the Attorney General.*"[45] The legal thrust of the argument could not be denied: English juries were almost as reluctant as American juries to punish sedition in the public press.[46]

It would be easy to brush aside the *Spy*'s argument as mere whig bombast, but to do so would miss the dilemma of Thomas Hutchinson and his fellow colonial governors. Implicit in the *Spy*'s editorial was the constitutional assumption that Americans were entitled to the procedural and institutional safeguards of English law. We must emphasize words. The *Spy* meant *English*, not *British* law. It would, American whigs implied, be a violation of their right to equality with other British subjects to punish a libel in Boston that England's attorney general would have ignored.

The argument was historically sound and legally convincing, yet it overlooked legal and political realities: time had overtaken the old constitution, Boston was no longer an extension of the English world where common law could function as at Westminster Hall or on the county assizes. If political realities were taken into account, comparisons should not be between Boston and London, but between Boston and Dublin.

It would not be until 1774 and passage of the intolerable acts that the British government acknowledged that to maintain its rule in the American colonies it would have to substitute part of the Irish for part of the Massachusetts constitution.[47] In the meanwhile, advised not to prosecute the *Spy*, the governor was told to make the best of a deplorable situation.[48] The British cabinet still envisioned Boston as New England, not New Ireland. American newspapers continued to publish Irish sedition while being judged by English law.

That was the dilemma faced by royal officials in prerevolutionary America. Left with American law they were expected to find English solutions to Irish problems.

6

In Defiance of the Threats[1]

THE CRIMINAL
TRAVERSE JURY

It is not law alone that we compare. It is lawlessness as well. If conclusions seem to be forthcoming we must not be in haste to draw them. Individuals may disagree about the meaning of law and lawlessness: whether the imperial rulers of eighteenth-century Ireland imposed a lawless rule or whether the whigs of Massachusetts were an irresponsible coterie of reckless law-breakers. It is a matter of definition and how one views the legitimacy of constituted power. During 1769 a militant whig such as Samuel Adams would have said that the imperial rulers of British North America were a lawless breed. Two centuries later we would be hard pressed to agree. All our evidence indicates they were rulers who ruled by the rule of law.

The legal theory of the whigs is more confused and more easily misunderstood. A look at events tells one story, an examination of attitudes may reveal another.

When we search for attitudes, not superficialities, there is a piece of evidence so pertinent that it must be reiterated: no man or woman was ever lynched by a political mob in prerevolutionary America nor was secret murder a weapon of the whigs. Historians have been intrigued by these facts. As noted before, some say they help explain how the American Revolution differed from other insurrections, especially on the European continent or in Ireland. It is a matter we must consider again. There is another side to the same evidence, however, that bears on the question whether the whigs of Boston and elsewhere were a lawless force. It reveals a feature of the American revolutionary scene obscured by tales of mobs and violence: the whig majority, even in Massachusetts, though using tar and feathers to punish political offenses left common-law crimes to the regular courts. They might not control those courts, at least not the judges, but they possessed enough leverage over the criminal process not to feel alienated from the judicial system and to abandon the established forms of law.

It would not do to exaggerate and suggest that everyone felt secure in life and property. Where a whig saw law, a tory might see anarchy. The fact that the mob was so easily raised obscured from view the equally pertinent fact that all the courts of law remained open and that no one interfered with the service of judicial process. Tories concentrated on the tar, the crowd, the threat of violence, and concluded that there was no law. Early in 1771, a London newspaper printed a letter purporting to come from Boston that painted a very gloomy picture.

> What is now the State of Society in the Town of Boston, that assumes to itself the Name of the Metropolis of America? No respect is paid to Government; no sense of Subordination; and from the want of some superior Power to cling to for protection, every Man is suspicious of his neighbour; whilst a few Demogogues harangue the People, and under the name of Liberty, lead them on to actions of violence, cruelty, and oppression; and Society seems altogether without order, without government; the Magistrate shrinks from his duty, and the Demagogues presume to dictate to the Judges on the seat of justice.[2]

We may assume the letter was not written by a lawyer, since lawyers had a taught perspective from which to judge judicial independence and even militant tories knew that in nonpolitical cases they could have their day in court and obtain a fair hearing for their clients. At almost the very time the letter was being published in London, Jonathan Sewall in Boston was saying that the picture it presented was false and that the opposite was true. There was no better spokesman for the tory side than Sewall, at least among the lawyers. He was a defender of Francis Bernard, a confidant of Thomas Hutchinson, the crown-appointed attorney general of the province, and a future loyalist exile. "I will venture to affirm, there is no spot on the globe, where *publick* and *private justice* is administered with more *equal impartial* hand, than it is here," he wrote of Massachusetts; "this is so evident, that the man who is not convinced of it, I am sure, must be blinded by *prejudice* and passion."[3]

We must be impressed by Sewall's words. He was writing at a time when Ebenezer Richardson was locked in the Boston gaol. Had Sewall not been so astute a lawyer he might have used the Richardson case to modify his assessment and score points against the whigs by showing it was not always impartial justice that they sought. When convictions served a political purpose the whigs made every effort to obtain them, and when failures occurred they would talk menacingly of more direct measures—threats that never materialized into action. The prosecution of Ebenezer Richardson is perhaps the most extreme instance of the Boston mob attempting to win a political conviction. Richardson, a native of Massachusetts, was associated with the customs service. While the commissioners of the customs would later deny he was one of their officers, Richardson had for many years, according to the *Boston Gazette*, "been known by the name of THE INFORMER." Whether he deserved that title or not, there is no doubt that he was an outspoken tory and one of the most unpopular men in whig Boston.[4]

On 22 February 1770, for reasons that need not concern us, Richardson was chased into his own house by a whig mob, composed chiefly of schoolboys. Surrounded on all sides, with the crowd growing every minute, his lower windows smashed, he took refuge on the second floor, alone except for George Wilmot, a sailor employed in the customs service, who had come to his aid. As the threats grew more menacing, Richardson panicked. Thrusting a gun through a second story window he fired a charge of bird shot, eleven of which struck and mortally wounded a young German boy named Christopher Seider (or Snider).

Reaction to the shooting was swift; bells started ringing and the mob broke into the house, seizing both Richardson and Wilmot. "The first thought was to hang him up at once," Thomas Hutchinson wrote, "and a halter was brought and a sign post picked upon, but one who is supposed to have stirred up the tumultuous proceedings took great pains and prevented it."[5] Richardson undoubtedly came nearer than anyone else in prerevolutionary Boston to being lynched. That he was not, Judge Peter Oliver believed, was evidence of how completely whig politicians controlled the mob and manipulated it to serve their purposes. "As they were pretty sure that they could procure a Jury for Conviction," he wrote, "so some of the Leaders of the Faction chose that he should be hanged by the Forms of Law, rather than suffer the Disgrace of Hangmen themselves."[6]

Still, the mob was to have a say as to Richardson's fate. Dragged through the streets of Boston and "cruelly abused by the Mob," he and Wilmot were taken before Justice of the Peace John Ruddock, who ordered them sent to Faneuil Hall. There in the presence of a thousand persons—a scene that must have foreshadowed revolutionary Paris or the mass trials of Communist China—they were publicly examined by four magistrates and committed to jail. When the boy died, they were indicted for murder.

There is no word to describe Richardson's trial except "political." The jury, selected in the same manner as a civil jury—by the town meeting—was composed largely of whigs who had been subjected to an unprecedented barrage of propaganda including a funeral that drew what for Boston were massive crowds. Great pressure was placed on the judiciary to rush Richardson into the dock. The whigs wanted their man tried before passions had time to cool. The judges professed to be frightened and when the Boston Massacre occurred, arousing public opinion to fever pitch, the task of protecting Captain Thomas Preston and his men was made easier by diverting attention to Ebenezer Richardson. He was offered as a sacrifice to political emotions.

By forcing the authorities to place Richardson on trial earlier than had been planned, the whigs had a victory of which to boast. They had humiliated the court and brought the agents of imperial rule to heel, but the judicial process had to run its course and there were surprises no one anticipated.

When Richardson appeared for trial he was without counsel, and reported he had been unable to find a lawyer willing to assume his defense. The court postponed the trial while it tried to persuade an attorney to defend him. Finding none willing to volunteer, the judges ordered Samuel Fitch, the advocate general in admiralty, to appear. Fitch attempted to withdraw, the judges would not accept his excuses, and finally he agreed, "saying that since the Court had peremptorily ordered him, he would undertake it, but not otherways."[7]

Today the most striking feature of this affair might be the reluctance of lawyers to appear for the defense. To an eighteenth-century English barrister it would have been that Richardson was entitled to representation. In England he would have been accorded none of the privileges for which he contended in Boston. In Massachusetts the right to legal counsel in felony prosecutions was a civil protection that no one questioned, no matter how unusual it might have been in the mother country. Proof comes not from the fact that an unwilling Samuel Fitch was forced to assume the duty. Proof lies in the attitude of the court and the public. The judges professed to have rushed to trial out of fear of mob violence, yet indicated no hesitation to postpone the proceedings when Richardson said he had no lawyer.[8] The whigs might suspect a delaying tactic, but no clamor was raised. It mattered not that the right was nonexistent in England. In Massachusetts not even a Richardson could be forced to defend himself without counsel.

When the case finally came on for trial the defense argued that Richardson had been attacked in his house by a mob. His life endangered, he was privileged to protect himself with reasonable force according to the circumstances, killing if necessary one or more of his assailants. The prosecution offered evidence to show that the crowd was composed of schoolboys; rowdy perhaps, but their insults and stonethrowing never endangered Richardson's life. Besides, the victim was a mere boy. If, in fact, anyone threatened Richardson it surely was not young Seider. By way of rebuttal, the defense replied that the youth was part of a Boston mob, an illegal enterprise. Thus, if his death was not justifiable homicide, it was at most only manslaughter. Even if Seider was an innocent bystander, it was contended, Richardson could not be guilty of murder as he had been justified in defending himself by firing his gun at the crowd. Thus the issues were all of a legal nature. There were no factual disputes, except the question of Seider's role as a part of the mob. Whether he was active or passive was immaterial. Richardson might be found guilty of manslaughter; that was the limit.

The judges agreed with the defense. Each instructed the jury "that if what the witnesses on both sides had sworn was believed," the homicide "could amount to no more than Manslaughter." Judge Peter Oliver went further, telling the jurors that as the homicide was justifiable Richardson had committed no offense, not even manslaughter. If anyone was to blame it was "the Promoters of the Effigies and the Exhibitions which had drawn the people together and caused unlawful and tumultuous assemblies." Or it was the justices of the peace who failed in their duty to suppress Boston mobs. It was a bold condemnation from one who later claimed the judges were in danger of assassination and the shouts of the crowd in the courtroom soon told Oliver of its displeasure. While he was delivering this charge and instructing the jury "that the Case was *justifiable Homicide*," Oliver wrote, "one of the Rabble broke out, 'D—n that Judge, if I was nigh him, I would give it to him'; but this was not a Time to attempt to preserve Decorum; Preservation of Life was as much as a Judge dared to aim at." [9]

Preservation of life was beyond the capacity of Peter Oliver and his fellow tory judges that day. Despite the clear instruction to the contrary, the Suffolk county jury returned a verdict of guilty of murder. The verdict, Judge Oliver later observed, "was guilty of tenfold greater Criminality than the Prisoner." [10]

While available documents do not furnish precise information about the chronological sequence of events, it seems apparent that the defense immediately moved for a new trial. The judges, not certain what they could do, adjourned without passing sentence. The delay stretched out over the summer, for it was not until the first week in September that the court took up the motion for a new trial. The jurors were called back and, in the presence of counsel, individually examined. What the judges learned only increased the legal dilemma. "The Foreman," Oliver recorded,

> with a sullen Pride of Revenge, replied "that he was not obliged to give any Reasons for his Conduct." The others shewed less of a Temper of sullen Revenge. One of them said "that he should have acquitted the Prisoner, had the killing happened in the Night instead of the Day." In either Case, the Law had justified the Prisoner. Some of them acknowledged, that, as they past thro' the Mob, from the Court to their Apartment, they were called upon to bring the Prisoner in guilty. One of the Jurors declared, that he thought him innocent, & had persisted all Night in that Opinion, against the united Sentiment of the other eleven; but in the Morning, after a tedious whole Nights Fatigue, his Bretheren overperswaded him to unite with them, by urging this Argument upon him, vizt. "that the Court had delivered their Opinion, in Law, that the Prisoner was innocent, & that his Life would be saved; therefore, that it was not worth while to stand out any longer." These Arguments alone, he said, prevailed with him to join with the others in their Verdict.[11]

The court was faced by a legal issue almost insolvable under eighteenth-century adjective law. The jurors had been exposed to a courtroom mob unusually noisy even by Boston standards, but it would not be said that the shouts of the crowd had influenced the verdict, for they had not been "mentioned in the Jury Room." [12] They had also found the facts in substance with the prosecution's case and might have held Richardson guilty of manslaughter, a verdict that every judge but Peter Oliver had told them was legally acceptable. The difficulty was that eleven members of the jury either misunderstood the law or deliberately misled the twelfth man. When they assured him (according to his testimony) that "if the verdict was not agreeable to Law the Court would not receive it," they were saying either that the judges could lower the offense from murder to manslaughter or they could grant Richardson a new trial. Indeed, if whig legal theory were carried to its logical conclusion, and the jurors were makers of law as well as triers of fact, then the argument used by the eleven jurors to win over the twelfth was practically a mandate for the court to grant a new trial.

Richardson's attorney brought to the court's attention some precedents sustaining the motion for a new trial. Unfortunately for the defendant, all of the cited opinions dealt with noncapital cases. English law did not permit new trials in capital cases. A criminal jury was as powerful as a civil jury; a criminal court, however clear the law, could neither direct the jury to return a verdict of not guilty nor overturn a verdict of guilty. The judges had no option but dismiss the defense motion. No matter what may have been said or intended in the jury room, the verdict delivered to the court had to be accepted. Moreover, as it was a capital case, the superior court had been the tribunal of original jurisdiction, and there was no higher court in Massachusetts to which to appeal.

With the jury omnipotent and themselves helpless to discharge a man they thought innocent of the crime for which he had been convicted, the judges might well have washed their hands of the matter, leaving Richardson to the constitutional mercy of the executive branch of government. Instead, they showed again that their fear of the Boston mob was not as great as sometimes depicted. They could have sentenced Richardson according to law and put Governor Hutchinson in the center of a political controversy by forcing him to suspend execution until the king's pleasure was learned. To save Hutchinson this embarrassment, the court postponed judgment, reprieving Richardson to await the king's pardon.

The pardon was a matter of course. Once London learned the facts, there was no doubt the home government would set Richardson free. Yet what should have been a simple, straightforward procedure proved complicated and exposed still more defects in the administration of justice within the eighteenth-century British empire. It was over a year after Richardson's conviction before Hutchinson received word of the pardon. Unfortunate as that delay may have been for Richardson himself (who had to remain in jail fearing for his life should the mob stir onto the streets of Boston) the form of the pardon proved even more unfortunate as it led to a further delay. Perhaps due to the difficulties of long-distance communication or, more likely, to British bureaucratic inefficiency, the pardon was written for a convict already sentenced and awaiting execution, not precisely applicable to Richardson, upon whom judgment had not yet been pronounced. It was a technical problem, but Hutchinson was a stickler for technicalities. While Richardson languished in jail, the acting governor wrote to London for clarification.[13]

Here we see another glaring deficiency in the administration of imperial justice during the eighteenth century. Due to distance it was more than a year after Richardson's conviction before his pardon arrived in Boston, and it had been prepared in a form that caused colonial officials to doubt their authority to execute it without supplemental documentation. In Ireland the problem would have been avoided. There, due perhaps to a longer history of political strife, the lord lieutenant enjoyed a larger degree of federal autonomy. Not only could he issue pardons on his own warrant over his signature, he could do so without consulting London (with convicted felons still enjoying the right to appeal to the king when he failed to act). The governors of the more distant colonies, in contrast, enjoyed less executive discretion.[14] Subject to closer supervision by the British ministry, they even depended on it to prepare the proper legal documents and when technical errors were made could not correct them. To expedite matters Hutchinson proposed that a royal warrant be issued authorizing him to pardon Richardson under the provincial seal. London would not sanction even this limited precedent and it was not until ten months after the first pardon had arrived that final, satisfactory instructions were received. By then Richardson had been in jail for two years.

There are other contrasts between the conditions of law in Massachusetts and in Ireland dramatized by the Richardson trial. One of course is the jury. It was selected by the same sheriff who selected the grand jury—"by our accuser" as John Philpot Curran said in one case.[15] "I cannot but feel the peculiarity of your situation," he told another criminal traverse jury. "Not a jury of his [the defendant's] own choice, which the law of England allows, but which ours refuses; collected in that box by a person, certainly . . . not very deeply interested in giving him a very impartial jury."[16] Curran's son tells us that when an Irish defense attorney of his father's generation addressed jurors in criminal trials, he knew he was speaking to "men whose feelings of humanity and religion were kept under by their political prejudices—that they had already foredoomed his client to the grave—that, bringing with them the accumulated animosities of past centuries, they came less to try the prisoner than to justify themselves, and make their verdict the vote of approbation upon the polities of their party."[17]

It must not be thought that jurors came only to convict. Juries could not only be packed with government supporters, they could be packed to favor individual defendants—defendants of a type who often would have been at a disadvantage before a Massachusetts jury. In one case described by Sir Jonah Barrington, an Irish judge, an army officer was indicted for a notorious murder. With the cooperation of the sheriff, ten fellow officers were placed on the jury, and although the presiding judge almost urged a verdict of guilty, they quickly returned a verdict of justifiable homicide.[18]

Richardson not only faced a hostile jury because he was of the government party, he saw his jury intimidated by the mob in open court. In Ireland the intimidation would have come from the other side. A few minutes after Curran rose to speak for the defense in the trial of Archibald Hamilton Rowan, charged with distributing a seditious pamphlet, a guard of soldiers was brought into the courthouse by the sheriff.[19] Surely the government intended to impress Rowan's jury in the same manner that the Boston crowd tried to impress Richardson's.

There are many examples of managed trials and partial justice in the history of eighteenth-century Ireland. One which involved a legal issue similar to Richardson's was the conviction of William Orr.[20] He was accused of administering the United Irish oath to two men, arrested, and kept in prison for over a year before he was brought to trial. At first the jury could not agree and was locked up for the night. The next morning it attempted to leave Orr to the court's mercy, a solution the judges refused to accept. At their insistence the jury rendered a verdict of guilty, accompanying it with a recommendation of mercy. Curran, who as usual was the defense attorney, moved for an arrest of judgment, producing a deposition signed by one juror stating facts similar to those in the Richardson case. The juror alleged that he had resolved to acquit Orr and had agreed to concur with the other eleven only when told that a verdict of guilty would not be followed by Orr's execution. Irish judges, unlike Massachusetts judges, could grant new trials.[21] They did so seldom and in Orr's case denied Curran's motion. He tried again and submitted additional depositions by jurymen relating that the panel had possessed two bottles of strong whiskey, and that some members "became very sick and unwell, which occasioned their vomiting before they gave their verdict."[22] The judges rejected these affidavits as well. William Orr was executed, professing his innocence and claiming that he had been convicted on the evidence of an informer.[23]

The Irish gaol, Curran asserted to the jury during his defense of Orr, was an eighteenth-century Irishman's "only place of security."[24] With the whig mob always a potential threat, we may doubt if Ebenezer Richardson felt secure as he waited for over a year in Boston's jail.

Thomas Hutchinson, now newly appointed governor of the province, also did not feel secure. Even after Richardson's proper pardon was safely in hand, he proceeded with caution, waiting seven days, until Bostonians were at their annual town meeting, before bringing the defendant into court to plea on bended knee, his release. Richardson was then set free and immediately fled the town. "The Rabble heard of it," Judge Oliver wrote, "and pursued him to execute their own Law upon him, but he happily escaped."[25] Perhaps taking their cue from Oliver, some historians have also suggested that Richardson would have been lynched had the mob caught him. Such speculation is doubtful, even if the Boston mob had been only half as well controlled as these same writers suggest.

Ebenezer Richardson had served his purpose and the whigs were far from bloodthirsty. Richardson alive was worth more than Richardson dead. Lynched he would have been a tool for tory propaganda to blacken the image of Boston in other colonies, already nervous over the excesses of the mob. Alive, Richardson represented justice cheated by a tory placeman, a picture the British completed by appointing him to the customs service at Philadelphia.[26] A political doggerel ridiculing the tory judges and distributed as a broadside by Paul Revere (with his engraving of the Boston Massacre) was more in keeping with the whigs' objectives.[27] We need only note the fate of Wilmot, Richardson's coindictee. He more clearly than Richardson seems to have been identified with the imperial customs service yet he was released without trial. His innocence was manifested. Whig law might demand its pound of flesh but it wanted the flesh to be guilty flesh.

Yet it has been claimed that Richardson's trial represents a miscarriage of justice, an example of the breakdown of law in prerevolutionary Massachusetts.[28] Perhaps it did; certainly for Richardson himself. If so, the perspective of history requires that we ask where the law broke down. The answer cannot turn on historical evidence but on our own bias, our legal prejudices or legal predilections, the predilections of a tory or the predilections of a whig. Of course a tory thought the Richardson affair a miscarriage of justice, and we may assume such even of a tory who would have said the trial of William Orr was fair because the politics were on the right side. A whig would have disagreed, and it is the whig perspective that deserves our attention. It has been either ignored or misunderstood for too long.

To appreciate whig attitudes it is best to recall a contemporary case, one in which another local man was accused of murdering several persons on board a ship off the Massachusetts coast. Because the common law did not extend beyond the line of low tide, the only tribunal in which the defendant could be tried was a special admiralty court, commissioned to hear charges of felony and piracy on the high seas. Thomas Hutchinson, a member of the court, was convinced of the man's guilt, yet due to another defect in imperial law had to order the defendant released from custody. The statute creating the special admiralty court had been so carelessly worded that doubts about its jurisdiction were created, and the judges felt they had to return a verdict of not guilty.[29]

Tories should have been disgusted at parliament's slovenly draftsmanship. Perhaps some were, but surviving records indicate greater disgust was expressed toward the fact that the defendant's escape from the penalty of the law was hailed by the more extreme whigs as a political victory. The special court of admiralty sat without a jury and the acquittal was more than the vindication of a man who may have been innocent.[30] It was a triumph of constitutionalism over prerogativism.[31] For tories with a different legal perspective than Jonathan Sewall, the glee of the whigs was disturbing evidence of the corruption of law and the judicial process. "We have become so long habituated to illicit trade," Thomas Hutchinson wrote on another occasion, "that people in general see no evil in it. Justices and grand juries, whose business it is to suppress riots and tumultuous assemblies, have suffered mobs against informers and to rescue seized goods, to pass unnoticed. Breach of law in one instance leads to others, and a breach of oaths at the customshouse is one cause of so frequent perjuries in judicial proceedings."[32]

The incidents of lawlessness troubling Thomas Hutchinson arose from disrespect for imperial law, not all law. It was a tory view that breaches of imperial law would lead inevitably to breaches of local law and a breakdown of respect for law in general. The whigs disagreed. True some had cheered at the release of a suspected mass murderer. Their dread of admiralty jurisdiction had blinded them to the possibility that the defendant might well be guilty and that there was no other court in which he could constitutionally be tried. True also, the same political passions blinded many whigs to the fact that Ebenezer Richardson might have been a bad tempered but legally innocent victim of circumstances. Concentrating on political manipulation of the judicial process, a tory would compare the two cases and conclude that justice in prerevolutionary Massachusetts was tainted; not so the whigs. Better, they would have said, to remember Ebenezer Richardson in company with John Mein, the editor of North America's best tory newspaper. He too had been attacked by a Boston mob. As he fled, a gun he was carrying accidently discharged. Seizing on a rumor that Mein had deliberately fired at the crowd, prominent whigs led by Samuel Adams obtained a warrant to arrest the editor "for having put innocent people in bodily fear" by shooting at citizens "lawfully and peacefully assembled together." [33] Mein never returned to Boston and soon his newspaper, a thorn in the side of the whigs, ceased publication. Thus was the predictable course of law reversed in Boston: the victim of the mob was forced to flee the law, while those who might have persuaded the crowd to desist obtained the law's warrant.

When we contemplate the fate of Ebenezer Richardson we might recall William Orr in Ireland or even the suspected murderer released by the special court of high admiralty. But if we think as a whig might have thought we recall John Mein. In both cases the whigs of Boston, by manipulating those instruments of the judicial process that they controlled, had rid themselves of a troublesome tory without a lynching.

7

Unless Laws Are Enforced[1]

THE LEGITIMACY OF WHIG LAW

A realist, not given to exaggeration, Thomas Hutchinson did exaggerate when he predicted a complete breakdown of law and order. The whigs did not agree for theirs was a different perspective. If Hutchinson was right, so were they. There is no evidence in prerevolutionary Massachusetts of a deterioration of respect for law, at least for that part of the law not associated with the political struggles. Fornicators and other criminals, when detected, could be as certain of indictment and conviction as they would have been in less turbulent times. If whigs committed perjury in those situations described by Hutchinson, they did not think that they were subverting the forces of law; rather they thought of themselves as frustrating the operation of illegal or unconstitutional statutes. Nor did they feel alienated from the criminal courts or the judicial process as did their counterparts in Ireland. When there were placemen, customs informers, other "enemies of liberty," or an Ebenezer Richardson accused of crimes, the whigs demanded the full penalty, as long as it was imposed by the common-law jurisdiction and not by admiralty or some other imperial court.

The premises upon which positive law was based in prerevolutionary Massachusetts Bay became one of the causes dividing the colony from the mother country. Regarding law as a reflection of community consensus, expressed through the community's control of its own institutions, the whigs of Massachusetts Bay could not help but define "law" differently than did British lawyers and laymen. Massachusetts whigs read Blackstone's *Commentaries* with comprehension and acceptance, but when Blackstone defined law as "a rule of action" he was not employing their definition.[2]

What Americans thought of law was significant as they also believed themselves capable of understanding and applying it, especially constitutional law. John Adams, for example, said there was no need for judges to instruct Massachusetts jurors on constitutional principles as they learned them from birth and knew them as well as any lawyer.[3] "It has been observed," he wrote, "that we are all of us lawyers, divines, politicians, and philosophers."[4] Every colonial American, George Otto Trevelyan has concluded, "thought himself, a lawyer." "Look into these papers," an English attorney general is reported to have remarked in 1768, "and see how well these Americans are versed in the Crown law. I doubt whether they have been guilty of an overt act of treason, but I am sure that they have come within a hair's breadth of it."[5]

Confident in their own knowledge of the law, Massachusetts whigs were not willing to have imperial officials interpret it for them. Colored as their views of constitutional law were by whig principles, their view of positive law also became colored. As the prerevolutionary controversy intensified, two distinct legal theories began to emerge. On one side was the imperial law applied by the royal officials and endorsed by the judges of the provincial superior court. On the other was whig law, supported by most of the local institutions of government, including the inferior courts, the magistrates, and the grand and traverse juries, both civil and criminal.

It is important to note the scope of whig law. It was not merely constitutional, but positive law as well. It should not be confused with the constitutional debate. Within the context of prerevolutionary America, there were at least three levels at which the argument of a dual law or a two-law theory could operate.

At the highest level was the constitutional argument. When American whigs asserted that the British parliament had usurped constitutional power when it passed statutes such as the Stamp Act, they were also asserting that such laws were unconstitutional and that their resistance was not only legally justified, it was constitutionally legitimate. Under the Stamp Act, for example, the colonial courts were not supposed to function without stamps as every legal document required them. Americans refused to purchase stamps and local judges were faced with a dilemma: whether to keep the courts closed or do business in defiance of an act of parliament. In Virginia, Edmund Pendleton resolved the problem by considering his oath as a judge to determine cases according to law. Since, he believed, parliament had no authority to enact a statute such as the Stamp Act, he could not regard it as a valid law. It would be a violation of his oath if he did not hold court for certain purposes and he did so, despite the act of parliament.[6]

There was nothing new in Pendleton's legal theory. It harked back to an earlier day, to men such as John Pym and John Hampden who had bid defiance of Charles I by appealing to the same constitution. The concept of whig positive law should not be confused with this ancient English tradition. Whig constitutional law stood on more honorable and historically defensible ground than did whig positive law.

Nor should whig law be confused with another American legal idea that has been employed to lend a coloring of legitimacy to self-help or violence. The

Regulators who took over the backcountry of South Carolina represent this strain of law. The British government, for political and constitutional reasons, refused to extend the provincial court system into new areas recently settled following the defeat of the Cherokee nation. Law-abiding citizens were being harassed by outlaws due to the absence of legally constituted processes of justice. In the name of law and order, in the full glare of public notice by issuing signed proclamations and acting in the open, community leaders set up a system of punishment and brought the situation under control. Whig law was not of this type; it represents no dichotomy between acceptable and objectionable violence, between the desire for order and respect for constituted authority. The mobs that tarred and feathered the customs officials of Boston in 1769 should not be equated with the vigilantes of San Francisco in 1851. If legal theory can distinguish both from southern lynch law, it does so for different reasons.

Unlike the vigilantes of California, the whigs of Massachusetts Bay had no quarrel with the quality of local justice or with the abuse of the executive power to pardon. Unlike the Regulators of South Carolina, they cannot be described as people who "unlawfully took up arms to establish lawful authority."[7] What characterized whig law was that in one degree or another it always represented or was protected by some agency of "lawful authority." Thus whig law must also not be confused with underground law. It was the whigs' control of certain government institutions for enforcing law—the justices of the peace and the jury—that gave whig law its claim to legitimacy, not any theory that it was people's law or majority law.

Whig law was not like Irish hedge law or Irish Republican law, it was not a law for settling disputes between whigs unwilling to resort to the royal courts. When it operated it did so against imperial law, and it was this fact that brought the constitutional argument into play. Indeed, the very nature of the British constitution—that it was unwritten and rested on custom, precedent, convention, and force—lent a degree of uncertainty to the powers of parliament. When opposing the claim of parliament to tax them or to subject them to its laws, the American whigs could assert that they were defending the ancient constitution and the rights of Englishmen. Their arguments were no mere sham thanks to the premises of the British constitution. They could be as sincerely held as the opposite theories of parliamentary authority championed by Lord North, Lord Mansfield, Thomas Hutchinson, and Francis Bernard.

The consequence for British rule due to the inherent vagueness of the constitution—its inability to furnish definite answers to controversies concerning rights and power—was not restricted to the lofty heights of constitutional debates. It filtered down from organic law and had impact upon both public and private law.

Whig law was first introduced into the constitutional controversy ·by American opposition to parliament's Navigation and Revenue Acts. Whig domination of local colonial juries made it difficult for imperial customs officials to obtain convictions for violations of these statutes. To remedy this defect in what it regarded as justice, parliament created vice-admiralty courts in all the North American provinces with judges appointed directly from London. As admiralty law was civil law, not common law, the court sat without a jury and factual issues were resolved by the judge. Free of any local veto in the form of a jury consisting of local men and with officials appointed and paid by the crown, the vice-admiralty courts should have been an effective and sympathetic instrument for the enforcement of imperial law. They never lived up to official expectations. From the very beginning, customs officers, for whom the vice-admiralty jurisdiction had been designed, discovered that the vice admiralty had not made them independent, of either local government or local law.

The vice admiralty was, of course, bound to be unpopular. It was, after all, a revenue court. More to the point was the fact that even in criminal matters it sat without a jury, becoming one of the prime symbols of British tyranny. Some colonial lawyers avoided association with vice admiralty, and customsmen could not always find competent attorneys to prosecute cases. In a few colonies there was no advocate general—the crown law officer in admiralty—while in others only young, inexperienced lawyers were willing to accept the position.[8] Massachusetts was an exception, for Jonathan Sewall and later Robert Auchmuty were capable lawyers, yet even with them at hand, the vice-admiralty court did not function as efficiently as its planners had hoped. It might supplement the common-law jurisdiction and be free of the common-law jury, but it was not free of the common law itself.

English constitutional theory came to the aid of American whig law in its struggle against the vice admiralty. When the British parliament created these courts it modeled them on the English high court of admiralty and on its jurisdiction. As a result, the colonial vice admiralty inherited admiralty's constitutional relationship to common law, and after both Cromwell's revolution and the Glorious Revolution, that relationship was one of inferiority. Common-law prerogative writs held the upper hand in England, and in Massachusetts the common-law courts stood in the same constitutional position as those in the mother country. For example, when an advocate general, seeking to collect revenue on smuggled molasses, had potential witnesses jailed by the vice admiralty to force their testimony, the superior court intervened with writs of *habeas corpus* and the prisoners had to be released.[9]

More menacing to the customs service was the king's bench power to stay vice-admiralty proceedings by writ of prohibition. As the highest common-law tribunal in the colony, the local superior courts assumed the same jurisdiction that in England was vested with king's bench. Even the tory judges of Massachusetts Bay were willing to issue such writs when they found that the imperial vice-admiralty court overstepped its prerogatives and was treading on common-law jurisdiction.[10] To do so was a constitutional tradition made sacred to English lawyers by Lord Coke's great struggle against admiralty at the beginning of the previous century, and an eighteenth-century American tory could be as dedicated as most whigs to the constitutional principle of the common law's supremacy.[11] There can be, however, differences in the use of the writ of prohibition: differences in kind as well as degree.

In the province of Massachusetts, where the high-court judges were tories, the writ of prohibition was not employed indiscriminately to harass the vice-admiralty jurisdiction. For the writ to have been a weapon of whig law, the whigs needed control of the superior court, and only in Rhode Island and Connecticut, thanks to their charters and their politics, did the whigs have that advantage. In Rhode Island, legitimate proceedings in which the vice-admiralty court had cognizance could be and sometimes were stayed by whig judges. Rhode Island, it must be remembered, was not a royal colony and the governor was not appointed from London. As a result, when passing acts designed to nullify imperial law, the assembly was free of the gubernatorial veto. During the Stamp Act crisis, for example, it passed a statute to indemnify local officials who suffered by disobeying the act, a statute that may explain why that colony could keep its courts open without interruption despite the fact no one used the stamps required by imperial law. In royal provinces, the governor would have vetoed such a law, and even if the assemblies asserted by resolution their intention to compensate anyone who suffered loss resulting from opposition to the Stamp Act, few officials would have felt safe knowing that the governor could and would veto any act of indemnification.

Rhode Island courts derived their power from the local assembly and with the assembly safely whig, the judges had every encouragement to use the writ of prohibition to prevent enforcement of the imperial revenue code. On those occasions when they did so, it became a matter of court against court, one imperial and civil law, the other local and common law, one accepting actions it was competent to hear, the other issuing writs to stay those proceedings.

Such rivalry would strike today's lawyer as odd or chaotic, yet an educated eighteenth-century layman, versed in English constitutional history, would have seen it as both historically logical and constitutionally justified.[12] Any superior-court judge who stayed proceedings valid under parliament's revenue statutes could appeal to English constitutional traditions and few would question his principles. The appeal might be a sham, the application of principles might be partisan, but the argument was nonetheless effective as it had the ring of constitutional familiarity. A whig judge in Rhode Island who sided with a merchant against the enforcement of the trade and customs acts could employ English constitutional law to evade British statutory law, and, as a result, the collectors of import duties, seeking to seize contraband or to libel carriers of illegal goods, could not always depend on the court that had been specifically designed to give them a forum and validate their actions.

The use of whig law for political ends may not have always been legitimate as sanctioned by legal precedent, but between competing legal cultures it is acceptance that creates part of the legitimacy.[13] There is every reason to believe that the citizens of prerevolutionary Massachusetts, whether militant whig or politically neutral, subscribed to the uses made of whig law by their local leaders. If they accepted the constitutional premises that underlay opposition to British rule, they could also accept the constitutional premises justifying manipulation of the legal process to oppose that rule. The same constitution that provided a coloring of legality for Rhode Island judges when they issued writs of prohibition staying vice-admiralty proceedings made it legitimate for local magistrates to refuse to enforce imperial law or for local juries to refuse to convict violators of parliament's revenue statutes. There was, after all, a long legal history sanctioning such opposition even to the point of violence. As early as 1701 no less an official than the attorney general of South Carolina publicly attacked a customs informer "and struck him several times, crying out, this is the Informer, this is he that will ruin the country." [14]

The British, of course, did not think of American law as different from Irish law; they did not think of the governance of their empire in terms of bicentric power but of unicentric power applying one law laid down by parliament; not of competing legal cultures but of one legal culture applicable to all of their colonies. "It is not likely," Thomas Hutchinson explained, "that the American colonies will remain part of the dominion of Britain another century, but while they do remain, the supreme, absolute legislative power must remain entire, to be exercised upon the colonies so far as is necessary for the maintenance of its own authority and the general weal of the whole empire, and no farther." [15]

Such a view of the law—and Thomas Hutchinson spoke for many tories—made compromise with the whigs difficult and, worse, it sowed a rhetoric dividing them even further. When one side spoke of "law" the other did not always credit the sincerity. Hutchinson, for example, could not accept that whigs were arguing law when denying the cabinet's power to govern by executive instructions. During 1771, while Hutchinson was governor, the Massachusetts assembly requested that it be permitted to meet in Boston as provided by the provincial charter. Hutchinson replied that he had instructions to convene the assembly outside of Boston and was powerless to receive it in the capital until his instructions were changed. In a public "protest," the lower house remonstrated "against all such doctrines, principles, and practices, as tend to establish either ministerial or even royal instructions as laws within the province." [16] The whig theory was that the charter rights of Massachusetts were the "law" and could not arbitrarily be set aside by instructions; that the governor was bound by "law" to obey the charter, not the instructions. Forgetting that the British constitution was whatever could be plausibly argued and forcibly maintained, Hutchinson was annoyed by the assembly's argument. "The most unfair, delusive part," he complained, "was their equivocal use of the word 'law,' and their insinuating that the governor considered his instruction as authorizing him to act contrary to laws, which, without such instruction, would be in force." [17]

An official capable of thinking "unfair" the use of the word "law" to describe a whig constitutional argument surely could not think whig law to be "law" when opposition to imperial statutes filtered down to the lower levels of the judicial process. There was, for Thomas Hutchinson, only one correct definition of law. "We," he told the March 1769 term of the Suffolk county grand jury, "who are to execute the Law, are not to enquire into the Reason and Policy of it, or whether it is constitutional or not. . . . I mention this, Gentlemen, because, from my own Observation, both in this and some other Counties, I have found Juries taking upon them to judge of the Wholesomeness of the Laws, and thereby subverting the very End of their Institution."[18]

The chief justice was referring to whig juries ignoring imperial law and for a loyal king's man imperial law was "the law," there was none other. Massachusetts whigs would have disagreed, not only because they did not see "the worst Sort of Tyranny" arising from juries acting independently of the court, but because they had been taught by English legal history that a jury unwilling to play a subservient role was the best shield the people had against tyranny. Indeed they would go further, and even moderate whigs such as John Adams could argue that juries following whig rather than imperial law were obeying the constitution, not ignoring it. "As the Constitution requires, that the popular Branch of the Legislature should have an absolute Check so as to put a peremptory Negative upon every Act of the Government," he wrote, "it requires that the common People should have as compleat a Controul, as decisive a Negative, in every Judgement of a Court of Judicature." Adams was not only stating whig theory, he was stating whig justification. To use the jury for political purposes might be an abu⸱⸱ of the judicial system under most circumstances, but not when combating the government's pretensions to unconstitutional power.[19]

Contentions such as Adams's served to widen the gulf between whig and tory. Thomas Hutchinson criticized Massachusetts juries not for exercising unconstitutional independence but for ignoring imperial law when they disagreed with it. Law from the imperial perspective meant the command of parliament. For the American whigs it still meant Lord Coke's custom and right reason.

Even when whig law expanded to the point that it absorbed all the agencies of government and brought an end to imperial law in a colony, the British did not recognize it as a legal accomplishment, only as a political reality. By December 1774, matters had progressed to the point in Virginia where the governor, Lord Dunmore, was faced by the reality. Local law had taken over from imperial law.[20] Ordered by London to assert the authority placed in his hands by the charter, Dunmore replied that "the power of Government . . . is entirely disregarded, if not wholly overturned." The whigs, he reported, had control of the judiciary and were using the civil courts to force British merchants to lobby for a change in imperial law much as the whigs of Massachusetts had earlier used the courts to discourage enforcement of the customs statute. Worse, whig law had now emerged from being a counter to imperial law as it had been in Massachusetts. It had become for most people the only legitimate law.

> Independent Companies, &c., so universally supported, who have set themselves up superior to all other authority, under the auspices of their Congress, the Laws of which they talk of in a style of respect,

and treat with marks of reverence, which they never bestowed on their legal Government, or the Laws proceeding from it. I can assure your Lordship, that I have discovered no instance where the interposition of Government, in the state to which it is reduced, could serve any other purpose than to suffer the disgrace of a disappointment, and thereby afford matter of great exultation to its enemies, and increase their influence over the minds of the people.[21]

For Dunmore there was a "legal Government" and hence the forces opposing it were illegal. When he described the dominance of whig law he did not think he was describing law but rebellion, the very antithesis of law. Yet for over a decade such legal activities as he described had been law for the more active whigs. Now, by his own testimony, they had become the law for enough of the population to bring imperial law to an end. The king's writ would not run again in Virginia. Those who doubt that whig use of the juries was law rather than an abuse of the judicial process might ask themselves when whig law became law. It was based on the same premises in Massachusetts during the 1760s as it was in Lord Dunmore's Virginia a decade later. The Declaration of Independence made it no more legitimate in British legal theory; the Treaty of Paris did. The treaty was retrospective, recognizing the lawfulness of acts previously deemed rebellion. Surely the work of the Virginia associations of which Dunmore writes fall in that category. What is the difference between them and the Massachusetts juries who earlier brought in whig verdicts?

Historians have suggested many causes for the American Revolution— economics, nationalism, home rule, and the fact that the colonists and the mother country had advanced to the point where they no longer agreed on the imperial constitution. To this list should be added the fact that they no longer agreed on the definition of "law" itself.

The function of whig law was to oppose or harass the enforcement of that part of British imperial law that American whigs viewed as unconstitutional. The legitimacy of whig law did not arise from the fact that it was local law, or democratic law, or a constitutional defense against an unconstitutional exercise. Rather, its essence lay in whig control of certain institutions of legitimate judicial, legislative, and executive governmental machinery, and their control was constitutionally legitimate.[22]

It may now be trite to say that law is the command of the sovereign, but that was the definition of Lord Mansfield, the leading British jurist of the prerevolutionary era, and it was the definition he followed when pronouncing whig law unlawful.[23] For the sake of argument we may accept its validity and ask who or what institution spoke with a sovereign voice in eighteenth-century Boston. The house, the council, the majority of magistrates charged with suppressing riots, the town meetings, and all other institutions of local government supported the mob either by positive action or by refusing to proceed against it. They were constitutional institutions of government as legitimate as the governorship, the chief justiceship, or parliament itself.

In the functioning of eighteenth-century constitutional legality, local institutions defined the meaning of "law" as much as did imperial institutions.

Until 1764 there had been little conflict, for objectives in America and Great Britain were largely the same. After passage of the Sugar Act of 1764, local law and imperial law began an intense competition, and with each crisis the gulf grew wider. It was not the Treaty of Paris that gave whig law a retroactive validity nor was it any notion of popular sovereignty. It was the eighteenth-century British constitution, itself the evolution of many uprisings from that of the barons who drafted Magna Carta to the contemporary John Wilkes. That constitution defined law by viewing it functionally—in terms of institutions, the social harmony achieved by common submission to generally accepted procedures, and the restraint and purposefulness inherent in the customary law, the ancient law, the "good law" of bygone times.[24]

8

By Consent of the Council[1]

THE IMPORT
OF LOCAL CONTROL

If we seek the definition of whig legality, we must be bold—as bold as were the whigs themselves when they asserted it. It took more audacity than courage for whig jurors to snub the king's justices with judgments of local law. There was something to lose by following imperial law, nothing by defying the court. Jury verdicts were a form of resistance against British rule: the issue that made a whig a whig. It was when they attempted to enforce their own law that some whigs became nervous. Their most visible instrument of coercion called for risks not every whig relished. There were enough whigs willing to employ it, however, so that it was used and used frequently—used to an extent that showed the British more than recklessness. It demonstrated that there were Americans ready to question tory definitions of law itself.

That instrument of whig law was the mob, an instrument of enforcement a lawyer would find hard to league with the jury, yet joined they must be if we seek to comprehend whig legal theory. The jury and the mob, though law-minded people might think of them as opposite expressions of the popular will, one legal, the other illegal, for the whigs of Boston went hand in hand.

During 1766, just as the Stamp Act crisis was on the wane, Thomas Hutchinson recognized that the mob had introduced a new element into the definition of contemporary law. As yet he did not see the mob as an extension of whig or local law against tory or imperial law, but rather as a challenge to the law, a sort of veto the whigs could exercise over law enforcement. "In the capital towns of several of the colonies and of this in particular," Hutchinson wrote a former Massachusetts governor, "the authority is in the populace, and no law can be carried into execution against their mind."[2] The current governor, Francis Bernard, had reached the same conclusion. From one end of the colony to the other that same year he was confronted by mobs or potential

74

mobs ready to "rescue" goods or vessels seized by customs officials for violations of the Trade Acts.[3] In Falmouth, at the line of northern settlement, a mob roughed up the customsmen, kidnapped a deputy sheriff, and "rescued" undutied goods that the officers, armed with a Writ of Assistance, were attempting to seize. Offering a reward, Bernard admitted to the lords of trade that such gestures had "now become a meer farce of Government." No one dared reveal the offenders. They were, the governor knew, a majority of the town. "Formerly a rescue was an accidental or occasional Affair; now it is the natural & certain Consequences of a seizure, & the Effect of a predetermined Resolution that the Laws of Trade shall not be executed."[4]

In fact, so "natural & certain" were the consequences, that the potential of the mob could be as effective as the result. Earlier that same year a vessel carrying illegal tea arrived at Barnstable down on Cape Cod and the customs agent, Bernard predicted, would not intercept it. "He durst not make any use of his Intelligence," the governor wrote, "as in his attempting to make a Seizure, he would be sure to hazard his Life in a great degree."[5] "I doubt whether, at present, any custom house officer would venture to make a seizure," Hutchinson concluded.[6] Bernard agreed. "That there has been no rescue lately is very True; & the reason is that there has been no Seizure."[7]

Riots in prerevolutionary Massachusetts were directed at many other facets of imperial government besides the customs service and have been described by historians of that era. Their details need not concern us. Two of the most famous—the riot against Andrew Oliver and the sacking of Thomas Hutchinson's house—are sufficient to illustrate the clash between imperial law and whig law as that clash was personified by the mob.

Oliver was secretary of the province and later would be Hutchinson's lieutenant governor. In 1765 he was also the designated agent for distributing stamps under the Stamp Act and it was that office which made him the object of Boston's original whig mob, the first tory hung in effigy from the liberty tree. A brick building belonging to him was torn down "without Axes or Hammers," a building people called "the Stamp office," believing it was to be used for stamp business.[8] Then the crowd divided, most going to Fort Hill where they started a bonfire, others to Oliver's own house to find the agent. Instead of Oliver, they encountered Chief Justice Hutchinson and Suffolk county Sheriff Stephen Greenleaf who, drawing their swords, arrested a few members of the mob. News of this event brought the remainder of the marchers down from Fort Hill. The arrested men were freed "and the two great officers of State fled." The rioters "took Possession" of Oliver's house, "went from Top to Bottom satisfied themselves with Good Cheer broke all his Glass Windows &c. and Three very valuable Looking Glasses and then returned to Fort Hill Where they were entertained with a good Bon Fire and Wine in flowing Bowls and at Eleven Clock dispersed."[9]

On that day Boston not only experienced its first political mob but was introduced to "mob law" as well. Two high officials, the chief justice of the province and the sheriff of the most populous county, had asserted their authority and arrested some rioters, only to have their prisoners released and their offices treated with contempt by superior numbers. For several hours, Boston had belonged to the mob—a mob not only unchallenged but unhurried. More pertinent for presaging future events, loyal tory Andrew Oliver, realizing that imperial law left him unprotected, sent word to the whigs that he was resigning as stamp agent. No stamps would be distributed in Massachusetts Bay. The crowd had seen to that.

The sacking of Thomas Hutchinson's house twelve days later was another Stamp Act riot. There was a rumor current that Hutchinson, advising the ministry how to raise revenue in the colonies, had favored an internal tax. In fact he had opposed it, warning London of trouble ahead. Perhaps other motivations lay behind the attack, yet the Stamp Act was certainly a factor. It was, after all, why mobs were on the streets that month and everyone knew that, as lieutenant governor and chief justice, Hutchinson would enforce any parliamentary statute whether he approved of it or not.

That evening, as Thomas Hutchinson sat down to supper, the houses of some customsmen and of an admiralty-court official had already been menaced or invaded by the rioters, and the chief justice had little cause to think himself immune. He felt safe, however, believing friends who assured him that "I was become rather popular" with "the rabble." Thus when the mob appeared he was unprepared and could do little more than get his family to safety and flee himself before his house was taken over. The mob's freedom of action may seem remarkable today. Just as revealing was its leisure. Recently, without tools, it had paused to tear down Oliver's small brick building; now it remained until almost daybreak to destroy Hutchinson's mansion: time enough, as the chief justice himself recounted, to be certain that "one of the best finished houses in the Province had nothing remaining but the bare walls and floors. Not contented with tearing off all the wainscot and hangings, and splitting the doors to pieces, they beat down the partition walls; and although that alone cost them near two hours, they cut down the cupola."[10]

Whig lawyer Josiah Quincy, Jr., called Hutchinson's mob a "Rage-intoxicated Rabble," and other whigs such as John Adams expressed shock, yet no one would be punished.[11] This is one important fact. Another is that the same rioters that night had entered another house and destroyed vice-admiralty records before moving on to Hutchinson's. A third fact is that from just after the time the Hutchinson family sat down to supper to near daybreak the next morning, the mob stayed in one place, methodically destroying private property. These three facts help explain why mob law could be such an effective instrument of whig policy in prerevolutionary Boston. The question that needs to be answered is, what were the conditions of law that made it possible for the mob to roam at will, proceed unmolested, and remain unpunished despite the opposition of all tories and the shock of many whigs.

Statute law was certainly adequate in Massachusetts, at least as adequate as any place in the common-law world. Riot, an aggravated form of breach of the peace or, in one instance, an aggravated form of attack upon public authority was as clearly defined in Massachusetts law as it was in British law.[12] When twelve men armed with weapons or clubs, or fifty men armed or unarmed gathered together a civil officer could in the king's name call on the crowd to disperse. Once he did so—reading the riot act, so-called—they had one hour to depart before becoming rioters, subject to severe penalties upon indictment and conviction.[13] It was a serious crime, and one which significantly Hutchinson sometimes listed first in his grand jury charge, ahead of thefts, treason, murder, and even seditious libel.

Because the "riot act," for reasons that will be outlined, was seldom invoked, Hutchinson usually instructed grand juries by English common rather than Massachusetts statutory law. The common law prohibited riot, which was defined as an uprising of three or more people performing what Blackstone called "an unlawful act of violence" for a private purpose.[14] If the purpose was public the crime charged was not riot but treason. When the act was not carried out or attempted the offense was unlawful assembly and if some effort was made toward its execution it was rout. "For your Direction, Gentlemen," Hutchinson told the Suffolk grand jurors in 1765, "Riots, Routs, and unlawful Assemblies are where there are any Number not less than three, where they come with an Intent to commit some unlawful Act—if they take not one Step they ought to be punished for this Intent [i.e., for unlawful assembly]; if they move forward, it is a Rout; if they commit any one Act, it is a Riot."[15]

The law was clear, the definitions easily understood, and the penalties—up to a year's imprisonment with thirty-nine stripes every three months and forfeiture of all property—were severe.[16] The instrumentalities of enforcement were what provided the difficulties. There was no police force during those days; constables and sheriffs did not do what today would be called police work. The constables' job was to summon jurors, not to keep the peace. The sheriff and his deputies were available for making arrests, though not trained for much except serving writs. For maintaining peace Massachusetts law depended upon citizen participation. Once an unlawful assembly or a rout turned into a riot and after an hour the assembled crowd failed to disperse, the official who had proclaimed the riot was authorized to order citizens to aid in arresting the rioters. It was a scheme of enforcement designed for British towns, not for controlling the political mobs of whig America. During the few times when Boston bystanders did offer assistance, they apparently set their own terms as volunteers.

On one occasion, for example, the sheriff of Suffolk county was aiding some customs agents to enter a room that had been closed to them by the owner of a house. A crowd of Bostonians surrounded the place. A statute similar to the riot act gave the sheriff authority to turn the gathering into a posse.[17] Those who disobeyed could be fined or punished and may even have been guilty of a contempt against the king's prerogative. Knowing the people would refuse to cooperate, the sheriff did not invoke the statute, probably because he would then have had to seek criminal penalties and would have been laughed out of court by the grand jury. Instead he asked the crowd if it would aid him. The answer was yes, the people would assist, but only if "the Custom house

Officers would go before a Justice and make Oath who their Informer was." [18]

The incident was more than a confrontation between a royal official and a Boston crowd. More to the point, it pitted whig law against imperial law. The sheriff and the customs men were searching for evidence that a revenue law had been broken. In their eyes the violator of the imperial statute was a criminal. In the eyes of the crowd the informer, not the smuggler, was the criminal, and they had a right to demand his name. Thomas Hutchinson had acknowledged the force of whig attitudes when he urged the Suffolk grand jury to keep its deliberations secret. All too often, he complained, jurors reveal the names of informers, who then become "odious," and never again risk either "Reputation" or "Property." "In Consequence of which many heinous Crimes will go unpunished, many wholesome Laws will be broken with Impunity." [19] There was no chance the grand jurors would heed Hutchinson's plea when even a lawyer of the standing of John Adams was sarcastic. The chief justice, Adams said, was using "warbling declamations to Grand Inquests, to render the characters of informers honourable and respectable." [20] If John Adams could think that, a Boston crowd could feel it had the right to make a sheriff name the informer before joining his posse. [21] It goes without saying that no posse was formed that afternoon.

The day following the sacking of Hutchinson's house, some of the leading citizens of Boston, including many whigs, formed a patrol to guard the town from further riots until the crisis ended. At the same time, an inquiry by the council determined that Ebenezer Mackintosh was the man most active in supervising the destruction of Hutchinson's property. A roughneck shoemaker, he had recently ended the traditional rivalry between the North End mob and the South End mob, combined them under his leadership, and delivered them to the service of Samuel Adams and militant whiggery. A warrant was issued to Sheriff Stephen Greenleaf, ordering him to apprehend Mackintosh. Going out of the council, Greenleaf spotted the fugitive on King Street, arrested him, and then discharged him returning to the council empty-handed. Once again, Greenleaf explained, whig law had intervened to prevent execution of imperial law. Several prominent men had told him that citizen patrols would not be out that night or any other night if Mackintosh was held. The choice was between setting the shoemaker free or facing more riots. Sheriff Greenleaf made his decision to the relief of almost everyone except Thomas Hutchinson.

"And did you discharge him?" Hutchinson asked the sheriff.

"Yes," Greenleaf answered.

"Then you have not done your duty," the chief justice said. [22] "Some of the council gave their opinion that the sheriff was inexcusable," Hutchinson wrote later, "but it passed over without any act of council to shew a disapprobation. To this feeble state were the powers of government reduced." [23]

"Some of the principal ringleaders in the late riots, walk the streets with impunity," Governor Francis Bernard wrote; "no Officers dare attack them; no Attorney General prosecute them; no Witness appear against them; and no Judges sit upon them." Bernard's theme was similar to Hutchinson's: that "the real authority of the Government is at an end."[24] It was a contemporary judgment from the tory perspective, and one the historian cannot accept. Both Bernard and Hutchinson would have been more accurate had they marked the Stamp Act riots not as an end but as a beginning—the beginning of the division in government between the forces of imperial and whig law.

Captain Mackinosh seems to have been the only leader of a whig mob arrested in prerevolutionary Boston, and he, it should be noted, was proceeded against by an executive warrant, not by a warrant from common-law courts. There were, of course, several explanations why the government did not initiate prosecutions. One of the most revealing is the fact that no more than one or two whig mobs were ever challenged by a "reading of the riot act"; not one apparently was proclaimed a riot. While any official down to the rank of constable might "read the act," Massachusetts practice seems to have left that task to the justices of the peace. There were numerous justices, located in every section of the province, some were lawyers and all men of local prominence. Economic and social standing was the criterion for they, in a full sense, were the local governments even more than their counterparts back in England. Their personal prestige was such that when they addressed a crowd their words would carry greater weight than would those of a constable or even the sheriff. The problem faced by government was that most of the justices were whigs or neutrals. While only a few are on record as using their office to aid the opposition to government, most either were afraid to challenge a political mob or refused to act because of their sympathies. It is said that throughout the American colonies during the prerevolutionary period, when the mob was abroad the magistrates kept out of sight lest someone call upon them to disperse the rioters.[25]

During May 1770 a customs tidesman in Boston seized a vessel for violation of the law. He in turn was seized by a mob, tarred and feathered, and then carted through the town. About a thousand persons took part and the affair lasted for almost four hours. No magistrate appeared to disperse the crowd and the riot act was not invoked. Acting Governor Hutchinson had been out of town. When he returned the next day, he assembled the justices of the peace and inquired why nothing had been done. One of them, Richard Dana, replied that he had felt himself "under no obligations to make inquiry, as no Complaint had been made in form."[26] There was no reprimand Hutchinson could make. Five years before, the same Dana had shown less respect for "form." When an earlier mob forced Andrew Oliver to renounce the office of stamp agent, Dana had administered the oath of resignation. His role in the ceremony—conducted at the liberty tree—was a violation of law, as he, a barrister, surely knew.[27] Dana was not punished; he could not even be removed from office. Somewhat neglected by history, he deserves more attention, for his career tells us much about the rise of whig power and the decline of royal authority. Remaining a justice of the peace until his death, Dana used his authority to protect whigs and rioters and to browbeat customsmen and soldiers of the king's army.[28] In many ways more effective than any Boston jury, he knew how to employ whig law to hamper enforcement of imperial law.

That such men as Justice of the Peace Richard Dana were whigs explains a good deal about the conditions of law in prerevolutionary Boston. Reading the riot proclamations was, after all, more than a matter of form. When justices refused to cooperate, government could not impose the maximum penalties provided by statutory law. Had that been the only consequence, whig control of the justiceships might not have mattered, for juries would not have convicted anyway, even if proclamations had been read and mobs had refused to disperse. But there was more to the problem than punishment. Without reading the riot act, whig mobs would not in technical law be rioters and those who had to cope with them were left in a legally ambiguous situation. Such was especially true for the military, which, unlike civilian authority, possessed the physical force capable of dispersing crowds, but with good reason hesitated to act even in self-defense. Whatever the fact situation, an army officer would have a difficult time establishing justification when he acted without the proclamation being read and members of the mob legally designated as "rioters."

The most memorable of Boston's prerevolutionary riots, the Boston Massacre riot, demonstrated the predicament. The British soldiers felt menaced by the mobs and when the strain on their nerves became too much, they fired on the crowd. They and their officer were charged with murder, as they might have been in any event when the decision was left to a Suffolk county grand jury. Yet the prosecution's case would have been more difficult and the whigs would have reaped less propaganda from the incident had the proclamation been read, the crowd refused to disperse, and those killed that night been technical, as well as actual, "rioters."[29]

Ironically, the Boston Massacre was one occasion when a justice had been willing to read the riot proclamation. In town that night was a Scots merchant named James Murray, a justice of the peace who possessed both tory convictions and the personal courage to confront a whig mob. It appears that he did intend to intervene when he heard that the mob was out, for when the soldiers were surrounded by the crowd a shout went up, "Here comes Murray with the Riot Act." Some members of the mob turned and pelted the approaching figure with snowballs, forcing Murray—if it was he—to beat a hasty retreat. No riot proclamation came to the aid of the military that night, for the whig mob had again decided the conditions of law on Boston's streets. Later in the year the assembly made the point more emphatic by refusing to renew the riot act.

The importance of the magistrates was convincingly demonstrated in the case of John Mein. He was the Boston tory editor whose gun accidentally misfired while he was fleeing from a whig crowd. It was he, it will be recalled, not the mob, who was accused of violating the law. The reason the whigs were able to transmute Mein from a victim of law violators into a fugitive from justice was their control of the office of justice of the peace. The same Richard

Dana who had administered the oath to Andrew Oliver issued the warrant for Mein's arrest. It was Dana and a few men like him who made whig control of the magistrates' office the most important fact of law and government in the struggle against British rule, more significant even than whig control of the grand and traverse juries. It is also no exaggeration to claim that in respect to no other legal institution did the conditions of law in prerevolutionary Massachusetts contrast more sharply than with those of eighteenth-century Ireland.

As previously noted, the justices of Massachusetts were not appointed by the royal governor and could not be removed at will. Local men, filling local offices and protected from imperial reach by a tenure virtually for life, they were identified with local interests and subject to local political pressures. In Ireland the justices were the shock troops of the Protestant occupation. Appointed by the lord lieutenant, they were, quite often, not men from the community, but military officers. William Sampson, a Belfast lawyer who later became a leader of the New York bar, called them "foreign mercenary soldiers," by which he meant they were English.[30] The practice of selecting army officers as magistrates, one lord lieutenant admitted, approached martial law, yet he felt it necessary as the soldiery were often "the only magistracy in real authority."[31] Whether army officers or landed gentry, the magistrates of eighteenth-century Ireland could be depended upon to support British rule.

During 1795, Catholics known as Defenders were fighting in the north with Protestants known as Orangemen. A few magistrates tried to punish those Protestants who were driving Catholics off their land, but there were many more who contrived with the Orangemen.[32] Thomas Russell, a former army officer with service in India, was appointed justice of the peace in county Tyrone. He retired within a short time. "I cannot," he explained, "reconcile it to my conscience to sit on a bench where the practice exists of inquiring what religion a person is before investigating the charge against him."[33] Partiality in justice would be a cause of the Rising of '98 and it was the magistrates who were the most partial.

Massachusetts justices were of a different breed. Due to them, Lord North charged in 1774, the governor was unable to exercise the crown's authority. "There must," he told parliament, "be something radically wrong in that constitution, in which no Magistrate, for such a series of years, had ever done his duty in such a manner as to enforce obedience to the laws."[34] By "the laws," Lord North meant imperial laws, not local Massachusetts laws. When the event in question was nonpolitical, unconnected with the controversy against British rule, the magistrates of the colony enforced the law as written with as much dedication as did the justices of the peace in England itself or in Ireland.

Another institution making it difficult for the governor to suppress riots was the council. Even had a riot been proclaimed, the governor could not act on his own authority as he needed the consent of the councillors. During the Stamp Act crisis, when the mob controlled the streets of Boston, Governor Bernard "considered whether it would not be proper to call in assistance from without," namely the British army and navy. Constitutionally he could not make the decision alone, which meant no decision could be made in Massachusetts.[35]

The council would not vote for British troops because the people did not want them. Besides, a majority of the council argued, the 120 provincial soldiers stationed on Castle Island and a naval ship in the harbor were sufficient to meet the emergency. The suggestion was ridiculous and the council knew it. The colonial militia could not be used as a police force against a popular party, as it sprang from the same population and, electing its own officers annually, was led by whigs.[36] True it could do police work and in some colonies did, at least when Indians or slaves needed policing. But in a political quarrel, certainly in Massachusetts, the militia was unlikely to be neutral. During the very Stamp Act riots that had prompted Governor Bernard's request to the council, someone had suggested that the militia be raised. The answer was that it had already risen. When the mob was out against stamp-agent Andrew Oliver, Bernard became alarmed enough to act on his own, sending a message to the colonel of the militia ordering him to beat an alarm. The colonel replied that any drummer who tried would be knocked down and his drum smashed before he could strike it. Besides, what was the use? The drummers were probably all up at Oliver's house, part of the mob.[37]

Three years later, when John Hancock's sloop *Liberty* was seized for violation of the trade laws, and a crowd turned against the commissioners of the customs, the same rule of law prevailed. No magistrate would read the riot act. For about the only time in Boston, however, effective military help was available, at least to an extent. A naval vessel towed *Liberty* out into the harbor, beyond the reach of the mob. But the navy could not protect the commissioners while on land. After Bostonians had pelted several customs officials with stones, and broken windows in three of their houses, the commissioners went to Bernard and asked if he would guarantee their safety.[38] He could promise no military aid, Bernard replied, because the council would not vote it.[39] The commissioners went into hiding and later transferred their operations to the fleet.[40]

As with most other legal matters during this era, Boston juries contributed to the reign of the mob. Along with the justices and the councillors, they explain why riots could be so potent a weapon for whig politicians, entailing small risks for handsome returns. After all, it did not matter as far as prosecuting members of a mob went that the the riot act had not been read. No proclamation only meant that the mob, if indicted, would have to be charged with a common-law crime. The same was true for the council. It might not ask for outside help, and hence the mob might have to be left unchecked while on the streets. The sheriff, however, might have arrested perpetrators. True, while the mob was still active whigs could employ the threat of more violence to free a man like Mackintosh, but passions cool and people became weary—the mob could not be kept out forever. Yet no rioters were convicted in prerevolutionary Boston, and again whig control of town meetings which selected jurors is the reason.

When weighing the significance of whig domination, it is well to remember that the grand jury operated under few restraints. If the whigs would not enforce the riot laws—whether common law or statutory—they could have used others. Rioting was not the only crime with which Mackintosh could have been charged. As Thomas Hutchinson told the Suffolk jurors shortly after his house was sacked, the mob had also been guilty of burglary, and that was but one of several alternatives not colored by political overtones. Moreover, the grand jury did not need to question witnesses. It was obliged to return indictments for "those Crimes which come within your own Knowledge, or where you have sufficient Inducement to think Persons have been guilty of Crimes, which have not been brought forward by any one."[41]

With the criminal courts unable to punish their tormentors, victims of the mob who wished revenge still had the civil courts open to them. Anyone, after all, could file a writ, though some did not dare. Their excuse, of course, was that the mob would take its own revenge upon them.[42] But we need not belabor the obvious. It is what we might not expect that tells us the most about the conditions of law in prerevolutionary America. Victims of violence did not have to rely on either the civil or the criminal courts for satisfaction. If it was reimbursement for loss they sought, they could apply to the legislative branch of government for compensation. One day Great Britain would have to grant pensions to exiled loyalists. In the meanwhile relief had to come from the colonial assemblies. As that meant whigs were asked not only to award enemies but confess lawlessness to a hostile British public it would have taken an exceptional case to get a favorable vote.

The exceptional case, of course, was posed by the destruction of Thomas Hutchinson's house. Most whigs seem to have agreed that the damage he had suffered was unjustified by any view of current politics.[43] When application for compensation was made on Hutchinson's behalf, however, the representatives in the lower house from outside Boston resisted taxing their towns for Boston's excesses. The matter might have reached an impasse, another example of the division within the government with the tory governor demanding payment on behalf of London and whig representatives refusing on behalf of the people. Then a compromise was reached, demonstrating once more how the whigs could use control of an instrument of government to nullify official policy and substitute majority law for government law.

Joseph Hawley, a leading whig lawyer from western Massachusetts, formulated the compromise. Clients of his had been indicted for rioting during the Stamp Act crisis and a Hampshire county jury, less political than the juries of Boston, had convicted them. The Hutchinson application for compensation provided an opportunity to free the men. Moreover, the tories led by Chief Justice Hutchinson were talking of indicting other rioters, and though the chances of success were slim, the whigs preferred that no trials take place. They did not want to give the tories a forum that would bare to the world the violence of the Boston mob and further expose the partisanship of Massachusetts juries. Down in Rhode Island, where the whigs controlled the governorship as well as the assembly, they had voted indemnity to all officers who disregarded the Stamp Act and suffered for it. Massachusetts could not do the same, for Governor Bernard would have vetoed the act. Now Hawley came up with the next best substitute. He proposed to pay Hutchinson compensation in a fair amount, attaching to the bill a provision granting indemnity to Stamp Act rioters in Massachusetts—not just those involved in the Hutchinson mob, but all rioters including his clients previously convicted in Hampshire county. Under almost any other circumstances, Governor Francis Bernard would have rejected the bill, but Hawley's tactics had him trapped. He either had to approve it or forfeit Hutchinson's compensation. He signed the bill, sending it to London where, laid before the king, it was disapproved. By then events had moved too far. The money had been paid, the rioters released, and even Chief Justice Hutchinson did not dare ask anew for their indictment. Once again the whigs had demonstrated that control of a local institution of government gave them the upper hand. Once again they had nullified imperial law.

9

The Seeds of Anarchy[1]

THE EXECUTION
OF WHIG LAW

Two centuries have come and gone yet still we marvel at the impotency of British imperial law when challenged by a Boston mob. And it is well to remember that crowd-enforced whig law was a "law" that operated upon people as much as upon governmental institutions. The customshouse was not burnt down. Individual customsmen were tarred and feathered. They were invariably minor officials, usually suspected informers rather than revenue agents, but they were necessary for the imperial service and we would expect London to protect them. The physical pain and mental suffering were bad enough, but to ask men to endure them without hope of civil damages or legislative compensation seemed to be asking too much.[2] Yet the more officials groped for a solution the more they found their predicament insoluble.

The customs commissioners stationed at Boston thought they had an answer, or they were so desperate they were ready to propose anything. They wrote the home government inquiring about means to force the "County, Town or District, where such offenses . . . [were committed] to make good the damages." The suggestion was not without precedent. England had methods of riot compensation fixing liability on local units such as boroughs or hundreds, but they depended on common-law procedures, which meant trial by jury of the venue—a whig jury, in other words. The commissioners were told nothing meaningful could be done.[3] Eighteenth-century common lawyers were not adept at devising alternative remedies that strayed from analogy. The best solution anyone offered was an old statute of Henry VIII granting courts within England jurisdiction to try citizens accused of committing treason outside the realm. It would have eliminated the nuisance of Massachusetts whigs on the jury, but with a high cost—financial cost and cost in time when transporting witnesses to London, and above all the political cost of furnishing the whigs a new constitutional grievance. It is indicative of the conditions of imperial law in eighteenth-century North America that this impractical response to a serious problem, applicable to neither felonies nor misdemeanors and never utilized, gave the opposition one more constitutional issue with which to alarm Americans and fan the fires of mutiny.[4]

The nearest Great Britain came to invoking the statute of Henry proved to be less than a gesture; it was a disaster. A Rhode Island mob boarded and destroyed the revenue schooner *Gaspee*, a clear act of treason. London appointed a commission of inquiry, and had it been able to obtain sufficient evidence the British intention was to try the perpetrators in England. Of course the commissioners gathered no testimony, but even had they done so the plan would not have succeeded; local law and local institutions blocked the way. Stephen Hopkins, chief justice of the colony, a shipbuilder and former smuggler, was making no idle threat when he boasted that not a person would be removed for trial outside Rhode Island. Once again the British were to learn that enforcement of imperial law in North America depended on a whig-held local office. The commissioners might uncover sufficient evidence to warrant prosecution, General Thomas Gage wrote, but "they will find no Magistrate who will regard or obey their Orders."[5]

We may gape again, not at the reality of Gage's fears, but at how even his assessment oversimplified whig contempt for imperial law. The dimension of institutional opposition went deeper than he suspected. Local whig law could not only check British imperial law, it could mock it. While none of the Rhode Island mob that burnt *Gaspee* was put to trial, the captain of the schooner was. Sued at common law for unlawful conversion resulting from seizures under the revenue statutes, he bore the expense of three trials in the local courts and had three judgments returned against him for a total of £363. In one of the actions, the plaintiffs asked for and the jury granted damages of £295, £5 short of the amount needed for an appeal to London.[6] In Rhode Island, if not all of prerevolutionary North America, when the mob was not running through the streets it was sitting in the jury box.

Law alone did not make the British ridiculous. Definitions of lawlessness had a role to play. When they heard of whig mobs imperial leaders did not think as whigs thought, they were preconditioned to leap to opposite conclusions. Learning that Suffolk county grand juries failed to indict political rioters, ministers in faraway London envisioned anarchy and terror; they could not see that a new legal system was emerging to challenge the old. Lord Hillsborough was typical when he concluded that Massachusetts had become "a Colony in which the exercise of all civil power and authority was suspended by the most daring Acts of force and violence."[7] Hillsborough read all the dispatches from Boston but he did not understand what he read. Whig mobs, as he said, may have been daring for their sauciness but not daring for the risks they took. Civil authority was not being destroyed, it was shifting into different hands. Law and order had not broken down. It was the law itself that permitted a mob to be used for political ends and there was order in its use. Without the councillors, the justices of the peace, and the grand jurors, the rioters who made Boston famous might have stayed off the streets. In a sense, the councillors, the justices of the peace, and the grand jurors were as much a part of the mob as were those who formed its ranks. The councillors who would not use troops against a "political" mob, and many of the rioters themselves, would have opposed a "lawless" mob.[8]

Recent historians from both extremes of the political spectrum have interpreted events much as did Lord Hillsborough. The prerevolutionary Boston mob was not a spontaneous outburst of political discontent, we are told by a historian who tends to view the eighteenth century from the tory perspective. It was the creature of a few men, marshaled for battle and sent into action at the command of Samuel Adams. Historians taking the opposite perspective—who see the mob as an expression of class divisions, not as puppets dancing to a tune played by any political leader—have, interestingly enough, adopted the same view of law. According to them, the people turned to unlawful violence, took to the streets of their own initiative, and forced a solution with the only means they possessed. "Upper-class leaders demanded legality and tried, sometimes by shady means, to suppress or distort the dissent." But the people at the bottom of the class structure stayed on the streets. It was they who, during the Stamp Act crisis, spoke out "against the British, against deference, and against colonial leadership, and they had won."[9]

Although these opposite interpretations shed some light on other issues, they miss the point in terms of law. Samuel Adams and other prominent whigs, when they condoned violence, did not regard the actions of the mob as "lawless." There were excesses, they would admit, but the use of force was not necessarily unlawful. Nor is there evidence of a class conflict on this point. So-called upper-class leaders may have demanded legality, but that legality was whig legality, not the legality of Hillsborough, Gage, and Hutchinson. Merchants and lawyers as much as seamen and artisans recognized the legitimacy of the mob, and there were poor people who agreed with Governor Bernard that defiance of constituted authority was unlawful. Whig legal principles were not dictated by economic status.

Eighteenth-century Americans unlike those of today could distinguish between lawless and semilawful mobs. As a form of public protest, mobs of the type that ran through Boston streets during the prerevolutionary era had been common for decades in the colonies.[10] Pauline Maier speaks of their "quasi-legal status" and Gordon S. Wood says that the mob tradition both before and after the Revolution led some Americans to believe that "sedition itself will sometimes make law."[11] Maier explains the theory of the mob's extralegality or legitimacy:

> Eighteenth-century uprisings were in some important ways different than those of today—different in themselves, but even more in the political context within which they occurred. As a result they carried different connotations for the American Revolutionaries than they do today. Not all eighteenth-century mobs simply defied

the law: some used extralegal means to implement official demands or to enforce laws not otherwise enforceable, others in effect extended the law in urgent situations beyond its technical limits. Since leading eighteenth-century Americans had known many occasions on which mobs took on the defense of the public welfare, which was, after all, the stated purpose of government, they were less likely to deny popular upheavals all legitimacy than are modern leaders. While not advocating popular uprisings, they could still grant such incidents an established and necessary role in free societies, one that made them an integral and even respected element of the political order.[12]

In a sense, this American attitude toward mob action was an extension of an old English tradition. In London and other places, as George Rude has shown, crowds usually went against political targets, not property, and "in the eighteenth century the typical and ever recurring form of social protest was the riot."[13]

The constitutional controversy gave added legitimacy to this tradition in Boston during 1760s and 1770s. After all, one of the topics being debated was local attitudes toward British law. John Adams was speaking as a lawyer, not a whig politician, when he asserted that a mob would be acting lawfully if it used violence against a British naval press gang commanded by a commissioned officer "without any warrant." The navy, not the crowd, would be an unlawful assembly. "If they were to impress an inhabitant, and carry him off for a sailor, would not the inhabitants think themselves warranted by law to interfere in behalf of their fellow citizen?"[14]

If a lawyer could find legitimacy in a mob acting to prevent an impressment that, if illegal, could have been corrected by the courts, it was not difficult for whigs to see the legitimacy in mobs opposing laws they thought unconstitutional and from which there was no appeal.[15] During 1770 Acting Governor Hutchinson sent a message to the assembly, protesting that a customs official had been tarred and feathered in Gloucester, yet no one had been punished. In its reply, the House of Representatives summed up the whig theory of the right to riot against unconstitutional statutes. The people of Massachusetts, the answer asserted, "seldom if ever, have assembled in a tumultuous manner, unless they have been oppressed: it cannot be expected that a people accustomed to the freedom of the English constitution will be patient, while they are under the hand of tyranny and arbitrary power; they will discover their resentment in a manner which will naturally displease their oppressors."[16]

There is no evidence to support the supposition that this legal theory was forced upon the assembly by lower-class elements impatient with what historians call "law." It had been good whig constitutionalism long before the Stamp Act crisis, as demonstrated by local support earlier during the eighteenth century for rioters who opposed press gangs or who prevented enforcement of such imperial statutes as the White Pine Act.[17]

There were, therefore, three aspects of the struggle which lent legitimacy to the whig mob. First was the open support or at least the forebearance of certain officials or organs of government such as the magistrates, the grand jury, the council, and the assembly. Second was the constitutional debate being conducted against the authority of parliament in a legal system in which there was no appeal except to parliament. Third, there was the competition between local whig law and British imperial law. It is this last aspect that Maier stressed when she concluded that the colonial mob "often appeared only after the legal channels of redress had proven inadequate. . . . Violence broke out only in local situations where no alternative was available." When imperial laws were involved, both the reality of distance and constitutional doubts contributed to the mob's sense of legitimacy, "and it was not unusual in these cases for local magistrates to participate or openly sympathize with the insurgents."[18]

We need not depend on whigs only. The tories, too, had something to say. A number of the most dedicated royal officials in prerevolutionary North America, whether they accepted it or not, recognized and reported the Americans' theory of the extralegality of some mobs. The riot that had forced Andrew Oliver to resign as stamp agent, for example, could even by a governor be put in one class, the wanton destruction of Thomas Hutchinson's property in another. Although they had occurred back to back, and had been carried out by mobs similar in membership, Francis Bernard wrote, "great pains are taken to separate the two riots, what was done against Mr. Oliver is still approved as a necessary declaration of their resolution not to submit to the Stamp Act; and . . . it has been publicly hinted that if a line is not drawn between the first riot and the last [Hutchinson's house], the civil power will not be supported by the principal people of the town. . . . And indeed, if the last riot had been the only one, the civil government would appear to be in full power."[19]

Even Thomas Hutchinson eventually conceded that "mobs a sort of them at least are constitutional."[20] Deploring attacks on customsmen by mobs "rescuing" undutied goods that had been legally seized, he recognized that a new source of authority was being introduced. "I imagine a few more such instances will make it settled law that no act but those of our own legislatures can bind us."[21]

When he said "legislatures" rather than "legislature," Hutchinson may not have been referring to colonial assemblies only, but also to the mob. In a letter to a former governor, he called the mob "the lowest branch" of current Massachusetts government, "partly legislative, partly executive." It was executive, for example, when it forced Andrew Oliver to resign, legislative when assembled in town meeting—"where Otis with his mobbish eloquence prevails in every motion."[22] Though saying he wrote for his friend's "amusement," Thomas Hutchinson was never more serious and seldom more perceptive. During the 1760s, Boston whigs had learned to use the town meeting as a legal mob or as a means to make a mob legal.

There was a difference—subtle but important—between a town meeting acting as a legal mob and a town meeting legitimizing a mob. Even Hutchinson may have recognized the distinction. In a letter to Francis Bernard, he defined the first—the town meeting as a legal mob. "When you consider what is called its constitution," he explained, "your good sense will determine immediately that . . . the majority which conducts all affairs, if met upon another occasion, would be properly called a mob, and are persons of such rank and circumstance as in all communities constitute a mob, . . . men of weight and value, although they wish to suppress them, cannot be induced to attempt to do it for fear not only of being outvoted, but affronted and insulted."[23]

An example of the Boston town meeting as a legal mob occurred during the controversy leading up to the Boston Tea Party. When Boston opposed the landing of dutied tea the town meeting became a "mob" as Hutchinson defined the word. The town was not legally authorized to meet at all, but Bostonians made their own law, not only meeting but meeting in continual sessions with every man present allowed to vote. Inhabitants of neighboring towns flocked in; no one challenged their right to be there; moderate voices were shouted down; resolutions were passed making demands with which the governor believed himself powerless to comply, compromise was impossible; and the Tea Party resulted.

An example of a mob made legal by a town meeting occurred in Boston during 1769 when H.M.S. *Romney* was the center of controversy. The immediate cause of raising the mob was seizure of John Hancock's sloop *Liberty*. When the whigs gathered to rescue it from the commissioners of the customs, *Romney* intervened, towed the vessel to safety, and then provided refuge for the commissioners when they fled Boston. Another cause for the riot and one perhaps more important was *Romney*'s press gang, a grievance capable of raising a mob in almost any eighteenth-century American seaport.[24]

Governor Francis Bernard appealed to his council to suppress the mob. He thought the situation fraught with peril and so did the councillors. But they did not see the causes that he saw and his remedy was not their remedy. Seldom did whig legal theory clash so sharply with imperial law. "With regard to what happen'd," they replied, "it seems to have sprung wholly from the persons who complain of it, by the plan laid and the orders given for making the seizure aforesaid, and carrying it away by an armed force. Which circumstance together with the time of day of seizing the vessel, it being then near sun-set, makes it seem probable that an uproar was hoped for, and intended to be occasioned by the manner of proceeding in making the seizure."[25] In other words, the council claimed, the commissioners of the customs had provoked the riot. They were responsible for it, not the rioters.[26] By employing the navy, they did more than irritate Boston; they had acted unlawfully for the navy had not been used for that purpose before.[27] In whig legal theory the fact that the imperial government had acted in an "unprecedent manner" furnished grounds for challenging the legitimacy of official actions.[28] The mob that sought to rescue *Liberty* was similar to John Adams's example—the mob that tried to stop an unlawful impressment. It was a legal mob.[29]

Frustrated at losing *Liberty*, barred from further direct action by the guns of *Romney*, the whigs called a mass meeting at "Liberty Hall," the area immediately surrounding the liberty tree. It proved to be a remarkably large turnout. "Vast numbers of the populace, and others," was how Thomas Hutchinson described them.[30] A crowd of about 2,000 was the estimate of a tory newspaper, which reported that after the people had assembled, they "adjourned" to Faneuil Hall. Another way of explaining the same event was that whig leaders marched their men down Main Street to Faneuil Hall. At that point they were a mob and could have been designated rioters had any authorized officer read the riot proclamation. In Faneuil Hall the large crowd again briefly adjourned to permit the selectmen "to call a legal town-meeting."[31] Warrants were issued, the meeting was convened, and James Otis was elected moderator. Thus the mob was transformed into a legal instrument of government; the meeting may still have been a mob, but it was now a mob made legal.

The first order of business demonstrated the fact that it had not ceased being a mob. It was proposed and adopted to adjourn to Old South meeting-house. The excuse was that the building was larger, but the true purpose probably was to impress the governor with a second parade of strength through Boston: a town meeting acting like a mob just as during the Tea Party troubles the mob acted like a town meeting.[32] If, in fact, Faneuil Hall could not contain all who had assembled, it was surely a sizable multitude.[33] That building, Samuel Adams reported, was "capable of holding 1200 or 1300 men," while Old South could hold five to six thousand.[34]

Once off the streets the meeting adopted a predrafted resolution in the form of a petition to the governor, suggesting that as they had fled Boston the commissioners of the customs should be ruled to have resigned their offices and asking Bernard to order *Romney* out of the harbor and to prohibit naval press gangs.[35] The negotiations were entrusted to a committee that the governor had to receive or risk having the mob on the streets for the third time that day. "The governor," Thomas Hutchinson was to write, "was struck with the strong insinuation of the consequences which would attend his refusal to comply with the prayer of this address. The council and house were sitting, but he was afraid that, by consulting them, he should increase his difficulty. The same men who had led this assembly were the men of greatest influence in the general assembly."[36]

While Governor Bernard argued that it was his duty to assist the customs commissioners until they had in fact resigned, and that he had no authority to order a naval vessel out of Boston harbor, he did promise to do what he could to halt impressments.[37] It was a concession he would not have made to an ordinary mob or a conventional town meeting.[38]

10

The Same Leaven
with the People[1]

THE LEGAL MIND
OF THE AMERICAN WHIG

It is well to linger a few pages more with the prerevolutionary American mob. There are those who may question whether it was less lawlessness than law. If there is doubt and we try to resolve it, we must be careful not to seek too much. To understand the whig legal mind it is not necessary to adopt whig legal theory. Its purpose was not to convert tories, it was to police whigs. Our problem is not whether the law of the mob was truly "law" but whether the whigs were sincere. It is attitudes we must examine, the attitudes of whigs not the attitudes of tories. If they did, in fact, believe they acted "lawfully" we may accept their judgment. Whether they were right or wrong is a consideration at best collateral.

If we search for attitudes, we can do no better than turn to instances in which whig law was executed by the mob. It was on those occasions that the whigs had to explain themselves either by their words or by their actions.

Perhaps it is well to start at a different locale if for no other reason than to remind ourselves that there were other mobs besides Boston's mob, and whig law ran in other colonies besides Massachusetts Bay. An incident that occurred in New York tells much about attitudes for there we find whigs engaged in an enterprise that was unlawful under imperial law yet distinguishing between lawfulness and lawlessness as they pursued their objectives.

During one of the nonimportation movements the whigs of New York proscribed certain products of British manufacture and voted that they could not be sold in the town. To prevent clandestine trade, merchants were directed to store prohibited items in a warehouse supervised by a whig committee. Some volunteered, others complied only after they were persuaded by a particularly violent mob.[2] It did no good to argue that nonimportation was a common-law crime; whig law had made it legal. Indeed, it had done more: those who imported British vendibles in violation of the boycott were criminals in the eyes of many Americans. It was they who violated the "law."[3]

One day a peddler was discovered in New York with contraband goods. The nonimportation committee demanded they be surrendered for storage and he cooperated. He was not "punished," a fact that seems to have disturbed some of the more fervid whigs. That night a number of disguised persons—we must assume they were whigs—broke into the warehouse, seized the merchandise of the peddler and no other merchandise, and burned it. The peddler thought he understood the message and fled town. The tories might have said he was well advised. Threatened by the "mob" twice in one day, he might be lynched the next. The whigs would have disagreed and it was their reaction that tells our story.

A tory would have termed the committee's pressure on the peddler, forcing him to suspend part of his trade and surrender his property, a "lawless" action. The whigs did not. But the burning of his goods they called "lawless" as it was contrary to whig "law." The committee issued a statement urging the public "to bring the Authors, Aiders and Abettors of so unwarrantable an Act to speedy Justice," and the unknown perpetrators were described as "lawless Ruffians."[4]

Had the "lawless Ruffians" been captured, a tory attorney general would not have been embarrassed by having to prosecute them. The crime of larceny was broad, and he would not have to prove that the nonimportation committee had "lawful" possession of the stolen merchandise. Nor would most whigs have been embarrassed in using the king's court to enforce whig law. They saw nothing inconsistent between the two as long as they were able to define what part of imperial law was constitutional and what part unconstitutional. It appears George Washington even thought that whig law in the form of nonimportation agreements could be pleaded in a common-law court to define or modify a contract. Ordering goods from London during 1769, Washington specified that "if there are any articles contained in either of the respective invoices (paper only accepted) which are taxed by act of Parliament for the purpose of raising a revenue in America, it is my express desire and request, that they not be sent." He even gave his reasons. He had joined an association "not to import any article which now is, or hereafter shall be taxed for this purpose until the said act or acts are repealed."[5] Had proscribed goods been shipped, we may conjecture, Washington would have expected a royal court to return a verdict of "no contract" if he were sued in *indebitatus assumpsit* for refusing to pay.

George Washington reveals whig thinking about whig legality but not on the central question that demands our attention. It is attitudes about the role played by the mob that will tell us most because the mob—not only in Boston but elsewhere in British North America—was the ultimate sanction of whig law. Whigs did not have to support the mob to accept the legitimacy of whig law, but if they did they surely were saying that whig law was legitimate. They were claiming—no matter what the reason—that the mob not only should act but had a right to act. We may assume this of the "inarticulate" at the bottom; we know it of the "articulate" at the top.

There are many defenses of mob action that could be considered, but to avoid detailing irrelevant facts it is best to consider only one—the one that does not have to be described—the Boston Tea Party, the most famous and important of the prerevolutionary American mobs. Significant also, it was the mob that whig legal theory did not justify in London as it was the mob the British would not abide, producing a reaction that forced parliament to undertake the reformation of whig law by passing the intolerable acts, the statutes that led directly to the Revolution and American independence. It is well to consider contemporary attitudes about that mob. Historians have stressed the British reaction, but American reactions may tell us even more.

The Boston Tea Party was staged by a mob, and the whigs did not deny it. The perpetrators were disguised as Indians, though still we wonder why. There were three tea ships in the harbor; and within what the Boston committee of correspondence described as "a very little time," they were emptied of 342 chests of tea.[6] In Great Britain the fact remarked on was the helplessness of the government, especially as Governor Thomas Hutchinson had a sizable naval force at his command in addition to the regular army troops stationed on Castle Island. The entire operation may have taken three hours yet the guns of the fleet remained silent. There were those in London who expressed surprise, even anger, yet we may ask if they should have censured men. The admiral could not be blamed as he had no authority to act without orders from the governor.[7] Hutchinson's critics might say he was at fault even though they did not know he had been away at his country home at Milton or how far Milton was from Boston. Yet he could not move without consent of the council and his councillors were one with the mob.[8]

In Boston a different fact was emphasized. It was not the impotency of imperial law but the execution of whig law that drew the comment. "It is worthy of remark," the next issue of the *Boston Evening-Post* would observe, "that although a considerable quantity of goods of different kinds were still remaining on board the vessels, no injury was sustained; such attention to private property was observed that a small padlock belonging to the Captain of one of the Ships being broke, another was procured and sent to him."[9]

Surely it is proper to stress whig words when we search for whig attitudes. If they do not tell us what Boston whigs were thinking, they tell us what Boston whigs wanted their contemporaries to believe they were thinking. They had mob action to justify and the only way they could justify it was by whig law. One may question their sincerity as they were pleading a case, but by way of replication another might ask if they really were. At least there is a question whether the whigs were trying to persuade tories that the Boston Tea Party was "legal" as earlier they had tried to convince tories that the Stamp Act was "illegal." Rather, when we consider the arguments they employed, the active whigs of Boston appear to be talking to more moderate whigs, telling them that the Tea Party had been a legitimate exercise of mob force because it had been confined within the principles of whig legal theory. If this is true then what they say provides a clue to the whig legal mind.

The defense stressed at the time of the *Liberty* riot was again repeated. The people had been provoked by Thomas Hutchinson and the American commissioners of the customs. The very fact that they had not called on the admiral to save the tea proved that they "connived at least at the destruction of the tea." They were responsible for the Tea Party. The whigs had wanted the tea returned to Great Britain, a solution to the impasse that the governor prevented.[10] The fact that Hutchinson lacked authority to allow *Dartmouth* out of the harbor[11] and could not employ the military without consent of the council was immaterial. The whigs had been left with no alternative. They had no choice but to stage the Boston Tea Party.

If there had been violence everyone but the whigs of Suffolk county would have been to blame, the governor, the customs commissioners, and even the consignees of the tea.

> The Body[12] having manifested an exemplary patience and caution in the methods it had pursued to preserve the Tea, the property of the East India Company, without its being made saleable among us, which must have been fatal to the Common-wealth, and to return it safe & untouch'd to its Proprietors, and perceiving that in every step they have taken towards this just and salutary purpose, they have been counter-worked by the Consignees of the Tea, and their Coadjutors, who have plainly manifested their inclination of throwing the Community into the most violent commotions, rather than relinquish and give up the profits of a commission or contract, and the advantages they have imagined from the establishment of an American revenue; and no one being able to point out any thing further that it was in the power of this Body to do, for the salutary purpose aforesaid, — It was moved and voted, that this Meeting be immediately Dissolved — and it was accordingly.[13]

Prior to the motion to adjourn, the meeting had learned that Hutchinson would not allow *Dartmouth* to depart without paying tax on the tea in her hold, and the signal had been given for the Tea Party.[14] Even then the emphasis was on order, and people were requested not to leave the meeting.[15] When several of the "Indians," on their way to the harbor, "approaching near the door of the assembly, gave the War-Whoop," some men in the galleries answered them, but not for long. "Silence was commanded, and a prudent and peaceable deportment again enjoined."[16]

Thus, from the beginning, the whigs maintained two standards by which they wanted their actions judged, the maintenance of public order and the preservation of private property. In all their accounts sent abroad over the days following the event, the whigs of Boston stressed and restressed the theme stated by the *Evening-Post*: the Tea Party had been "transacted with the greatest regularity and dispatch." Tea had been jettisoned into the harbor, they admitted in private letters as well as official statements, but the mob had taken the "greatest care not to injure in the least" any other property on board the three vessels.[17] The Boston committee of correspondence in a circular letter reporting the Tea Party gave as much weight to the fact that private property had been respected as to the fact the tea had never been entered at the customshouse for purposes of taxation. We should not be surprised that when New York held its own tea party a few months later the same evidence was emphasized. The whig crowd threw the tea into New York harbor "without doing any damage to the Ship or cargo."[18]

We may think them somewhat hypocritical, but they were not. By whig definitions the tea that was destroyed had not been private property.[19] Most Bostonians seem to have agreed that the aspect to be underscored was not the destruction but, as Samuel Adams said, that it had been carried out "without the least injury to the vessels or any other property."[20] Even contemporary tory accounts made the whig point. The argument was best stated by the Boston committee: "Our Enemies must acknowledge that these people have acted upon pure & upright Principle."[21]

Perhaps the Boston whigs did not care about London, for they surely knew the ministry would not "acknowledge" those "pure and upright principles." The fact that counted was that the argument was accepted not only in Massachusetts but throughout whig America. Stating that they "do highly approve of the proceedings of the numerous assembly of the people of Boston, and the neighboring towns," the inhabitants of Dedham voted "as the opinion of this town that the respectable body of men there assembled, acted with the greatest prudence and caution, and did their utmost to preserve the property of the East-India Company." If any culpability existed, it rested on Hutchinson and his tory cohorts "who prevented their upright intentions from taking place."[22]

The whig legal doctrine was summed up in the Dedham resolution. The justification for mob violence was the necessity created by stubborn tory ill will. Order, lack of violence, and respect for "private" property were the hallmarks of legitimacy when executing whig law. It was restraint that made crowd action legitimate, and restraint was enforced by limiting activities to the constitutional grievance of the tax on tea.

It is important to understand that appearances were not an accident. They were the manifestation of the whig law enforcement as well as of whig law itself. Besides acting with a limited purpose, the whigs policed the execution of their law. Men with weapons were present, "watching for Spies (as they called them)" according to an eyewitness, and making certain none of the tea entered private hands rather than the harbor.[23] One man caught violating whig "law" was punished by the application of typical whig sanctions. He had ripped the lining of his coat and vest and, "watching his opportunity had nearly fill'd 'em with tea, but being detected was handled pretty roughly. They not only stripp'd him of his cloaths, but gave him a coat of mud, with a severe bruising into the bargain; and nothing but their utter aversion to make *any* disturbance prevented his being tar'd and feather'd."[24]

Orderliness, respect for private property, and limited objectives were not the only tests whigs used to establish that the Boston Tea Party had been a legitimate execution of law. Another was popular approval. "The next Day," a Boston newspaper reported, "Joy appeared in almost every countenance, some on Occasion of the Destruction of the Tea, others on Account of the Quietness with which it was effected.—One of the Monday's papers says, That the Masters and Owners are well pleased that their Ships are thus cleared." [25] "You cannot imagine," Samuel Adams reported to Arthur Lee, "the height of joy that sparkles in the eyes and animates the countenances as well as the hearts of all we meet on this occasion; excepting the disappointed, disconcerted Hutchinson and his tools." [26]

For "Hutchinson and his tools," of course—for the tories of America and Great Britain—there could be no validity to the theory of legality within illegality. Private property had been destroyed and the British imperial system defied. Whig law was becoming more dangerous for now it was bordering on open rebellion. Though admitting he was in a "forlorn state," Governor Hutchinson "thought it necessary to keep up some shew of authority, and caused a council to be summoned to meet at Boston, the day after the destruction of the tea." [27] He was not certain what the council would do, "probably it may issue in a proclamation promising a reward for discovering the persons concerned, which has been the usual proceeding in other instances of high-handed riots." [28] He appreciated, however, the strength and acceptance of whig law: "a proclamation, with a reward for discovery, would have been ridiculed." [29]

When the governor's council met it would not give Hutchinson even his useless proclamation. The councillors expressed their approbation at the Tea Party, and the only measure they advised was that the attorney general "make diligent inquiry into the offense afforesaid in order to discover the offenders, and that he lay his discoveries before the Grand Jury . . . for prosecution." [30] "The attorney-general, therefore," Hutchinson wrote, "was ordered to lay the matter before the grand jury, who, there was no room to expect, would ever find a bill for what they did not consider as an offence." [31]

Hutchinson was right: the Suffolk county grand jury would return no presentment not merely because the people approved the Tea Party but because they did not think the destruction of the tea a crime. Considering his high toryism it was a remarkable feat, but no one better summed up the whig legal mind than did the governor himself. "The people had done every thing in their power," he explained to a friend in Britain, "to get rid of the tea, but could not do it, and were under a necessity of destroying it, and they had better pay for it than suffer the duties on it to have been paid. This, I assure you, was said where, of all other places in the government it ought not to have been said." [32]

Hutchinson was speaking of the council but he had not needed the councillors to teach him the finer points of whig advocacy. He had heard the argument of necessity many times before. The governor even knew that he would be blamed for forcing the whigs to use violence, an important element in the whig theory of legal necessity that bears repeating so we may see how it was explained by Samuel Adams. [33] "You will observe," Adams wrote Arthur Lee in London, "that the people were resolved that the tea should not be landed, but sent back to London in the same bottom; and the property should be safe guarded while in port, which they punctually performed. It cannot therefore be fairly said that destruction of the property was in their contemplation. It is proved that the consignees [of the tea], together with the collector of the customs, and the governor of the province, prevented the safe return of the East Indian Company's property (the danger of the sea only excepted) to London." [34]

For Samuel Adams, whig law was hard law. "I think," he wrote in another letter, "we have put our enemies in the wrong; and they must, in the judgment of rational men, be answerable for the destruction of the tea, which their own obstinacy had rendered necessary." [35]

Adams was extreme only in his desire to fix blame on Hutchinson, not in his law. Most other whigs agreed with him that a theory of the mob's legality was supported by the doctrine of necessity. Some of these whigs were at the highest levels of government. The councillors are our salient example. Ordering their agent in London to defend Boston on the grounds that submission to parliamentary taxation would be similar to "rivetting eternal shackles on themselves and their prosterity," they told him to argue that the Tea Party had been "no assumption of government, but flowed from the great law of nature, self-preservation." [36]

The argument of necessity had been part of the political controversy ever since the Stamp Act riots. Taxation by parliament was the chief issue at the constitutional level and whig constitutional law had been developed to combat it. The people of Great Britain understood the constitutional debate, but generally in the past, the execution of whig law had been presented, even to English whigs, in terms of a lawless mob. Now the whigs made an effort to explain that the mob was not lawless, that it was in fact "the people" acting as a last resort.

The Tea Party, one Bostonian wrote in a letter reprinted by the *London Chronicle*, was justified because there was no alternative. The body did everything possible to have the tea returned, but the consignees, the ship owners, and the customs officials would not listen to reason. [37] Another newspaper correspondent could even question whether the property of the East India Company deserved the consideration the whigs had shown when they attempted to save it by having it shipped back. "I think the affair of the tea is, in general rather ill understood; and that the Constitution of *England*, the fundamental law of property, and the inalienable rights of human nature, seem to have been but little regarded in this dispute, concerning *American* taxation." If one gave attention to the constitution, it could be asked whether the tea belonging to the East India Company was private property entitled to protection under common law. "Ought it not rather," the correspondent concluded, "to have been considered as that identical property, that very engine, by which the enemies of *America* meant to subvert its privileges, and by introducing along with it an unlimited and discretionary right of taxation, totally to annihilate *American* property? Certainly property so circumstanced . . . had lost those sacred sanctions which are the defence of common property, and may figuratively be said to have changed its very nature, and to have become an instrument of war." [38]

There is no need to multiply arguments. If the whigs have not presented their theory of legitimate mob action by now, they probably will not succeed. Yet there is one source from which we have not heard and to whom it is worthwhile to harken: a whig lawyer of more ability than Samuel Adams, a whig lawyer of standing and reputation within the legal profession. It is not surprising that the best argument for the legality of the Tea Party came from the leader of the whig bar in Suffolk county.

> The question is, Whether the destruction of this tea was necessary? I apprehend it was absolutely and indispensably so. [The ship owner] could not send it back. The Governor, Admiral and Collector and Comptroller would not suffer it. It was in their power to have saved it, but in no other. It could not get by the castle, the men-of-war, &c. Then there was no other alternative but to destroy it or let it be landed. To let it be landed, would be giving up the principle of taxation by parliamentary authority, against which the continent have struggled for ten years. It was losing all our labor for ten years, and subjecting ourselves and our posterity forever to Egyptian task-masters; to burthens, indignities; to ignominy, reproach and contempt; to desolation and oppression; to poverty and servitude. [39]

It is important to realize what we have been reading. John Adams wrote these words, but he did not write them for propaganda. He was not pleading the whig case before the bar of British public opinion. He was recording private thoughts in the privacy of his diary. [40] Adams was a lawyer, a conservative lawyer, and it is significant that as he meditated alone in his study on Brattle Square he found, as did so many other whigs, that constitutional legality was at times determined by political necessity. The stakes were vital and made the game worth playing, but it was up to the British what game was played. If parliament pushed, the Americans would resist. They would not resist if parliament did not push.

11

Disjointed and Independent of Each Other[1]

THE CONDITIONS OF IMPERIAL LAW

We have been stressing strengths and weaknesses—American strength and imperial weakness. There is a danger that the picture drawn may be distorted. The emphasis has been on the American side: an emphasis implying that the failure of British imperial law arose from an inability to compete with local institutions strongly entrenched in the colonial legal system. Imperial law may seem weak because it has been juxtaposed against a tenacious Massachusetts law.

The tale of the conditions of law in the prerevolutionary era could be told by comparing colonial barriers to imperial initiative but that would be only half the story. Imperial legal impotency was not the work of whigs alone. The Americans were pouring salt on a self-inflicted wound. British propensity for a legislative botch contributed much to the imperial strait, perhaps even more than did whig enterprise.

We must not think only of power or even the appearance of power. We must think of lawyers and what they could do with law. Even had they been able to manipulate or neutralize local American institutions to the degree their colleagues in Ireland manipulated Irish institutions, royal officials in North America would not have ruled with the same firm hand. All too often, they would have found, the law they were expected to enforce was unenforceable.

A British military officer viewing the martial status of his empire during the prerevolutionary era saw the triumph of his profession. It was an empire won on the Plains of Abraham and on the oceans of the world, seemingly invincible among the powers of Europe. A British civilian viewing the scope of that same empire, stretching from Hudson's Bay, through the islands of the Caribbean, across to the mighty fortress at Gibraltar, and on to the unlimited riches of India, saw order in its diversity, security in its vastness, and prosperity in its regulated trade. A contemporary British lawyer viewing the laws of that empire would have seen only chaos. Indeed, had that English barrister or Scots advocate looked deeply, he might have concluded that the conditions of imperial law explained why Americans were saucy and becoming saucier.

British imperial law may have been the law of the empire but it had not been formulated to rule an empire. It was a flaccid law—flaccid in two senses that lent an aura of legitimacy or extralegality to the violence of whig mobs. One was an abulia in enforcement that opened imperial law to challenge. The other was a flaw in formulation exposing it to emasculative questioning. It was in many respects a "confused" law, more easily broken than upheld, as easily ignored as obeyed.

The imbroglio marking eighteenth-century British imperial law was due to the quality of legislation. Statutes were either poorly drafted, conflicted with other statutes, or failed to indicate whether they were applicable to the North American colonies. Lawyers were often puzzled, not a comfortable condition for lawyers. British officials were as often nonplussed and their situation was worse. Carrying out imperial policy, they found themselves on the defensive, charged with unlawful conduct for attempting to enforce what they believed was the law. Their problem was not that a reading of the statute books before acting told them one thing, later a whig jury told them something else. Too often a reading of the statutes told them little or nothing. There were even times when statute books told British officials less, and less was worse than nothing.

If one has to enforce law it is awkward to find that law unclear, disheartening to find it contradictory. A glance at the law of impressment may show us why oftentimes eighteenth-century British officials proceeded with more caution than one would expect of agents of imperialism. Naval press gangs were vital to an empire depending upon its navy to maintain the lines of communication and enforce imperial discipline. Yet when operating on the American mainland during the eighteenth century, they raised more mobs inflicting greater violence than any other grievance, including the Stamp Act. Considering both the importance of impressment and colonial opposition, one would approach the governing statutes expecting them to be definitive and the authority of press gangs beyond challenge. Instead, that law was so vague that opponents of impressment could pose issues of legality and when press gangs came ashore treat them as "rioters" unlawfully using violence against local citizens. Mobs raised to attack a press gang became defenders of law and their violence the lawful violence of a *posse comitatus*. The king's sailors were the "illegal" mob, and it was they, not members of the "legal" mob, who generally were lodged in American jails.

There were many fact situations that could be cited to demonstrate how the mob's sense of being a legal force preventing unlawful impressments was used to excuse antiimperial violence. But the problem of the vagueness of the law and consequent defensiveness of British officials can best be summarized by considering Corbet's case, an especially noteworthy litigation as it did not take place in a common-law court. No mob was involved, a fact that helps clarify the legal issues and reveals the confused nature of the law. Rather a naval lieutenant, obeying orders issued by the highest naval authority in the colony, Commodore Samuel Hood, boarded a Massachusetts-owned brig and attempted to impress four merchant seamen. Avoiding the use of force or a display of arms, he sought neither married men nor Massachusetts citizens. In fact, there were no Americans on board the brig.[2] The crew was Irish, and by custom Irishmen were always fair game for British press gangs.

Four crew members hid themselves in the forepeak, a small space under the weather deck between the stern and the main hold, refusing to come out. Even the mate of the merchantman would testify that the fugitives knew they were resisting impressment and intended to do so.[3] Telling the master of the brig he would take all four, the lieutenant ordered the bulkhead torn down. Both John Adams, who would defend the men, and Thomas Hutchinson, one of the judges, believed that at some point the naval officer defied them and stepped forward, to be killed by a harpoon that one of them, Michael Corbet, drove at him with all his force (as Corbet had threatened to do). In fact, he seems to have remained passive, directing the operation at an unhurried pace, while sitting on a pile of salt.[4] Surely from the evidence it was a simple case of murder. The lieutenant while performing his duty had been killed by men knowingly and intentionally resisting with deadly force the commands of one of his majesty's officers.

This case was far from simple however. For one thing, the homicide had been committed on the high seas, beyond the jurisdiction of the common law. It was a matter for admiralty, but not the provincial admiralty court which heard no criminal business or the imperial vice-admiralty court as it had criminal jurisdiction only over petty offenses at sea, not over acts that on land amounted to felony. The only competent tribunal was the Special Court of Admiralty called pursuant to a commission for the trial of piracies, with its members appointed by London. Thus when the judiciary convened to try Michael Corbet and his three fellow Irishmen, the bench consisted almost entirely of loyal tories and reliable placemen, among whom were Governor Francis Bernard, Lieutenant Governor Hutchinson, Admiralty Judge Robert Auchmuty, and Commodore Samuel Hood. The only whigs associated with the trial were John Adams and James Otis, advocates for the defense.

Adams, who took the lead, moved for trial by jury and the court dismissed the motion.[5] There was much debate, however, for the question was more cloudy than we might expect. It is indicative of the conditions of imperial law that the statutes conferring jurisdiction on the admiralty left in doubt whether trial was by common- or civil-law procedure. Imprecise draftsmanship was the reason.[6] The commissioners could do little more than guess what parliament had intended, not knowing if their verdict would be overturned on appeal. Yet the fact that they did rule against the jury—against a grand-jury indictment as well as trial by traverse jury—tells us something of how they valued the admiralty jurisdiction. The court, led by Hutchinson, was not about to give the whigs a voice in the one criminal tribunal under imperial control.[7]

In the end the ruling did not matter, nor did several other legal ambiguities that remained unresolved.[8] John Adams needed only one statutory defect to force even Thomas Hutchinson to acknowledge that the lawmakers of parliament had made the court's situation untenable. Prepared to defend imperial law, the commissioners were to find their legal redoubt in an indefensible position.

The issue of law that John Adams exploited was whether the lieutenant had been in command of a legal press gang at the time he had been slain by Corbet. Put another way, the question was whether the Irish seamen had been resisting an unlawful imprisonment. The answer depended on the powers of the navy to impress and on whether parliament had enacted legislation restricting those powers. Despite its importance to Great Britain and its fleet, the matter had been hanging fire for years. Surely American antiimpressment riots and American arrests of press gangs had been reported to London, yet the British government had done nothing to clarify the law, perhaps trusting that executive instructions would settle the difficulty. Recently Lord Hillsborough had written Bernard that in the cabinet's view impressment was legal in America.[9] His word may have been good enough for a colonial governor seeking authority to cooperate with a naval press gang, and he may have thought it sufficient for a court of law. It might have been in Ireland, though we may wonder. In North America it was not enough. John Adams had cited higher authority during the controversy over the impressment activities conducted by H.M.S. *Romney*. It was a statute passed by parliament in 1707. "No Mariner," it provided, "or other person who shall serve on board . . . any . . . trading ship or vessel, that shall be imployed in any part of America . . . shall be liable to be impressed or taken away, or shall be impressed or taken away by any officer or officers, of or belonging to her Majesty's ships of war." Never repealed or superseded, the statute covered the four defendants, for although they were not American seamen they had been serving aboard an American-owned ship engaged in the colonial trade, or so Adams would argue.[10]

Both sides called their witnesses. The prosecution sought to show that the slain lieutenant had acted reasonably, and there was no legal cause justifying the homicide or reducing it from murder to manslaughter. The defense, in turn, depended on its evidence to demonstrate that everyone involved in the incident knew that the boarding of the brig had been for the purpose of pressing seamen, not to search for customs violations. Adams intended to base his case on the argument that impressment was illegal under the statute of 1707. Even if a long-established custom gave Commodore Hood the authority to issue impressment orders, thus providing the lieutenant with the color of law (and a possible defense had he been sued in trespass), the men still had a right to resist.[11]

Barely had John Adams in his summation begun to elaborate this view of the law than Thomas Hutchinson interrupted to call an adjournment. The court went into closed conference for at least four hours, perhaps overnight. When the commissioners returned, Governor Bernard, as president, announced, "The Court have considered the evidence in support of the libel against you, and are unanimously of opinion that it amounts only to *justifiable homicide*; you are accordingly acquitted and discharged from your imprisonment."[12] A silence followed and then, John Adams later wrote, Judge Auchmuty "squealed out, 'The judgment of the Court is unanimous' and not another word was said."[13]

The commissioners of the Special Court of Admiralty never explained the reasoning for their sudden decision. John Adams was certain that they wanted to avoid ruling on the antiimpressment statute of 1707. Thomas Hutchinson gave a different explanation. "It appeared," he later wrote, "that neither the lieutenant nor any of his superior officers were authorized to impress, by any warrant or special authority from the lords of the admiralty." The prisoners were legally justified in defending themselves and had to be acquitted for even "at common law, the killing would not have amounted to manslaughter."[14]

Once again Thomas Hutchinson had demonstrated his capacity for formulating legal arguments. Yet it must be doubted if the acquittal rested on so narrow a point as the fact that while the lieutenant acted under orders from Hood, the commodore himself had none from the lords of the admiralty. John Adams's explanation makes more sense. The tory court could not get around the statute of 1707.

A recent writer has expressed doubt whether the statute of 1707 was the controlling factor, asserting instead that Adams adduced convincing evidence for the defense, which the court accepted.[15] That evidence, however, proved only that the defendants had not committed common-law murder. The lieutenant had forbidden the use of weapons and had seized the pistol of one of his subordinates after it had been fired.[16] Weighing that fact, the commissioners might have ruled that he was unarmed. Thus Michael Corbet, the man who killed him, could have been held guilty of murder under a statute of James I providing that a stabbing "though done upon sudden provocation," was punished without benefit of clergy when the victim did not have "a weapon drawn."[17] That statute was in force in Massachusetts, and as the court had ruled that common-law definitions were controlling, the statute could have been used to convict Corbet of murder.

That Corbet was not convicted of murder under the statute of James I may, of course, be due to the fact that the commissioners were unaware of it, or that they doubted if it was applicable to homicides committed on the high seas, or they were not certain that impaling a naval lieutenant on a harpoon fell under the definition of "stabbing." None of these possibilities is likely, however, and beyond much doubt the court did not apply the statute due to an English precedent known to Massachusetts lawyers. The rule was that a defendant who used a dagger to kill an armed man could not be convicted of murder under the statute of James, if the victim at the time of the stabbing had been restraining the defendant's freedom to a degree that, in trespass, would have constituted false imprisonment. There was a common-law privilege to resist unlawful restraint. If death resulted from the use of force unreasonable under the circumstances, the defendant could be guilty of manslaughter but not of murder.[18]

This precedent is the most likely reason that the court did not apply the statute of James I to Corbet. By pleading the defense of unlawful imprisonment, John Adams would have forced Hutchinson and his colleagues to rule on the lawfulness of the impressment and that ruling would have turned on the question whether the lieutenant had been acting legally under the statutes of parliament. The best explanation why the statute was not applied is that the court wished to avoid ruling on that question.

If the court did not wish to rule on the legality of impressment, it would not even hold Corbet guilty of manslaughter under that precedent. For the same reason, it could not convict him of manslaughter as that crime was defined by the general principles of common law. By these principles the grounds for manslaughter were even stronger than had the court used the precedent. In fact, were it not for the question of the legality of impressment, it would be difficult to understand why Corbet was not convicted of manslaughter.

No one had a constitutional right to resist authority that had color in law. Resistance had to be reasonable. The lieutenant had been performing a duty that every British, Irish, and American seaman knew was established by custom. He was not threatening Corbet's life, only Corbet's freedom, and Corbet's use of a deadly weapon, given the facts, was not sanctioned by common law.

Corbet knew that his life was not endangered. Resisting impressment not death, he committed homicide by employing a degree of force not lawfully justified considering the circumstances. Yet Corbet was not convicted. Rather he was released and the court gave every indication that it was deliberately avoiding a public explanation.

To have held Corbet guilty of murder under the facts, the commissioners would have had to rule the impressment legal. To have convicted him of manslaughter under the same facts, they would have had to find the impressment illegal by statute whether or not sanctioned by custom. By acquitting him not only of murder but also of the lesser offense of manslaughter, they were avoiding all controversy about the legality of impressment. To make that conclusion, says one legal historian, is to imply "without much evidence, that the court would rather have maintained the legality of impressments . . . than to have done justice."[19] Depending on how you define "justice," such certainly seems to have been the case.

Sitting on that tribunal was Commodore Samuel Hood, the very man who had ordered the impressment in question. He had issued such orders before and would continue doing so, yet he voted for acquittal. Hood must have realized that if the decision became a precedent, any seaman signed on an American vessel who, on land as well as on sea, resisted a press gang commanded by a commissioned naval officer, even if he defended his freedom with more violence than necessary, would not be answerable to imperial law. Hood should have pressed for a conviction. Instead, he tried to push the case from public memory. The Massachusetts council, standing on whig principles, refused to pay the expenses of the Special Court of Admiralty. Hood paid them personally. When one of the acquitted defendants went to civil court and sued a midshipman who had been a member of the press gang for an injury received during the fracas, Hood intervened to settle out of court. He even wrote John Adams offering his client a cook's position worth £30 a year. He could not risk trial before a Boston traverse jury. The Corbet case would have been tried a second time, as the midshipman, to escape tort liability, would have been advised to establish the performance of a lawful duty.

There is no other conclusion to be drawn from the evidence. As a commander of the fleet, Hood had an important and sensitive assignment. His decision in Corbet's case made his task even more difficult, and only doubts about the statute of 1707 can explain his vote to acquit. Like Francis Bernard and Thomas Hutchinson before him, he found that the very law he was supposed to defend could often be more of an embarrassment than an aid.

We must be careful not to go too far. The point that should be stressed is not that Adams's argument regarding substantive law prevailed; the significant point is that the court did not wish to rule on it. To have done so could have been costly. By any fair reading of the statute, the commissioners would have had to hold illegal the current naval practice of impressing seamen aboard American vessels serving the colonial trade. That ruling would have been more than a whig triumph. It would have added the navy to the boiling pot of contemporary politics, leaving it little choice but to find new recruits ashore where press gangs would surely raise mobs, and whig magistrates could proclaim the officers and their men to be rioters. That may be another reason why Commodore Hood was persuaded to overlook the homicide of one of his lieutenants.

The admiralty court had been created to do a specific job, vital to a seagoing nation. It had been handicapped from the start of the trial by the need to define its adjective and substantive law, legal issues that these Irish seamen could raise because they had competent legal representation. Even had they convicted Corbet and his fellow defendants for murder, or Corbet alone for manslaughter, the commissioners were not certain that trial without jury would be upheld on appeal—if appeal were allowed. In the end they did not even dare rule on the legality of a substantive law that their court had been designed to enforce. Under some legal systems vagueness in the law is resolved in favor of the government. In Great Britain and Ireland it might have been as well, but not necessarily in Massachusetts. Again we see one consequence of transferring English law to the colonies without adding the imperial rule that characterized government in Ireland. For in Massachusetts, like Ireland, defendants were entitled to legal representation in criminal trials. In England they had to defend themselves without the aid of barristers. The greater authority possessed by Irish judges as well as the fact that in Ireland the government not the people selected grand and traverse jurors served to balance whatever advantage council in Ireland might bring to the defense. This was not true in Massachusetts where defendants enjoyed a right Englishmen could not claim, yet were tried by a procedure English, not Irish, in origin: rules formulated for a trial in which the accused defended himself without professional aid. In England and Scotland, moreover, there were no appeals from felony convictions. In Massachusetts with the help of a lawyer, a defendant such as Corbet could question the validity of a statute at the trial stage and, if he lost there, might get a second opportunity in a higher court.

The drafters of imperial statutes served the army even more poorly than the navy. When, following the riot over the seizure of John Hancock's sloop *Liberty*, the Boston mob drove the commissioners of the customs out of town, forcing them to take refuge first with the fleet in the harbor and later at Fort William and Mary on Castle Island, the British ministry, acting on its own authority, ordered General Thomas Gage to send troops to their rescue. This action was precisely what Governor Francis Bernard had long hoped for, although unable to make an official request as the council would "never advise it let the case be ever so desperate."[20] The whigs, he believed, would be tamed by the appearance of military force.[21] General Gage and his officers shared the governor's confidence—a taste of military discipline would temper the politics of Boston's unruly whigs. They did, however, fear they might be met by armed resistance. When instead they were greeted by hostile silence, some tories thought the worst was over; not so General Gage. The fact the people had not fought them, he wrote to Commodore Hood, meant only that the troops could expect more opposition from "law & gospel, than sword and gun."[22]

Thomas Gage turned out to be a better prophet than general. He knew his American whigs and he knew how they could manipulate law—both imperial and local common law.

Again statutes enacted by parliament proved a hindrance rather than an aid to imperial policy. Again poor draftsmanship and doubts as to whether a law applied in the colonies produced embarrassment for British officials. As with the commissioners of the Special Admiralty Court, the officers of the king's army found themselves fighting or avoiding statutory and common law more often than enforcing it.

The army's first need was housing and housing was its first legal difficulty. Under the pertinent parliamentary statute, the Mutiny Act, the duty of finding adequate quarters was entrusted to civil authorities in each colony: not to the governor alone but to the assembly, local officials such as the justices of the peace, and the courts of common law.[23] It was a policy dictated by British constitutional principles requiring civilian control of the military, a policy tested in Ireland where civilian control had more shadow than substance: where the persons upon whom the statute depended were members of the Protestant gentry, a group that in turn depended upon the army to keep down their Catholic tenantry. Now it was to be tested in Boston where, General Gage well knew, civilian control was all substance and little shadow.

In 1768, after their men had landed, the army officers applied to the council for quarters within the limits of Boston proper. Adopting the role of provincial lawyers, the councillors responded to the military's demands by pointing out that there were barracks designed for a thousand men on Castle Island. That was where the harbor fort, called Fort William and Mary or Castle William or the Castle, was located close to the deep water of the channel—the very place Governor Bernard and General Gage did not want the troops stationed.[24] True the barracks there were of poor wartime construction and badly out of repair. True, also, they were on an island a few miles from Boston proper. Legally, however, the Castle was part of the town and as the Mutiny Act required that barracks be filled before other quarters were requisitioned, the councillors told the army's commanding officer he would first have to go there before expecting aid from them.

An impasse had been reached, serious enough for Thomas Gage to make a visit to Boston. He had encountered a similar situation in New York that had taken two years to resolve. In Massachusetts he was not going to have even that slow success.

While the intent of the Mutiny Act was clear enough, some of its wording was not. Colonial officials, one clause specified, were "to quarter and billet the officers and soldiers in his Majesty's service, in the barracks provided by the colonies." If there were no available barracks, substitutes such as "inns, livery stables, ale-houses, victualling houses, and houses of sellers of wine by retail" were to be requisitioned.[25] The council, Gage reported, interpreted these words as requiring not only that all barracks within a town be filled before other housing be requisitioned, but "That whatever Place in a Province The King's Troops should be ordered to, that they could not be quartered in that Place, till all the Barracks in the Province, however distant from it, were first filled with Troops." It was a reading of the act, Gage argued, "which rendered it of no Effect"; an "absurdity" that "absolutely impeded the March of Troops through the Province, as well as the King's Right to order his Troops to any Town or Village."[26]

Considering only law and ignoring politics, General Gage had a point. The council's interpretation of the statute was ridiculously narrow, especially in view of the conditions of the barracks, the purpose for which the army had been posted to Boston, the fact Castle William could hold only about one-fourth of the men expected, and that plans called for it to be fully occupied when all the soldiers arrived. But the rules of statutory construction were not of service to the king's men that day. Whig arguments prevailed because the whigs held the veto. There was no authority higher than the council to which the army could appeal.[27]

The councillors' obstinacy meant more than a refusal to provide quarters within Boston proper. If the barracks on Castle Island were unoccupied, the whigs could claim, any troops stationed in the town would not be lawfully there. If so, the army, until it moved to the Castle, failed to satisfy the Mutiny Act, and it followed the colony was not obliged to furnish various items that, in addition to quarters, were specified in the statute. Moreover, there was no need to call the House of Representatives into session so public funds could be appropriated to finance the colony's requisitions for there would be no requisitions. Not that General Gage expected cooperation from that

108

whig-dominated body. "It depends too much upon the temper and whim of an Assembly," he had complained of the Mutiny Act. "One may perhaps grant, the Next not, One provides consent, Another refuse. So that it can never be certain Whether the troops can obtain Quarters or not?"[28]

We must not misjudge the army's concern. It did not need appropriations from the House of Representatives to hire quarters. Money was not the problem. The problem was posed by the justices of the peace and the role the Mutiny Act assigned them to play. They were the civil officials directed to requisition quarters. The decision of the council, therefore, meant more than an excuse for whig magistrates to refuse to do their duty.[29] It meant that even a tory justice, realizing that whig law had ruled the troops were not lawfully in Boston, would be less than energetic if asked to cooperate. After all, he would not have to seek legal advice to learn that a whig lawyer could draft a civil writ making him personally liable for trespassing on private property. It was that reality that made the army concerned. If the magistrates would not enforce the statute the military was in a dilemma: the Mutiny Act left officers little discretion to proceed on their own.

Do not think of the army moving into houses against the owner's wills. The Mutiny Act did not permit the military to billet either officers or men in private homes, not even if other types of buildings were filled. The army had no thought of violating the law. Its dilemma was that if it obeyed the statute and placed troops only in public structures or inns, the terms of the Mutiny Act were such that an officer quartering men anywhere within the town might face a whig court, his very career in jeopardy.

Again we can only wonder at the conditions of imperial law. Had American whigs truly wished to be free of British rule they would have found it difficult to draft statutes more favorable to their cause than those drafted and enacted by a parliament hoping to perpetuate that rule. Had the Mutiny Act been well written, at least for the realities of North American politics, it would have contained provisions penalizing obstinate colonial officials. It did, in fact, have clauses along these lines, but the lawmakers of parliament, intent on preventing abuse and avoiding friction between the army and civil authorities, framed them in such a way they gave more aid to the whigs than to the soldiers of the king.

Local common-law courts had jurisdiction under the Mutiny Act; hardly the tribunals General Gage would have selected. Not only were juries unlikely to convict but, as he pointed out, "the penalty on the Magistrate for not quartering the troops being only five pounds, renders a prosecution of little consequence."[30] Gage had asked for more severe measures—"a large Fine upon any Justice of Peace, Mayor or other Magistrate"—but the ministry had not responded.[31] The justices of Boston had been more or less correct when they told him "that the Act did not require them to quarter troops, or words to that Effect."[32] The mutiny statute did not require them to quarter troops because the courts of jurisdiction were their own courts and martial measures to compel compliance were not permitted.

The other side of the coin would have been to allow military people, when all else failed, to make requisitions on their own authority. On this point the Mutiny Act of 1765 was almost self-defeating. Penalties levied against army officers for violating the law were the opposite of those levied against stubborn civilian magistrates. They were so severe that no officer in Boston dared on his own authority occupy, let alone requisition, quarters. It had been ordained by parliament that any officer who took upon himself to quarter soldiers in any way other than provided by the act, or who used "menace or compulsion," would upon conviction before two justices of the peace, "be *ipso facto* cashiered, and shall be utterly disabled to have or hold any military employment." [33]

Even for the eighteenth century the cashiering proviso was harsh, and military officers could expect such a penalty to be invoked only in cases of gross abuse. It was somewhat of a dead letter in most places, that is, except whig Boston and other parts of North America. Even there the threat would not have been great had parliament provided for trial at court-martial. Instead jurisdiction was vested at common law, which meant that an officer who assigned shelter to his troops might find himself compelled to answer charges before two Boston justices of the peace or a whig traverse jury.

When requesting that the Mutiny Act be reformed, General Gage had complained that army officers had been "sent to Jail for being in the Quarters which had been alloted to them." [34] The statute parliament gave him did not improve matters and may have made them worse. Writing to the Earl of Hillsborough from Boston about the cashiering proviso, a frustrated Thomas Gage left us one of the best extant summaries of the helplessness felt by tories when face to face with whig law.

> I would take the Liberty My Lord to represent, that the Clause in Question, is by no means calculated for the Circumstances of this Country, where every Man Studys Law, and interprets the Law as suits his Purposes. And where the measures of Government are opposed by every Evasion and Chicane, that can be devised. An Officer of Rank and long Service may be cashiered, by the Management of two Justices of the Peace, the best of them a keeper of a paltry Tavern, who shall find Evasions to disobey the Clauses of the Mutiny Act they dislike, and to pervert the Sense and Meaning of others to serve their Designs against him. [35]

It is impossible to disagree. An officer who attempted to quarter troops ran the risk of losing his commission.

Surely Governor Francis Bernard and the army's commanding officers took the cashiering clause seriously, a fact demonstrated when they started assigning the soldiers to barracks. Forced by the council and the justices of the peace either to locate on Castle Island or find their own quarters in Boston proper, they tried to make the best of a frustrating situation. Some of the men were placed in publicly owned buildings, and the army used crown funds to rent space for the remaining men and for the officers, and to purchase whatever supplies could not be obtained from the commissary in Halifax.

The whigs were now on the defensive. The legal maneuvering by the council may have been a whig victory, but considering the major issue it was at best a delaying action. The taxpayers of Massachusetts Bay might have escaped paying for the military occupation, but the overriding political reality was that the troops were being housed and Boston was to become a garrison town. It was at this juncture that the whigs sought to invoke the cashiering penalty. When the army officers began to quarter their troops, the whigs threatened them with arrest. Once again the argument turned on the fact that the Castle must first be occupied. The cashiering provision directed that quartering of troops could not be "OTHERWISE than is limited and allow'd in this act." That clause, the whigs contended, meant that until the barracks were filled the officers would not be billeting their men according to law.[36]

Under the statute an officer placing men into housing could be protected from prosecution in two and perhaps three ways. The governor and council might appoint "a proper person or persons . . . to take, hire and make fit" the quarters. Should they fail to do so, the law directed the justices of peace to perform the task.[37] Apparently officers could also escape the cashiering clause if a magistrate certified the appropriateness of hiring private quarters.[38] All three solutions were impossible in Boston as they required cooperation of either the council or the justices of the peace.

Now it was the tories' turn to shade the meaning of statutory law and employ legal technicalities. They had to or the troops would not have been housed without every officer facing possible prosecution. Outflanking the whigs for the only time during his administration, Governor Bernard gave "a particular Warrant to a Commissary, against whom no Action could lye, to quarter the Soldiers in the House, fitted up for their Reception"[39] In other words, he appointed a civilian straw to place the troops in their barracks, freeing army officers from any apprehension that they might be charged by the Suffolk grand jury with illegal actions or (and this was not likely) sued in tort for trespass.

Governor Bernard's solution was simple; a mere technicality that might seem silly today though it probably appeared rational and essential to the officers it was designed to protect. Indeed, the use of the strawman is not important in itself. What is revealing is that Bernard believed it necessary to resort to such a legal dodge. That he did demonstrates the extent to which the governor and his tory advisors respected whig control of the justices of the peace and of the Suffolk county juries. The desperation they must have felt may to some extent be measured when it is recalled that the usually cautious Bernard solved his dilemma by making an appointment that the Mutiny Act, if it did not say so directly, at least implied required consent of the council.[40] Moreover, the fact that the military looked to the governor for a prior solution shows how seriously everyone regarded the cashiering proviso. The conclusion must be that the army officers were unwilling to rely upon the executive pardoning power. They needed immunity from prosecution or apparently they could not perform their duties in whig Boston.

Indeed, the concerned officers of King George's army may well have asked themselves not only whether they could do their duty but whether they had any duties to perform. The answer lay less with the determination and resourcefulness of the king's men than with the law.

We learn something of the imperial legal mind directing affairs from faraway London when we consider that perhaps none of the leaders of the British government gave much thought to law—to what the troops were to do or even what they could do once garrisoned in Boston. The assumption seems to have been that their very presence would make a difference: the mob had been allowed to run wild because it had no opposition; now there was a police force on hand and riots would be suppressed. The Earl of Hillsborough surely had such expectations in mind. The troops, he told General Gage in his orders, "will strengthen the hands of government in the province of Massachusetts Bay, enforce a due obedience to the laws, and protect and support the civil magistrates and the officers of the Crown in the execution of their duty."[41] A month later, writing Governor Francis Bernard that soldiers were on the way, Hillsborough expressed fatigue at hearing of Bernard's helplessness before Boston mobs. "Full responsibility thus rests with you," he warned, "and terror and danger in execution of your office will not be an excuse for remission of duty."[42]

Hillsborough apparently believed that Bernard now had the means to maintain the king's peace and enforce the laws of parliament. Lord George Sackville knew better. "They talk of vigour, and two regiments are embarked for Boston," he wrote two months later, "but . . . applying this military force . . . is a point of such delicacy in our constitution that I doubt much of its being properly executed."[43] Events would prove Lord George Sackville nearer the mark than Lord Hillsborough.

Not all responsibility was placed on the unwilling shoulders of Francis Bernard. The man who had to contend with what Sackville termed the "delicacy" of the British constitution was Major General Thomas Gage. As commander-in-chief of the king's forces on the continent, Gage occupied an office of such a nature "that the incumbent might be called the principal representative of the British Empire in North America."[44] Like Lord Hillsborough he believed that a show of military forces backed by strong parliamentary action would end "the Mutinous Behaviour of the People of Boston" and "reduce them to their Constitutional Dependence, on the Mother Country."[45]

After his troops had been in Boston for almost two years, General Gage was less confident. "No Laws can be put in Force," he warned the war secretary in London, "for those who shou'd execute the Laws, excite the People to break them and defend them in it. Nothing will avail in so total an Anarchy, but a very considerable Force, and that Force empower'd to act."[46] Gage was lamenting whig law and whig control of the justiceships of the peace. They produced what he, and most other tories, called "anarchy." But his basic complaint was that he and his fellow officers did not have authority "to act." The cause was neither whig law nor whig magistrates, it was the British constitution.

As Thomas Gage understood the constitution and as he interpreted it through his orders to subordinates, the law gave the military a subaltern role in political disputes. To act against crowds the army needed directions from a civilian officer or could not act at all. The colonial governor would not do. Orders from him were not enough for soldiers to use their weapons. Troops were not to fire unless a civil magistrate on the spot gave the command. In Massachusetts that meant whigs, about the same as saying that the soldiers, when confronted by civilian rioters, would never fire, a fact Gage knew only too well. The one exception to the rule of civilian superiority was open rebellion. Then the commander-in-chief could act on his own authority.

The troops had not been in Boston long before the men in charge discovered that the constitution deprived them of any chance to be an effective force. After about a year, their commanding officer requested permission to employ the soldiers as necessity required. Gage replied that he agreed with the arguments that the officer made; he too expected fresh riots at any moment; he knew that most Bostonians were fond of "anarchy & licentiousness"; and that the "tyranny of the people appears to be confirmed in opposition to order and justice and every mark of a regular government." He could not, however, direct his men to suppress rioting unless requested by some civil authority. "Had I proper authority to act in these cases," he assured his junior colleague, "I should have interfered in matters that occurred here [New York] lately, Wherein I think everything has happened but a declaration of war against Great Britain. . . . You will feel the same indignation & resentment which such proceedings must occasion in the breast of every Briton here, who has the least love or regard for his country, but if they do not rouse a proper spirit at home, what can we do here?"[47]

That, indeed was the question not only whigs but tories had been asking. What could the troops do now that they were stationed on official duty in Massachusetts Bay? For once both sides gave the same answer—the military could do little or nothing.

The whig answer had a whiggish warp: the army could do nothing, for it had no constitutional function in law enforcement. "Nor," the Massachusetts house argued, "can there be any necessity for it; for the body of the people, the *posse comitatus*, will always aid the magistrate in the execution of such laws as ought to be executed."[48] It did not have to be said that there were laws that "ought not to be executed" or that those were the laws the army had come to enforce.

The tory answer had a familiar savor, redolent to a whig, effluvial to an imperialist. Coming first from the commissioners of the customs, it was unencouraging for the future of British rule in North America. They had been largely responsible for the troops being sent—it was to protect the commissioners as much as any other consideration that persuaded the British cabinet to order the occupation of Boston. Before the troops arrived, the commissioners had fled the town and taken refuge at Castle William. Until they were protected, they had argued, they would not be safe in Boston and would not go back. The idea seems to have been in the minds of the ministry that the troops, if they accomplished nothing else, would at least protect these revenue men and make it possible for them to perform their duties. Governor Bernard at first accepted this theory. "We have got two Reg[iments] from Halifax landed at Boston," he optimistically wrote to Lord Barrington. "So that the Persons of the Crown Officers are safe as I believe; tho' that is still doubted." [49]

Among those who doubted were the commissioners themselves. Secure behind the guns of the Castle, with leisure to weigh whig law against tory order, they came to the conclusion that while the people of Boston did not want them in town they would be wiser to stay away. Even Thomas Gage could not coach them back, When he tried they asked who would guarantee troops would be used to protect them. "The Governor and Lieutenant Governor were present," Gage reported, "but neither could be answerable." [50] The governor and lieutenant governor were saying what they had said before. They could guarantee the safety of no British official, for the reins of government were not in their hands.

Again we should be careful not to oversimplify the problem. Bernard's difficulty arose as much from the formal institutions of imperial law as from the veto whig magistrates held over military action. Power was constitutionally there but it was constitutionally restricted. It was not a matter, as has sometimes been said, that a governor was unable to impose martial law without the consent of the council. If that were true elsewhere, it was not the rule in Massachusetts Bay. Under the colony's charter Bernard had "full Power by himselfe . . . to use and exercise the Law Martiall." His authority was limited, however, to "time of actuall Warr Invasion or Rebellion," precisely the type of emergencies when Gage could act on his own and did not need marching orders from the civil branch of government. Even if a revolution were proclaimed, martial law would not have solved the dilemma faced by Bernard and Hutchinson. For the charter further provided that while the governor alone made the decision to declare martial law, he "shall not . . . grant Comissions for exercising the Law Martiall upon any [of] the Inhabitants of Our said Province or Territory without the Advice and Consent of the Councill." [51] The army might have been free to function independently of civilian control, but the whigs on the council would not have allowed the governor to supersede the common law by appointing reliable king's men to the courts of martial law and arrests would have been meaningless.

In Ireland the constitutional rule was different. Martial law was routinely imposed and the lord lieutenant set military policy. Irish tradition was not that the forces of government refused to employ troops. Rather, in Ireland the army was the force of government, freely and often applied. It is true that, as in Great Britain and North America, soldiers were not supposed to fire on civilians without the orders of a civil magistrate, but in Ireland that part of the constitution was easily suspended. Before the eighteenth century came to a close, one of Britain's most distinguished officers, Sir Ralph Abercromby, would resign as commander of the king's forces in Ireland, charging that the Rising of '98 had been due more to excesses committed by the troops than to

French propaganda or plots by the United Irishmen.[52] The lord lieutenant of the kingdom, the Marquis of Camden, had issued a proclamation of "Martial Law and Free Quarter," which not only some legal historians, but many rebel leaders said was the cause of the insurrection.[53] "The basic principles on which Ireland was governed," the biographer of Wolfe Tone has written, "were martial law, free quarters, and house-burnings. The first meant that the will of the military officers superseded the law of the land; the second that in places where the people failed to obey the order to deliver up their arms, the troops were billeted on them and instructed to live well at their expense; the third that houses in which arms were found were burnt."[54] Officers were not only authorized but instructed to act without waiting for a civil magistrate, and the abusive exercise of power seems unbelievable even within the notorious context of British government in Ireland. It was a policy of excessive military rule that General Abercromby refused to tolerate. Both the yeoman militia and the regular forces, he declared in a memorable general order, were more dangerous to their friends than to their enemies, and he forbade his officers to take any police action without the presence and authority of a civil magistrate. His objective was to restore internal discipline among the troops and bring the army under the rule of law.[55]

While it has been suggested that the lord lieutenant sympathized with Abercromby's orders,[56] he gave no public indication of support. In fact, the rule of civilian law was not the constitutional policy of Dublin Castle: martial rule, as set forth in the proclamation, was. "Under that proclamation," the lord lieutenant wrote the general, "the military received orders to act without waiting for a civil magistrate. . . . That necessity exists, and since it does exist, it appears to me that the proclamation must be acted on."[57] Refusing "to sanction the cruel orders of the Viceroy, which he could not dispute," General Abercromby relinquished his command and departed from Ireland.[58] In North America no army officer would resign for that cause because no colonial governor could issue those orders.

The commissioners of the customs, when they refused to return to Boston, were not asking that Irish military law be imposed on Massachusetts. Martial law was one solution they would not have rejected, but they were not seeking the impossible. All they wanted was some assurance, now that troops were on hand, that the military would be called upon to act should it be needed. They were requesting a pledge that Bernard, Hutchinson, and even General Gage could not give. As so many times before, the difficulty lay with the justices of the peace. Magistrates who would not try to disperse mobs by reading the riot act were not likely to take the more drastic legal step and call for force to suppress riots. The troops might be in Boston but they would remain of marginal utility unless the justices of the peace would employ them.

If imperial law could not depend upon the magistrates to call out the troops, only two alternatives remained. One was the sheriff but no lawyer was certain what martial authority he possessed.[59] During the New York tenantry riots, magistrates had accompanied the troops even though a sheriff was present. While other explanations are possible, it was most likely that the sheriff was there to take custody of civilian prisoners, the magistrates to lend legality to whatever force was exerted. Besides, in most Massachusetts counties—if not most of those in North America—the sheriff leaned more toward the whig than the tory persuasion.[60]

A second alternative to the justices would have been the governor. It was undisputed that he could order out troops if the council consented. What was not certain was whether the governor had the power to act without consulting the council. Authority might be implied either from his commission as captain general of the province, from his instructions, or from the fact that he, like the justices of the peace, was a magistrate.

Both Francis Bernard and Thomas Hutchinson had no doubts on the question, and each steadfastly based his conduct on the premise that he had no constitutional power to apply force against civilians unless the council concurred. Former Governor Thomas Pownall disagreed as did at least one other member of parliament who had served as the chief executive of a North American colony.[61] In truth, no one knew the law for it had never been formulated—an amazing commentary on the conditions of imperial law in eighteenth-century North America.[62] In emergencies bold men might have acted, a possibility that excluded the cautious, fearful Bernard. Hutchinson was more the type to take risks but not on legal questions. Without clear instructions from London he rested on precedent, leaving the constitution precisely where he had found it.

Thus we see in summation the conditions of imperial law in prerevolutionary America. Imperial law was often contradictory, when not contradictory it was often vague, and even when clear (as in its requirement of civilian control of military police actions) it was often self-defeating. Whig law in contrast was dynamic in its pretensions and energetic in its enforcement. We need only recall the Boston mob to realize the difference. When it had business on the streets the nearness of the troops was no deterrent. One fact alone furnishes the measure of the army's effectiveness as a police force: no person was tarred and feathered in Boston until after the troops arrived and were stationed within the town limits. The process often took several hours, with the tory victim carted through the streets, providing the authorities with both ample time and the choice of several locations to test the peace-keeping capabilities of the soldiers. They never did. Thomas Gage's biographer summed up the times in a single sentence when he wrote, "More than one Boston merchant was forced to sign the nonimportation agreements under the very nose of the British Army."[63] Ebenezer Richardson was paraded through the streets to Faneuil Hall under that same nose. After the Boston Massacre, General Gage admitted that the situation was hopeless and the fault lay not with the military but with the law. "When the Troops first arrived indeed at Boston," he wrote to his superiors in London, "the People were kept in some awe by them; but they soon discovered, that Troops were bound by Constitutional Laws, and could only Act under the Authority, and by the Orders of the Civil Magistrates; who were all of their Side. And they recommenced their Riots, tho' two or three Regiments were in Town, with the Same unbridled Licentiousness as before."[64]

Boston had become an occupied town but the occupiers were not in control. They had been sent to intimidate and it was they who were intimidated. They were expected to police but it was they who would be policed.[65] Massachusetts whigs were not cowed by the presence of the army. The presence of the army made whig law more jaunty, final proof for persuading Americans that imperial rule was backed by little force.

British troops stationed in North America would have to await open rebellion before they found a constitutional role to play. If anything, the occupation of Boston aided the cause of Samuel Adams by uniting even more firmly the bulk of the population behind the whig leadership and adding one more grievance dividing the colonies from their mother country. To be a force an army must be able to act, and the army commanded by Thomas Gage was not allowed to act. Too many laws and too many constitutional inhibitions stood in its way. To send troops into a province where there was no government able to employ them was not a decisive action. It was an act of provocation. If Francis Bernard and Thomas Hutchinson were expected to govern by the aid of military force, they needed a different constitutional tradition or the troops that landed during the autumn of 1768 were too few. Under the eighteenth-century British constitution, those troops were far too many.[66]

12

The Government
They Have Set Up[1]

THE EMERGENCE
OF WHIG GOVERNMENT

Adjectives may be misleading. When we look closely eighteenth-century British imperial law seems less than imperial. So too we may wonder whether whig law was the law of a political party only. When we contemplate the run of its writ and the force of its judgment we may ask if, even before Lexington and Concord, it was not the law of an emerging nation or the law of at least one American province.

Consequences have a way of multiplying results. The ambiguities of British constitutionalism, the anemic conditions of imperial law, and local control of most governmental institutions did more than furnish American dissidents with means to keep the agents of British rule at bay. They encouraged the gestation of several *sui generis* channels of legislative and executive authority that in the fullness of time would supplant the institutions of the old order. To put it another way, law and the conditions of both imperial and local law help explain why—as Thomas Gage stated somewhat prematurely during 1769—"an imperium" had been "set up and at length established, without the least Shew of Opposition."[2]

With legislatures, juries, and most other instruments of local government in the hands of whigs, the British by 1769 retained what governance they exercised over North America largely through those offices, both imperial and local, subject to royal or proprietary patronage. In all the provinces, except the charter colonies of Connecticut and Rhode Island, the most important of these offices was the governorship. While it is true that most provincial councils sharply curtailed the discretion of both royal and proprietary governors, all executive authority was in their hands. As a result, executive power in North America was stronger—at least in constitutional theory—than in Great Britain. The various acts of settlement following the Glorious Revolution, limiting the executive prerogative at home, had not been extended to the colonies. The governors could, for example, veto acts of the assembly, a check that the king no longer held over parliament. Thus, even though the whigs dominated most of the lower legislative houses, they could not emulate parliament's recent assumption of executive authority, exercised through control of the cabinet. To counter the executive authority of the governor, the whigs had to develop institutions, independent of the assembly. The first step was the nonimportation associations.

Nonimportation was designed to promote American whig policy by placing an embargo on selected British merchandise. While some historians believe that it was economic in origin, the whigs claimed that it was intended to force repeal of certain imperial statutes: during 1765 the Stamp Act; during 1769–70 the Townshend duties; and during 1774 the intolerable acts.[3]

The mechanics of nonimportation need not be detailed. It is British reaction that tells us about the conditions of law. From his office in New York Thomas Gage recognized the danger posed by nonimportation associations and thought it a threat to the unity of the empire.[4] From his seat near Boston Chief Justice Thomas Hutchinson, looking at the same event from the perspective of constitutional law, saw a menace even more alarming: the first stirrings of whig legislative activities independent of the imperial constitution. For in New England, the nonimportation movement had been initiated by the town meeting, a legal institution that the whigs could easily employ to cover any program of opposition to British rule with an aura of semiconstitutionality and the appearance of legitimately sanctioned legality.

The whigs were employing a legal institution, but under imperial law they were employing it illegally. A town meeting had no more constitutional authority to sanction nonimportation than did a grand jury in the counties of Delaware or a mass meeting of citizens in Savannah.[5] Yet it was a constitutional body that a dynamic whig legal theory could expand into new areas both legislative and executive if not checked by British law. It was the Boston town meeting that set the example for usurpation of legislative functions when it voted during October 1767 to encourage local manufactures and not to purchase enumerated items from abroad.[6] Two years after the Boston agreement went into operation, the town meeting's potential as an executive as well as a legislative branch of government was demonstrated when it coerced obedience to its edicts by voting that the names of merchants previously proscribed be published in newspapers and entered on the town records.[7] The purpose they said was "that posterity may know who those persons were that preferred their little private advantages to the common interest of all the colonies" and "so those who afford them their Countenance, or give them their Custom, must expect to be considered in the same disagreeable light."[8] It was action of this sort along with mass visitations by groups numbering up to a thousand men that persuaded the sons of Thomas Hutchinson to end their defiance of nonimportation and surrender for storage merchandise they had recently received from British shippers.[9] In some other New England localities the town meetings went further toward making nonimportation part of local government policy. In Marblehead, for example, the meeting voted to use town funds to pay freight costs when sending contraband goods back to Great Britain; in Portsmouth, New Hampshire, the town meeting forced compliance by threatening to revoke the license of any tavern keeper who permitted proscribed merchandise to be displayed for sale in his establishment.[10]

Perhaps the whigs of Boston, unlike those of Salem or Portsmouth, were troubled by constitutional doubts concerning the town meeting's power to enforce nonimportation or, if they were not, they may have thought it best to free Boston of any hint of illegality. They soon abandoned the regular town meeting as the forum for sponsoring nonimportation and gathered in what at first were called merchants' meetings. The change was largely of form, not substance or personnel. The merchants' meetings, Thomas Hutchinson explained to Lord Hillsborough, were as effective as town meetings. They "are called and held by adjournments, whose resolutions are come into, Committees appointed, and other proceedings had in as formal a manner as in a body corporate legally assembled and known and established by the Constitution; and those meetings have had such effect that . . . most of the Traders who until now had firmness to stand out have joined in the subscription to import no goods."[11]

Hutchinson put his finger on the essence of the whig theory of constitutionality when he stressed that these "merchants' meetings" were "held by adjournments." While more effective work could have been accomplished by small committees, the lack of constituted authority and their own legal predilections persuaded the whig leadership to recall the people into frequent sessions. From the tory point of view, the purpose was to reinforce decisions with the sanction of a mass vote which, if no more legal, carried the threat of coercive enforcement by aroused public opinion. From the whig perspective—or at least from that of Samuel Adams—the importance of the meetings lay in the emergence of a counter constitution to which appeal could be made should the British attempt to enforce imperial law.

By late 1769 or early 1770 the pretense that these affairs were merchants' meetings was abandoned, and a new name adopted: the "Body" or the "Body of the Trade, and others."[12] In strict constitutional law the "body" was no more legal than other mass gatherings or such contemporary movements as the Regulators who attempted to enforce law and order in the back country of the two Carolinas. But due to the inability of imperial government to suppress it and also to the fact that it met openly and regularly during times of crisis, the "body" had the future before it.

Today the regularity and openness of the meetings, as well as the appeal for public consent, seem to be the hallmarks of the "body," distinguishing it from a mob. During the 1770s other features were marked. As an unfriendly correspondent observed in *The Massachusetts Gazette & Post Boy*: "A body meeting has great advantage over a town meeting, as no law has yet ascertained the qualification of the voters; each person present of whatever age, estate or country, may . . . speak or vote at such an assembly; and that might serve as a skreen to the town where it originated, in case of any disastrous consequence."[13]

It may be asked which was the greater factor for creation of the "body"—the desire to broaden the franchise or the need for a legal "skreen." While it is possible that both considerations played a role in the decision to substitute the "body" for the town meeting, it is unlikely that many whigs thought Boston protected from punishment by the fiction that illegal action was the responsibility of the unofficial "body" rather than the regular town meeting. True, Thomas Hutchinson three years later would tell London that the "body" not the town meeting was fomenting the Tea Party crisis on the advice of an attorney, thought to be John Adams. The lawyer, Hutchinson wrote, "left the audience to suppose he thought it a matter more proper to be taken in hand by the people who assembled without colour of Law."[14] Hutchinson had not been present and was reporting hearsay. Even so, what he said sounds more like political than legal advice. Other colonies, disenchanted with the Boston mob, might react less favorably to violence if it did not have official sanction. To suggest, on the other hand, that the British government could take punitive action against a town meeting but not against the "body" was legally unrealistic. A lawyer of the caliber of John Adams would not have said so. If any whigs believed it possible, the Port of Boston Act, which punished the town for the staging of the Tea Party by the "body," could disabuse them.[15] Imperial law may have been weak, but it was not trapped in absurd technicalities.

The second consideration mentioned by the correspondent in *The Massachusetts Gazette & Post Boy*—the extension of the franchise—is the better legal explanation for creation of the "body." The purpose was not to increase representation within Boston proper. At a regular town meeting the whigs were in control and could see to it that all their supporters were permitted to participate. Thomas Hutchinson complained that it was "very rare that any scrutiny is made into the qualification of voters."[16] He estimated that there were only about 1,500 "legal voters in the town," yet on one occasion at least 3,000 had participated—"their newspaper says 4,000."[17] What a "body" meeting, unlike a town meeting, could do was admit residents from other communities, thus increasing the weight of public opinion behind its decisions. The threat of doing so may have been a factor persuading Hutchinson to yield to town demands during the Boston Massacre crisis.[18] The threat would become a reality during the controversy leading up to the Tea Party.

The legal or constitutional importance of the nonimportation association—whether the earlier merchant-oriented agreements of the Stamp Act period, the more vague programs ostensibly based on public consent aimed against the Townshend duties, or the continental reaction to the intolerable acts in 1774—was that they provided whig leaders with their first significant experience with executive authority independent of imperial prescripts. They not only made regulations governing nonimportation,[19] they attempted to enforce them and to a remarkable degree were successful. As Lord Dunmore in Virginia explained to the earl of Dartmouth during December 1774, "They inspect the trade and correspondence of every merchant, watch the conduct of any inhabitant, may send for, catechize and stigmatize him if he does not appear to follow the laws of their Congress."[20]

The emergence of whig law enforcing nonimportation is a fascinating tale so far neglected by historians though this is not the place to tell the story. What interests us is that tories realized a new executive power was on the rise and nothing could be done to quash it. "Owners and masters of ships," Thomas Hutchinson lamented, "submitted to have the manifests of goods on board examined by committees; and merchants who would have procured resistance against the search of a custom-house officer, legally authorized by a writ of assistance, acquiesced in a search made by such committees."[21] Hutchinson could not avoid describing the work of these committees in terms of law, especially after he learned that some merchants were smuggling "legal" tea into Boston by way of Halifax to avoid detection by the committees of inspection. "Tea from Holland may be lawfully sold," he wrote, "it's a high crime to sell any from England."[22] Smuggling "illegal tea" from Amsterdam was more open, and apparently less risky, than smuggling "legal tea" upon which duty had been paid at Halifax.

Public ostracism was the chief sanction used to enforce nonimportation. Names of violators were spread throughout the community by printed broadsides or published in local newspapers.[23] If holdouts were stubborn the whigs would threaten violence. In Boston the favorite whig persuader was the mass visitation. Instead of releasing a mob, the "body" would adjourn to reassemble at the culprit's house or place of business.[24] When we realize there were many merchants and lawyers of prominence and fortune who took part we learn much about the nature of whig law and implications of mob violence. Their Irish counterparts would not have joined a mass visitation, they could not always risk public ostracism.

During the Volunteer movement that occurred in Ireland at the time of the American Revolution, there were also associations to abstain from purchasing British goods until certain commercial restrictions detrimental to the Irish economy were repealed. As in North America a decade earlier, some of these agreements were entered into by the grand juries, while others were drafted by county meetings and signed by citizens in the more important towns. "It was proposed," Lecky tells us, "in imitation of the Americans, to publish in the newspapers the names of those traders who had infringed the agreement, but this proposal, which would have probably led to much crime, was generally reprobated, and soon abandoned."[25] In few other decisions does the distinction between Irish and American society, and the conditions of law in those British dominions, stand in such stark relief. The merchants of Ireland could not afford to stigmatize publicly profiteers without risking violence and murder. In America the whigs could not only publicly label nonsubscribers "enemies to the liberties of America" and urge people to treat them "with the contempt they deserve," they could, if necessary, apply force without fearing Irish consequences.[26]

On one occasion the Boston "body," with lawyers in its ranks, even "visited" the home of Thomas Hutchinson. Warning them they violated imperial law, he, nonetheless, submitted to their demands and persuaded his sons to surrender contraband merchandise. He was then acting governor and hoped that his concession would restore the "peace of the town."[27] Instead the whigs became more bold and soon had the "body" debating political issues unrelated to nonimportation.[28] It was a dangerous turn; the mob had become an organized pressure group that could marshal public opinion in a guise that people would soon equate with the town meeting. Even if the governor refused to receive its petitions, a potential legislative body was emerging. Hutchinson had to take steps, but how? The council refused to support him and when he convened the justices they replied that the people "were greatly agitated and disturbed, from a sense of danger to their just rights and liberties." That was why they met in "tumultuous assemblies," and the magistrates "were of opinion that it was not incumbent on them to take any measures for interrupting the proceedings."[29]

Again Hutchinson was confronted by an argument based on whig legal theory. Under imperial law the meetings, as he argued, might be "unwarrantable," but the defense of whig principles furnished its own validity. Besides, the lieutenant governor noted, "Several of the justices attended the meetings and voted for the measures."[30] In addition to those "several Justices of the peace who ought to execute Law, [there were] several professed Lawyers and a great number of Inhabitants of property together with three of the Representatives of the Town and a mixed multitude warmed with a persuasion that what they were doing was right and that they were struggling for the Liberties of America."[31]

Left to his own authority, Thomas Hutchinson decided that he was empowered to act, if only feebly. He sent the sheriff to Faneuil Hall with a message outlining his version of the law. "Body" meetings, he declared, were unjustified, "by any authority or colour of law," and he warned the people "of the penalties to which they made themselves liable" and ordered them, "in his majesty's name, forthwith to separate and disperse" and "to forbear all such unlawful assemblies for the future."[32] The proclamation was read, and after a short discussion it was voted that "it is the unanimous opinion of this body after serious consideration and debate that this meeting is warranted by law."[33] In conclusion the resolution added that the "body" was "determined to keep consciences void of offence towards God, and towards man."[34] The king's law was not a factor.

The problem goes deeper than a confrontation between whig government and royal government, with local institutions nullifying the power of London's representative. The conditions of imperial law were a factor. We may be certain that under no circumstances would Hutchinson have persuaded the council, magistrates, or "body" to agree with his law. Yet, we may wonder if he did not suffer from the added handicap of not knowing how to argue his case. In his proclamation he called the "body" meetings illegal and in his reports to London said he knew them "to be against the Law," yet it seems he was not certain just what statutes were being violated and may have thought none adequate to meet the emergency.[35]

It was a remarkable situation, and we may be amazed, yet it should be remembered that a colonial governor was far from London. Even when legal advice was available, it could not have been as authoritative or confident as opinions the king's ministers received from England's law officers. The attorney general was usually a provincial trial lawyer with a limited library, while the judges—and it was proper for a governor to consult them—did not always have legal training. Hutchinson, himself, was not a member of the bar, yet he had to make decisions based on law—or guess what the law was. Small wonder that we find Hutchinson asking if he had sufficient authority to interdict "body" meetings. "An Act of Parliament for the severe punishment of all who shall in like manner offend for the future, will be necessary," he warned later that same year.[36]

Legal ambiguities did not arise from the meetings themselves. With cooperative magistrates and juries they could have been dispersed as riots. The challenge was the nonimportation agreements and their enforcement. When the Boston town meeting first proposed nonimportation against the Townshend duties, Hutchinson, himself, noted that by unanimous vote it was resolved to proceed "by all prudent and legal measures."[37] Unlike Hutchinson, the whigs were not asking whether the associations were unlawful. They probably did not care. Whig law was broad enough to embrace the concept that there could be "legal measures" taken by an illegal enterprise.[38]

At first Hutchinson thought that nonimportation violated the *praemunire* statutes. But these laws were narrow in scope and the only pertinent one—making it an offense to question the authority of the king and parliament—was limited to supporters of the House of Stuart and to those who denied the right of parliament to determine the rules of succession.[39] The nonimportation agreements did not fall in that category. Nor did they violate current common-law offenses against restraint of trade. Commercial combinations appear to have been unlawful only when directed at raising prices or controlling wages.[40] If anything, nonimportation was concerned with encouraging labor and by policing profiteering it sought to stabilize, not raise prices. Treason was a stronger possibility, as it was treason for individuals to "make an Insurrection in order to redress a public grievance, whether it be a real or pretended one, and of their own authority attempt with force to redress it." Nonimportation satisfied this crime, at least in part, for it was a combination that had as its purpose the reform of the revenue laws.[41] But one of the definitions of riot covered the same activities, and if Hutchinson could not get convictions for the lesser crime he would not be able to charge the "body" with insurrection.[42]

William Henry Drayton may have pointed out one violation when he charged that subscribers to the South Carolina association had set themselves up as a legislature.[43] Andrew Oliver, soon to succeed Hutchinson as lieutenant governor, said much the same: nonimportation appeared to him "little less than assuming a negative on all acts of parliament which they do not like."[44] It was a common-law crime—a contempt and misprision against the king's authority—to do anything that would weaken his government.[45] When the Massachusetts House of Representatives voted resolutions questioning parliamentary supremacy, parliament had answered by declaring the resolutions "illegal, unconstitutional, and derogatory of the rights of the Crown and Parliament of Great Britain."[46] If Hutchinson thought of these votes during the period when the nonimportation subscribers were subverting the laws of parliament, he may also have recalled that no members of the Massachusetts house had been charged with crime.[47]

There was even more to recall, much more for a royal official in Massachusetts Bay. Imperial government had previously reacted to whig manifestations of legislative authority and its reaction had been so infirm as to make it look ridiculous. Though their nonimportation regulations were in fact "statutes" intended to bind the reluctant as well as the volunteer, the whigs probably had not feared prosecution. During 1768 they had learned, once again, that the British lion had more roar than bite.

When it was discovered during 1768 that the British ministry had decided to station regular army troops in Massachusetts Bay, the whigs of Boston saw an issue with which to arouse the colony. Gathered in town meeting, they petitioned Governor Francis Bernard to call the general court into legislative session. Bernard, of course, had no intention of doing so, but recent events gave him an excuse to plead that he was unable to comply. On 11 February the Massachusetts House of Representatives had circulated a letter to the assemblies of the other colonies denying the right of parliament to tax North Americans and questioning the policy of granting royal salaries to the governors and the refusal of London to appoint local judges with a tenure of good behavior. Bernard had been ordered to prorogue the assembly and not to reconvene it until the letter was rescinded. As that had not been done, he replied, he was without authority to call the general court into session.[48]

The town meeting refused to accept the governor's answer. Assembling again on 13 September those present resolved, according to Hutchinson, "that raising, and keeping, a standing army in the town without the consent of the inhabitants, in person, or by their representatives, would be an infringement on their natural, constitutional, and charter rights."[49] Convinced they had a constitutional grievance, blocked by the governor from voting instructions to their representatives in the legislature, and perhaps agreeing with Samuel Adams that the law of self-preservation gave them the right to act, the whigs assembled in the Boston town meeting took another step in their increasing defiance of British imperial rule. They issued a call for a "committee in convention" to convene later that month, elected representatives to that convention, and directed the selectmen to invite the other towns of the province to send delegates.[50]

The convention or "committee in convention" met as scheduled with, Thomas Hutchinson estimated, representatives from about ninety towns in attendance. The principle of election by local town meetings made the convention a representative body and hence constitutional under whig theory, not under imperial law. The meeting has been described by a recent historian in terms of British constitutionalism when he referred to it as "an extralegal convention" with the delegates "participating in a *de facto* assembly of the House of Representatives called by the town of Boston, not the governor."[51] Thomas Hutchinson was more specific, "That it was a high offence," he wrote, "was generally agreed."[52] He meant that British officials agreed and he was right; in fact many termed it "treason."[53]

When the convention sent a message to Bernard urging him to convene the assembly, he warned the delegates to depart without transacting business. He was, the governor replied, willing to believe that those who had issued the call were unaware of the seriousness of the offense and that those attending had not considered the penalties they could incur if they continued to sit. "A meeting of the deputies of the towns, is an assembly of the representatives of the people to all intents and purposes, and calling it a *Committee of Conventions* will not alter the nature of the thing."[54] Coming from Bernard this was stern talk, much stronger than Massachusetts whigs were used to hearing from him. More likely than not, his words were written by Hutchinson, who later summarized them by saying that Bernard admonished the whigs "instantly to separate, and threatened, if they refused, more publickly to assert the prerogative of the crown."[55]

The law laid down by Bernard and Hutchinson was valid British imperial law. To erase any doubts on that score, consider the Irish comparison. Ireland during the eighteenth century would experience several conventions called to discuss constitutional grievances. Some of these would be permitted, especially when the British were powerless to suppress them, the outstanding example being the conventions of the Irish Volunteers. Armed to defend the nation against the French during the American Revolution, their officers' corps became a forum for urging parliamentary reform and for a brief while, until the regular troops returned from America, had to be tolerated. Also Irish constitutional practice allowed small meetings (conducted usually by merchants, Catholics, or municipal corporations) to pass resolutions and submit petitions without fear of prosecution. But bodies consisting of elected delegates, such as the Massachusetts convention of 1768, were prosecuted whenever possible.

In England it was constitutional for a sheriff to call a meeting of his county for the purpose of considering a petition for redress of grievances. The Irish sheriffs during 1784 seem to have thought they should enjoy the same privilege. At that time one of the various eighteenth-century movements for parliamentary reform was at its height in Ireland, and the sheriffs of the kingdom issued a call to a national congress that would draft a petition to the British government reflecting Irish public opinion. The sheriffs of Dublin summoned a meeting to elect delegates. The attorney general of Ireland, John Fitzgibbon, sent them a message laying down the law. "I must inform you," he wrote, "that if you proceed to hold any such election, you are responsible for it to the laws of your country." Should they persist, Fitzgibbon assured them, "I shall hold myself bound, as the King's Attorney-General, to prosecute you in the Court of King's Bench for your conduct, which I consider to be so highly criminal that I cannot overlook it."[56]

When the Dublin meeting convened High Sheriff Stephen Reilly read the letter and announced that, obeying Fitzgibbon's injunction, he would not take the chair. When the crowd began to hoot its disapproval, Fitzgibbon, himself, stood up and repeated his threat to prosecute the high sheriff if he either presided or held the meeting. As a result, the gathering dispersed, ending expectations of a national congress that would initiate a program for parliamentary reform.

It is probably unfair to compare Francis Bernard and Thomas Hutchinson to John Fitzgibbon. His law may have been their law but his power was not their power. While both condemned the convention of 1768 after it met, neither threatened to prosecute the town meetings that elected delegates, although Hutchinson did entertain some hopes of proceeding against the selectmen of Boston for issuing the call.[57] In Ireland, on the other hand, the strength of imperial law was not limited to suppressing meetings before delegates were elected as Fitzgibbon soon proved. Despite the fact that Sheriff Reilly, acknowledging his error, had backed down and not presided over an election, the attorney general decided that law had been violated. He instituted proceedings against Reilly in the form of an attachment as for contempt of the court of king's bench for calling an illegal meeting. The prosecution was based on the legal theory that, as the sheriff's power was an emanation of royal authority, Reilly could be punished in a summary manner by king's bench as that was where the king was supposed personally to reside. The defendant was found guilty and sentenced to a fine of five marks or a week's imprisonment.[58] When parliament met, a member moved "That the proceedings of the Court of King's Bench in attaching the Sheriff, and punishing him in a summary way, as for a contempt, was contrary to the principles of the Constitution, as depriving him of his trial by jury, and is a precedent of dangerous tendency." The motion was defeated by a vote of 143 to 71. A few days later the leader of the movement for parliamentary reform, Henry Flood, brought forward a resolution, "That the practice of attachment for contempt of court stands in the same ground of law in both kingdoms, and ought not to be extended further in Ireland than in England." Again the motion lost, this time by a vote of 120 to 48. During the first debate, John Philpot Curran, Ireland's great defense lawyer, insisted that the case should have gone to a grand jury. Fitzgibbon's answer would have astonished Thomas Hutchinson, though he might have envied the authority with which it was stated. The case could not be laid before a grand jury, Fitzgibbon replied, because to have done so would have meant that it was submitted to a jury of the sheriff's own choosing.[59]

Eight years after he had convicted the high sheriff of Dublin, Fitzgibbon had an opportunity to show just how tough law could be in Ireland. Catholics were agitating for parliamentary representation and their activities were directed by a group of leaders known as the Catholic Committee. It had never held a national congress but the lord lieutenant was sure it possessed nationwide power and his alarm was so great that he almost attributed to the Committee an Irish version of American whig law. "The Committee," he warned the cabinet in London, "already exercise the functions of Government, levy contributions, issue orders for the preservation of the peace—a circumstance perhaps more dangerous than if they could direct the breach of it. Their mandates are taken by the lower classes of people as laws." [60]

While this description was grossly exaggerated, the viceroy's alarm had some justification. The Catholic Committee had announced plans to hold a convention in order to draft a petition for political emancipation with delegates elected to that convention from every county of Ireland. Some Protestants were outraged by Catholic audacity; resolutions of protest were passed by grand juries and municipal corporations swore to protect the kingdom against insurrection. "As universal as is the Catholic demand for it [representation in parliament] so is the determination of the Protestants to resist the claim," the lord lieutenant wrote, expressing less alarm that Protestants might use violence "to preserve the peace" than he had at the prospect that the Catholic Committee was able to preserve peace without violence. "In Down a thousand Protestants are in arms, but to preserve the peace, and their object is to keep the Catholics down. They are arming in Monaghan on the same principle, and Volunteering will become general if Government will not act."

The Protestants might be arming but the lord lieutenant did not think they posed the danger. When he wrote asking for government action he expected action against the Catholic Committee. For advice he turned to John Fitzgibbon now lord chancellor of Ireland and raised to the House of Lords as the earl of Clare. Fitzgibbon agreed that the government had to crush the Catholic convention without delay. Proposing that they issue a proclamation against unlawful assemblies, Fitzgibbon also suggested warning Catholic leaders privately should they hold elections they would be prosecuted. Both he and the lord lieutenant were confident they could stop the Catholics if supported by the British cabinet. They were perplexed when William Pitt, presumably because he could spare no additional troops for duty in Ireland, informed them that the Catholic convention would have to be tolerated. It was, therefore, held—the first elected assembly of Catholics in Ireland since the parliament of James II.

As events turned out, the Catholic convention was hardly seditious. More comparable to the American Stamp Act Congress than to the nonimportation meetings, it had no thoughts of legislating. Professing loyalty to the king, the Catholics drafted a petition of grievances and appointed a committee to present their case in Great Britain through constitutional channels. Still, the convention represented a form of organized opposition not usually tolerated in Ireland. Later that year, the United Irishmen—disgusted at parliament's failure to enact reforms and at the tameness with which the Catholics had pressed their demands—called a convention of their own to speak for the country. Fitzgibbon would not permit it to take place. He introduced in parliament a bill declaring that the assemblage of persons calling themselves representatives, under any pretense, to be illegal. Not limited to gatherings *prima facie* seditious, it banned every elective or representative meeting. Assemblies such as the Catholic convention, which had no other purpose but to draft petitions, were now unlawful on the theory they might be used to violate the peace.[61] "The real object of the measure," Fitzgibbon's biographer wrote, "was to prevent public meetings in favour of Parliamentary reform," a purpose less easily defended when we recall that the House of Commons was in no sense a representative body.[62] "If," Curran told a criminal traverse jury the next year, "the people say, let us not create tumult, but meet in delegation, they cannot do it; if they are anxious to promote parliamentary reform in that way, they cannot do it; the law of the last session has, for the first time, declared such meetings to be a crime."[63]

Lord Chancellor Fitzgibbon, to be sure, was in a decidedly stronger position than was the governor of Massachusetts Bay. He could both push coercive legislation through parliament and enforce it. Had Bernard an Irish convention act at his disposal, the whigs of Boston would not have been concerned—unless it provided for trial outside the colonies or before a noncommon-law court. Still, had there been a statute such as Fitzgibbon's in Massachusetts, we may imagine that Bernard and Hutchinson would have responded with more decisiveness than they did. As it was, uncertain about the law, their response was not only confused, it was meaningless.

The convention had been a "Failure," Bernard admitted, "But shall so open & notorious an Attempt to raise a Rebellion remain unpunished because it was unsuccessful?"[64] Whatever was done had to be severe and he rejected as "very gentle" a scheme favored by Lord Barrington to impeach and bar from future public office the selectmen of Boston who had called the convention.[65] Rather, the governor insisted, now was the time to end disloyalty in Massachusetts by reforming the provincial government, making it more like Ireland's and less like Connecticut's.

The problem, Bernard believed, was one of constitutional law, for it was the constitution that had been violated. Therefore, he turned to the criminal side of constitutional law: the doctrine of forfeiture. "The Question will be whether the Meeting of the Convention & the Council's acting as a seperate Body from the Governor amount to a Forfeiture of the Charter." His answer was yes—"a general Forfeiture of the Charter on the Part of the People, is incurred."[66]

No matter what they hoped would be done—whether it was a forfeiture of the charter or common-law prosecutions—at the very least the royal officials in Massachusetts expected parliament to punish the selectmen of Boston. Hutchinson surely anticipated London would make them pay some penalty for, he tells us, "pains were taken to obtain, and preserve, some of the original letters signed by them."[67] When parliament did act, he was stunned by its constitutional timidity. Instead of taking command, parliament tossed the problem back into the powerless hands of Governor Bernard.

New criminal or forfeiture statutes may have been needed, but parliament did not enact them. Instead it passed a series of resolutions, condemning the conduct of the Massachusetts house, the council, the town of Boston, and the province in general. The series ended with two resolutions, probably drawn by the crown's law officers, labeling the convention both illegal and unconstitutional. In addition, an address of loyalty to the king was moved and accepted by both houses of parliament, pledging support "in such measures as may be found necessary to maintain the civil magistrates in a due execution of the laws within your Majesty's province of Massachusetts Bay." [68] These words satisfied Thomas Hutchinson. [69] It was the procedure adopted for punishing the whig leadership that was the letdown. The king was to direct Governor Bernard "to take the most effectual methods for procuring the fullest information that can be obtained, touching all treasons, or misprisions of treason committed within his government" so that offenders could be arrested and brought to England for trial "pursuant to the provisions of the statute of the thirty-fifth year of the reign of King Henry the eighth." [70]

The tameness of the proposal would have disgusted John Fitzgibbon just as it shocked Thomas Gage. "What better Information can Governor Bernard give?," he asked. "What Evidence can he procure so authentick or so strong as their own Publications?" [71] It is doubtful if any other action demonstrating the impotence of imperial law so discouraged the tory faction in eighteenth-century North America as did this address to the king by parliament.

Gage was not the only British official to believe that evidence sufficient to obtain convictions for sedition was readily available and that there was no need for more investigation. For some unexplained reason, parliament disagreed and instead of ordering the instigators of the convention arrested, it asked for "the fullest information that can be obtained." The request had to mean that parliament wanted direct testimony from cooperative witnesses. If so, Bernard complained, the address to the king was nothing more than a futile exercise in loyalty.

> A simple Order to me to make Enquiry into the Proceedings, which have incurred the Penalties of Treason or Misprision of Treason, will have no other Consequence that [sic] to show the Impotency of Government; unless I am armed with some extraordinary Power to oblige Persons, whom I shall require to undergo an Examination, to submit to it. But I have no such Power at present; otherwise I should have exercised it long ago. And if I was to call before me, even by special Orders from the King, ever so many Persons knowing of the seditious & treasonable Practices of the Faction here, & was to *beg Leave* to ask them a few Questions, I should be answered, as it is said the Secretaries of State were by [John] Wilkes', "You have leave to ask as many Questions as you please, but I *beg leave* to give no Answer to any of *them*." [72]

Bernard's letter should not be passed over lightly. It is not what he writes but why that makes it worth quoting. He has taken trouble to say something that should not need saying. His problem appears no different from that of any official seeking common-law evidence by common-law means. An uncooperative witness has a right to be uncooperative and cannot be made to testify against himself. Surely Lord Barrington, the man to whom Bernard wrote and a member of the British cabinet, could be expected to know as well as he the limitations on his power to force people to make statements. Yet Bernard apparently did not assume that he did, even though Barrington was a colleague of the men who had questioned John Wilkes and received the answer that Massachusetts whigs would likely echo. We will never know what Bernard intended, but there is one explanation that does wash and washes well. He probably believed Barrington and the other ministers did not realize how tightly he was bound by law. As imperial officials they were more accustomed to dealing with sedition in Ireland than dealing with sedition in North America. It is not far-fetched to suspect that parliament, when it voted its address to the king, was thinking more of the conditions of law in Dublin than in Boston and did not reflect that Bernard, due to the conditions of Massachusetts law, would be unable to comply.

Had Francis Bernard been lord lieutenant of Ireland and received a request for "the fullest information that can be obtained," he would not have to write Barrington about "the Impotency of Government" or complain that "I have no Power." He could have obtained as many witnesses as London requested—including their sworn statements—by ordering the sheriff to whip the desired information out of anyone suspected of possessing it.[73] In fact, Irish sheriffs often did that on their own, without prodding from either the British or the Irish parliament.

Ireland's history furnishes many stories but one will do to contrast Bernard's law with Irish law. During 1798, when there was fear of widespread insurrection, Thomas Junkin Fitzgerald, the high sheriff of county Tipperary, used flagellation to obtain "confessions" or information from many persons, some of whom he suspected, without evidence, of knowing rebel plans. One of the men to whom he administered up to 100 lashes was not only innocent, but influential enough to sue him for damages in a civil action. During the trial Fitzgerald declared in a "vehement" speech that "while sheriff he felt himself authorized to take every mode of obtaining confessions, and that in order to discover the truth, if every other mode failed, he had the right to cut off their heads." Fitzgerald was referring to the fact that there was an indemnity act making such conduct exempt from civil suit, but the plaintiff successfully argued that it did not apply where torture was malicious and the victim above suspicion. The jury returned a plaintiff's verdict for £500 and the presiding judges expressed the opinion that much larger damages would not have been excessive. Fitzgerald appealed to parliament where the government pushed through a bill reversing the decision and making similar suits void in the future unless the jury found that the complained of torture had been administered maliciously and not with an intent of suppressing rebellion. Moreover, even when juries did find maliciousness the trial court was empowered to set the verdict aside.[74]

Had Governor Bernard ordered Sheriff Stephen Greenleaf of Suffolk county to obtain the information sought by the British parliament, the sheriff would have refused. Of course he would never have used Irish methods; torture was not the British style in North America and Bernard would not have expected it. But even had the sheriff held a suspect for questioning, he would have exposed himself to a suit for trespass. If the writ were carefully drawn—if it did not mention that the defendant was a sheriff acting in his official capacity—the Massachusetts court, unlike the judges of Ireland, could not have dismissed the action or reversed the verdict. No legislature was likely to free Greenleaf from liability as the Irish parliament freed Fitzgerald. Had he paid damages the British cabinet might have reimbursed him, yet that was only a possibility and he still had to live in Boston unprotected from the mob.

We have marveled at the conditions of eighteenth-century British imperial law before and now we must do so again. If the statute of Henry VIII was a weak response to a serious challenge, its weakness went deeper than Bernard's helplessness. The crown lawyers in London apparently advised parliament it was the answer to Massachusetts sedition. We might think they could have come up with a better solution, but that is only half the puzzle. The fact is that the attorney and solicitor generals did not even know if the statute would do the job. It was so vaguely drafted that lawyers disagreed whether it extended to a colony settled after it had been enacted. Even as late as 1774, Hutchinson heard doubts expressed in London legal circles whether the statute of Henry covered any part of North America.[75]

Better than any other imperial official, Thomas Hutchinson understood the legal dilemma. Timidity by parliament had strengthened the whig cause. It had threatened to employ an unenforceable statute, and the very threat had added a grievance to the list of constitutional complaints and spurred the whigs of other colonies to bolder militancy. The failures to suppress conspiracies such as nonimportation or conventions such as that of 1768 or the Stamp Act Congress were depressing indications that British rule in North America might soon come to an end.[76] Parliament would have to act, and act with vigor, or "the government of this province will be split into innumerable divisions, every town, every parish, and every particular club or connexion will meet and vote, and carry their votes into execution just as they please."[77] The convention of 1768 was a dangerous precedent but not for the reasons that had led the crown lawyers in London to label it seditious. The gathering had been illegal, true enough, but the peril came not alone from a colonial-wide assembly usurping the functions of the general court. More menacing were the facts that it had been called by the Boston town meeting and had been endorsed by town meetings held in over ninety communities. The people had accepted the constitutional theory that great issues of state could be debated and voted on at the lowest levels of government. Each voter had a forum in which to raise and discuss questions of obedience and opposition to imperial rule. The threat was not to Great Britain alone but to the very existence of orderly government. Fragmentation and anarchy lay behind the ultimate conclusion—every man his own legislator.

Only after he had passed into exile was Hutchinson to learn how far popular sovereignty could be carried by the people of his colony. It threatened not merely imperial law, but the execution of any law represented by courts and lawyers. "I received intelligence a few days ago," he wrote Lord

Dartmouth early in 1774, "of town meetings held in the county of Berkshire . . . to form combinations against the payment of Lawyer's and Sheriff's fees in Actions at Law, because they thought the established fees by the law of the province were too high. Success in the opposition to the supreme power over the whole, leads the subjects of subordinate powers to conclude they may also shake off such subjection whensoever they are dissatisfied with them."[78]

Those meetings in Berkshire county did not represent whig law. Rather, they were whig law carried to such extremes that whig leadership could not tolerate them—as Shays' Rebellion later proved. Even Samuel Adams, despite his popular sympathies and suspicion of lawyers' law, would vigorously aid the suppression of that insurrection against the courts. During the 1770s, while the issues were still constitutional and not economic, when it was a matter of home rule against imperial rule, not merely a few farmers seeking to protect their property against creditors seeking to foreclose, Samuel Adams saw none of the dangers that alarmed Thomas Hutchinson. "Let every Town assemble," he wrote during 1772. "Let Associations & Combinations be everywhere set up to consult and recover our just Rights."[79]

Samuel Adams's policy would triumph over Thomas Hutchinson's fears. Slowly the legal concept introduced by the nonimportation meetings and the convention of 1768 would be expanded into new areas. The committees of correspondence belong in the same category.[80] Hutchinson labeled them "glaringly unconstitutional," yet he could not suppress them despite the king's command.[81] The night of the Boston Massacre the people, assembled in town meeting, appointed a committee to demand that the troops be removed to Castle Island. Fearful that if he did not act whigs from other Suffolk county communities would swarm into Boston and reinforce the local meeting, Acting Governor Hutchinson received the committee knowing that he had created a dangerous precedent. The committee might speak for a constitutional body, but it spoke on an issue beyond its constitutional competency and made an unconstitutional demand.[82] Three years later the Boston Tea Party crisis took the whigs one step further. His hands tied by imperial statutes, Hutchinson was unable to meet the demands of the town meeting. The event he had prevented during the Boston Massacre now came to pass. The town meeting was dissolved only to convene again as a "body" meeting open to all whigs. The Boston "body," originally created to enforce nonimportation, now spoke for Suffolk county and had an executive committee that maintained an armed guard about the tea ships. The Continental Congress carried the principle to its conclusion. The royal governors were ordered to prevent elections to the Second Congress, yet they were held openly and few if any delegates feared arrest. The final step would be to revive the convention idea and use it not to petition or protest but to take over the government of Massachusetts Bay.

When the Massachusetts provincial congress met, Hutchinson's successor, Governor Thomas Gage, knew what to expect. "I shall not be surprized," he wrote during October 1774, "as the Provincial Congress seems to proceed higher and higher in their Determinations, if Persons should be Authorized by them to grant Commissions and Assume every Power of a legal Government, for their Edicts are implicitely obeyed throughout the Country."[83] It was, he said, a few months later, "a Rebellious Meeting" and before long the example spread to all the colonies.[84] "There is scarcely a Province that has not overthrown it's constitution, a Shew only of their antient Governments appears to be kept up, but all Powers both Legislative and executive are lodged in the Hands of Congresses and Committees."[85]

From the hindsight of history the progression from nonimportation to convention to congress may seem inevitable. Perhaps it was. Perhaps the conditions of law that tolerated the seed cannot be said to have nourished the flowering. John Fitzgibbon, the earl of Clare and lord chancellor of Ireland, would not have agreed.

13

The Oppression of Centuries[1]

THE IRISH COMPARISON

John Fitzgibbon, the earl of Clare, belonged to eighteenth-century British-ruled Ireland. An imperialist of the imperalists he was at home in the poverty-ridden grandeur that was the Dublin of George III. Whig Boston would have destroyed Fitzgibbon much as it destroyed a better man than he—Thomas Hutchinson, who passed into exile following his failure to suppress the Boston Tea Party. The legal world of an American colonial governor had not been made for a lord chancellor of Ireland. British imperial law would not fail in eighteenth-century Ireland as it failed in eighteenth-century Massachusetts Bay. A Tea Party staged in Waterford, Belfast, or Galway would have brought swift, effective retaliation. Had he been Irish, Samuel Adams would not have mocked a proclamation of a lord lieutenant as he mocked the proclamation of Governor Thomas Gage. He would have obeyed, fled the kingdom, or rotted in jail.

The fact that imperial law could and would have been enforced in Ireland was not the only legal distinction that should be marked between eighteenth-century Ireland and eighteenth-century colonial North America. The way that people thought about law, how they defined it and viewed its place in society must also be recalled if we wish to learn why the two most important English-speaking parts of the first British Empire took divergent paths to rebellion and independence.

When American whigs opposed imperial law with a nonimportation agreement or such action as the Boston Tea Party, they sought for legal roots giving their opposition a touch of legitimacy. To sustain their side of the constitutional controversy, it was essential to maintain that the British, not they, were departing from law, to avoid the taint of illegality, even if only for their own satisfaction.

THE OPPRESSION OF CENTURIES

When the discontented of eighteenth-century Ireland thought of opposing British imperial law, they had little incentive to develop an Irish version of American whig law. A large percentage of potential Irish rebels were too far removed from the law itself to care what legal coloring others might attribute to their actions.

The legal, social, and economic worlds in which the eighteenth-century American lived were beyond the comprehension of the average Irishman. The economic difference alone could explain the contrasting attitudes toward legality. In our search for the Irish comparison historians who favor the economic intepretation of history might tell us to look no further. In Ireland's economic oppression we will find the explanation. Ireland had a tradition for violence because the Irish had more to be violent about. One may agree with the conclusion without agreeing that the search ends there. The question of why Ireland was so wretched a land remains and much of the answer lies with the conditions of law, certainly for the average Catholic.

"The law stood at his cradle, it stood at his bridal-bed, and it stood at his coffin," Henry Grattan said of the Catholic.[2] He meant of course the penal code. "In this country," John Philpot Curran charged, "penal laws have tried beyond any example of former times: what was the result? The race between penalty and crime was continued, each growing fiercer in the conflict, until the penalty could go no further, and the fugitive turned upon the breathless pursuer."[3]

In prerevolutionary North America local law did not force the citizen to turn on the government official for it oversaw a different way of life. Wealth was not concentrated in a few hands, the class structure was fluid, there was little cause for class conflict. The story of eighteenth-century Ireland—indeed, of nineteenth-century Ireland—can be told in terms of such discord. The Irish had a long tradition of social strife; in a sense, conflict conducted with violence was Ireland's version of whig law.

We may doubt if an American whig would have considered most Irish actions directed against imperial rule to be law. When the Irish equivalent of the dissatisfied American whig struck back at the system, the resort was usually to violence and, in its mildest form, the method was the destruction of property, pure and simple. The history of eighteenth-century Ireland is colored by agrarian movements based on retaliation against economic oppressors and premised on acts that in America would have been lawless by any standard, even the most liberal and the most whiggish.

The Houghers who appeared in Connaught during 1711 are an example. They apparently were landholders or sympathizers of landholders, who held by the insecure tenure of short leases that characterized Irish-Catholic tenantry. Their object was to scare off merchants investing surplus funds and other interlopers engrossing land, and their method was to hamstring cattle. The conflict was legal as well as economic: a conflict between two laws. For the English purchaser of Connaught real property it was a matter of sound economical use: turning marginal farmlands supporting a number of families into pasture returning higher dividends to a single investor. For the Irish tenant it was a matter of eviction.[4] As in Boston it was also a question of divergent legal definitions, one arising from imperial law, the other from folk law. The peasants who had always cultivated the land thought of it as their property, the owner of the fee had a different law to which to appeal, and there were no local institutions as in Massachusetts Bay to stay the hand of imperial judgment. The peasants turned to violence, and what has been described as a skillfully organized body of men protested the expansion of pasture by destroying cattle and sheep and terrorizing the entire province of Connaught.[5] They were not the same as American whigs destroying tea, yet their objective had a ring of similarity and public opinion was on their side. If they were Catholics, and surely most were or their leases would have been more secure, they had the sympathy of some Protestant neighbors, for few were caught, fewer punished, and only one or two executed. More to the point, they were successful—remarkably successful. For over fifty years stock breeders stayed clear of a province where their capital was unsafe. "No cattle-farmer remained in the West save those who consented to the laws and customs of Connaught."[6]

The government showed greater energy but little more success a half century later dealing with the Whiteboys. Again expansion of pasture was the chief cause: when the British parliament removed restrictions of the importation of Irish cattle into England whole villages in Tipperary were swept away.[7] In retaliation the Whiteboy movement rose up—men who roamed the countryside at night wearing white smocks—a movement that has been called "the precursor and the parent of all subsequent outbursts of Irish agrarian crime."[8] It was particularly brutal and soon took up the additional grievance of the tithe, paid to support a church to which few of those taxed belonged.[9]

The Whiteboys were guilty of few murders, but they did commit torture and destroyed an immense amount of property. At first the government was helpless, for the movement was cloaked in a conspiracy of silence, and landlords turned to armed force and nightly patrols. Parliament's response, in 1765, set a pattern for the future—a law creating new crimes and imposing harsher penalties. All persons who went by night in parties of five or more men wounding, beating, tying up, or otherwise assaulting other persons, destroying property or digging up ground, or who rescued felons from custody, were liable to death. If offenders were not given up or some evidence obtained concerning them, grand juries were empowered to levy on the local barony in which a Whiteboy crime had been committed a sum to compensate the injured victim—precisely the law that London had been unable to give customsmen tarred and feathered by Boston's mob. Another clause, borrowed from the penal code against Catholics, authorized a magistrate to summon before him people suspected of swearing an illegal oath and, if they refused to answer, to imprison them for six months. Thus a single Irish magistrate, acting on his own suspicion, was invested with more arbitrary power than was possessed by the entire government of Massachusetts Bay. Still, the statute, we are told, did little to end Whiteboyism. "The name of those who constructed it will never be known, and they were evidently men of some education and no small organising ability, and they created a system of intimidation which in many districts became the true representative of the Catholic peasantry, and which often made it much safer to violate than to obey the law."[10]

Ten years after the first Whiteboy bill, an additional statute was enacted by parliament amending the capital code to include such offenses as disfiguring human beings, sending threatening letters, compelling men to quit their farms or employments, or concealing Whiteboys who had committed capital crimes. Those who refused to answer an inquiring magistrate were now liable to unlimited imprisonment.

The Whiteboys were still active in 1787 when Fitzgibbon was attorney general. "I am well acquainted with the Province of Munster," he told parliament, "and I know that it is impossible for human wretchedness to exceed that of the miserable tenantry of that Province. I know that the unhappy tenantry are ground to powder by relentless landlords. I know that far from being able to give the clergy their just dues, they have not food or raiment for themselves; the landlord grasps the whole."[11] A frank and objective appraisal, one might say, surely an argument for legal, social, and economic change. Not so when the speaker was John Fitzgibbon. His solution was an even harsher law containing one provision empowering magistrates, at their discretion, to destroy any Catholic church in which tumultuous assemblies had been held or unlawful oaths administered and to forbid the reerection of a chapel so demolished within three years. Parliament found this clause too arbitrary even for Ireland and Fitzgibbon was forced to withdraw it, but the remainder of his tumultuous assemblies bill was enacted, including in its scope the riot act, previously unknown in Ireland. Magistrates were empowered to order any meeting of more than twelve persons to disperse and anyone failing to obey was liable to be shot. Attacks on clergymen or on established churches were made felony, while conspiracies, terrorism, administering unlawful oaths, seizure of arms, and efforts to silence witnesses were all punishable by death.[12] It was Fitzgibbon's first significant contribution to the criminal laws and set the tone of the policy he would promote as long as British-ruled Ireland retained a separate parliament.

It would not do to think of Catholics alone. Violent reaction to laws promulgated by an unrepresentative legislature was common to most sectors of Irish society, urban as well as rural, Protestant as well as Catholic. Even rural violence was not confined to Catholics. The Hearts-of-Oak movement, Presbyterian in membership, arose in Ulster to protest levies by grand juries forcing householders to labor on the public roads. When the law was modified the Oakboys disappeared. The comparable Hearts of Steel or Steelboys were more serious and more symptomatic of what troubled Ireland. In 1770, Lord Donegal, a landowner in county Antrim, demanded heavy fines for renewal of leases. Many tenants could not meet his terms and were replaced by others.[13] "A precedent so tempting and so lucrative," writes the historian Froude, "was naturally followed. Other landlords finding the trade so profitable began to serve their tenants with notices to quit. The farmers and peasants combined to defend themselves. Where law was the servant of oppression, force was their one resource."[14]

Eighteenth-century Irish government was simply not oriented to act on behalf of the Ulster tenantry even though, as most of the victims were Protestant, few officials doubted the landlords were in the wrong. "The law may warrant these proceedings," the lord lieutenant's agent in the area wrote, "but will not justify them. Should the causes of these riots be looked into, it will be found that few have had juster foundations. When the consequences of driving six or seven thousand manufacturing and laboring families out of Ireland come to be felt, I question whether the rectitude of these gentlemen's intentions will be held by the world a sufficient excuse for the irresponsible damage they are doing."[15] He was thinking of economic consequences and human suffering, but there was also a potential consequence he may not have had in mind, soon to be reported to London by an exasperated Thomas Gage. For the year of the Ulster evictions was 1772 and many of these Irish Presbyterians were to migrate to Pennsylvania where they swelled the ranks of the whig army.[16]

Not all eighteenth-century violence in Ireland was rural. Riots in towns were common, but unlike North America were met by force and rioters were sometimes punished.[17] In 1784 the Dublin mob adopted the Boston technique of tar and feathers.[18] Parliament reacted with a special statute, providing that anyone guilty of tarring and feathering would be flogged through the streets. When the first conviction was obtained an enormous crowd gathered to protest the execution of sentence. Stones were thrown, the soldiers fired into the howling mass; one man was killed; three or four wounded; the people disappeared; and the whipping was completed.[19] An event that could not have occcurred in Boston seemed almost normal in Dublin. "I am determined," the lord lieutenant reported, "that the execution of the law shall not be wantonly resisted, as far as my power can have influence."[20] Unlike the governor of Massachusetts Bay, he possessed both the power and the influence.

The power and influence of eighteenth-century Irish officialdom were not always employed to suppress unlawful violence. Sometimes it was used to support one side, especially when the quarrel was between Catholics and Protestants. Sectarian strife was not unusual in Ireland and only one example need be cited to illustrate its effects on the conditions of law.

Trouble occurred during the last decade of the century in the southern sections of Ulster, especially in county Armagh. While several causes contributed, the major complaint was that Catholics were successfully bidding for leases on lands previously held by Protestants. Protestant farmers organized themselves into armed bands, called Peep-o-Day boys, which raided the homes of Catholics trying to frighten them into leaving the county. Their object, wrote Thomas Addis Emmet, "was to scour the Catholic districts about the break of day, and strip the inhabitants of fire-arms, alleging that they were warranted in so doing by the Popery Laws."[21] The local magistrates, or at least most of them, apparently agreed. Unprotected by the established law, the Catholics set up a counter organization—the Defenders—and clashes between the two groups were frequent and sometimes fatal. It was then that the sectarian color of eighteenth-century Irish law became most manifest.

The magistrates, who largely ignored the violence of the Protestant Peep-o-Day boys, turned the full force of their authority against the Catholic Defenders and the law they laid down was often lawless law. Without trial, without sentence, "without even a colour of legality," the justices sent men they suspected of being Catholic Defenders to serve in the navy—"a tender sailing along the coast to receive them." [22] More than 1,000 Irishmen, almost all farmers, met this fate. It was, Lord Lieutenant Camden wrote his superior in London, "A measure which, I am afraid, is not very defensible, and to which I have taken the utmost care not to give either my own individual consent or that of Government." Camden was embarrassed by the illegal actions of his subordinates, and we might sympathize with him if he were a Francis Bernard or a Thomas Hutchinson facing an uproar not of his making, knowing that soon the whigs in the House of Representatives would be raising a hue and cry against imperial rule and imperial injustice. But Camden was not in Massachusetts Bay, he was lord lieutenant of Ireland where the law seldom got out of hand. It was indiscretion that troubled him, not illegality. "I am afraid some of the magistrates have been incautious enough, not to carry on this measure so secretly as to have escaped the notice of the public," Camden explained in a remarkable discussion of legality in British-ruled Ireland. "It has certainly, however, done much to quiet the country, and I shall of course take care to protect these gentlemen as far as I am enabled with propriety to do so." [23]

Camden is telling us all we need to know concerning the rule of law in eighteenth-century Ireland. The "gentlemen" he would protect were not the victims of lawless legality but the magistrates who had made a mockery of law. He will act with "propriety," but considerations of propriety in contemporary Irish law meant legalizing the illegal. "I think it probable," he wrote his chief secretary, "that a bill of indemnity may be necessary to cover the magistrates, who have exerted themselves so zealously and yet so indiscreetly." [24] When one victim of official illegality sought a writ of *habeas corpus* to escape naval service, parliament passed Camden's act of indemnity, not only freeing the magistrates from criminal or civil liability, but legalizing the illegal sentences previously imposed. As Henry Grattan commented, "the poor were stricken out of the protection of the law, and the rich out of its penalties."

Another law, the Insurrection Act of 1796, made the previously illegal procedure legal. After petitioning the lord lieutenant to proclaim their districts "to be in a state of disturbance, or in immediate danger of becoming so," magistrates were empowered to send without trial any man whom they suspected of being "an idle or disorderly person" to serve in the fleet. They could do the same with any "persons who cannot upon examination prove themselves to exercise and industriously follow some lawful trade or employment as a laborer or otherwise," "all persons found assembled in any proclaimed district, in any house in which malt or spiritous liquors are sold . . . after the hours of nine at night and before six in the morning," and "any man or boy" caught in a proclaimed district hawking "any seditious handbill, paper or pamphlet, or paper by law required to be stamped and not duly stamped."[25] Once his district was proclaimed, the discretion of a magistrate over individual citizens was almost without limit.

The Defenders were effectively crushed. During the next few months the Catholics of Armagh and neighboring counties experienced not only persecution but violent persecution—over 5,000 were driven out, "to hell or Connaught."[26] The Peep-o-Day boys had served their purpose and soon passed into history; their place as Protestant vigilantes taken by a new and more permanent group, the Orange lodges, the founding of which it has been said was destined "to produce as much sectarian bitterness in Ireland as the Ku Klux Klan has done in America."[27]

Ireland was moving toward the "Rising" and the Orange lodges help tell us why. It was not their activities that made the difference for by now Ireland was almost immune to violence. It was not even that they constituted a clear violation of the insurrection act yet flourished openly. It was the government's attitude—giving an appearance of supporting the Orangemen—that tipped the scales.[28] Catholics who had not lost faith before now told themselves that Irish law would never be used to protect them. The United Irishmen, an organization of Protestants seeking constitutional reform, began to listen to its more militant members who favored armed rebellion as the government seemed committed to a policy of arbitrary rule by brute force.[29]

It does not matter that the suspicion was probably wrong, that the government had no official connection with the Orange lodges. Law administered for the benefit of the few, applied unequally to the many was the essence of the United Irishmen's complaint. The bulk of the kingdom's population was alienated from the legal process.[30] It was becoming difficult for the discontented of Ireland, even men like Arthur O'Connor who were Protestant landowners or lawyers, to emulate the American whigs' search for lawful legitimacy, more difficult still to share their respect for the rule of law. "The whole framework of society, and all the moral principles on which it rests, seemed to be giving way," the English historian Lecky wrote of the Defender movement and its philosophy of meeting violence with violence. "Habits of systematic opposition to the law were growing up; outrages, sometimes of horrible cruelty, were looked upon merely as incidents of war, and savage animosities were forming."[31] Irish crime, another historian tells us, "assumed the character of legitimate war."[32] Back during 1766, Francis Bernard had used the same analogy—"I am obliged to maintain a political Warfare with the Popular party"—to describe his troubles in Massachusetts Bay.[33] But Bernard's warfare was far different from Irish warfare as the imperial law at his disposal was not the same imperial law that ran from Dublin Castle. Both invoked opposition, but they did not create the same degree of alienation. Also using the analogy of "warfare," Walter Hussey Burgh, a lawyer and chief baron of Ireland's exchequer court, was one of the kingdom's few rulers to acknowledge that law was a cause of social strife. "Talk not to me of peace," he said. "Ireland is not in a state of peace; it is *smothered* war. England has sown her laws like dragons' teeth, and they have sprung up, armed men."[34]

We may be surprised that other lawyers did not say the same. It is easy for historians to draw lessons missed by contemporaries. The men who ruled eighteenth-century Ireland on behalf of London did not ask the questions that we would ask or even Thomas Hutchinson might have raised. Instead they wondered if they were not too lenient toward their Irish subjects.

During the summer of 1798, while rebellion was raging throughout the kingdom, John Fitzgibbon summoned the imprisoned leaders of the United Irishmen to testify before a secret committee of the House of Lords. One of those to appear was Thomas Addis Emmet. Fitzgibbon asked him if he thought the government had been "very foolish to let you proceed so long as they did" before arresting him. Emmet, like Fitzgibbon, was a barrister and his rebellious energies had been directed at a reform of the law. He must have reflected on the fact that his close associates within the United Irishmen were constitutionalists, not anarchists, who worked, as had the American whigs a generation earlier, for a return to what they thought was the old constitution, hoping to bring about reform in an orderly manner without violence, bloodshed, or revolution.

> No, my Lord, whatever I imputed to Government, I did not accuse them of folly. I knew we were very attentively watched, but I thought they were right in letting us proceed. I have often said, laughing among ourselves, that if they did right they would pay us for conducting the revolution, conceiving as I then did, and still do, that a revolution is inevitable, unless speedily prevented by large measures of conciliation. It seemed to me an object with them, that it should be conducted by moderate men, of good moral charcters, liberal education, and some talents, rather than by intemperate men of bad characters, ignorant, and foolish; and into the hands of one or the other of those classes it undoubtedly will fall.[35]

14

A Most Dreadful Ruin[1]

THE LEGAL MIND OF BRITISH-RULED IRELAND

The people of eighteenth-century Ireland were a divided race and as time progressed they would divide even more. We think of English against Irish. They thought of Saxon against Celt. The very words they spoke dramatized the dichotomy. Those who made the laws had one language, those for whom laws were made another.

"It has been the misfortune of this country," William James McNevin, a member of the United Irish leadership, told the Secret Committee of the House of Lords, "scarcely ever to have known the English natives or settlers, otherwise than enemies, and in his language the Irish peasant has but one name for Protestant and Englishman, and confounds them; he calls both by the name of *Sasanagh*; his conversation therefore is *less against a religionist* than against a *foe*." John Fitzgibbon interrupted. "I agree with Dr. M'Nevin," he said. "The Irish peasant considers the two words are synonimous; he calls Protestant and Englishman, indifferently, *Sasanagh*."[2] McNevin thought the fact evidence of something wrong with law and government. For Fitzgibbon it meant that greater vigilance was needed and harsher penal statutes should be enacted.

On one point both men concurred: a large number of people were alienated from the law, but they did not agree on how to cure a social malady. McNevin's tonic was representative government through constitutional reform; for Fitzgibbon that was a toxin certain to corrode the imperial mien. "The gentleman has intimated that there is a general disposition to resist the laws gone forth among the people, and therefore we should not coerce them," Fitzgibbon had told parliament in 1784 when he was attorney general. "This is reasoning worthy of the cause. But it is not founded in fact. If it was, it would be the very reason for coercion."[3]

143

Thus in John Fitzgibbon was the legal mind of British-ruled Ireland personified. At the center of that mind lay the concept of coercion. Whenever opposition threatened, the laws should be made more restrictive and control tighter. Such was the legal program of the earl of Clare and such was the program he persuaded the Castle and the parliament to continue as the governing policy of Ireland.

In the Ireland of John Fitzgibbon there were many forces of sedition that needed coercion, and none seemed to trouble him more than the United Irishmen. It is well, therefore, to ask their purpose so we may see what the legal mind of eighteenth-century Ireland considered dangerous.

The United Irish society was at first not a secret organization. Meetings were held in public and the leadership signed their names to all manifestoes and documents. What it sought, at least originally, was parliamentary reform. "We have no national government," its constitution declared, "we are ruled by Englishmen, and the servants of Englishmen, whose object is the interest of another country, whose instrument is corruption, and whose strength is the weakness of Ireland; and these men have the whole of the power and patronage of the country, as a means to seduce and subdue the honesty of her representatives in the legislature."[4]

From such an indictment of Irish government one might expect a call for independence, a rallying of the nation, and an overthrow of British rule. The United Irish were not so bold; they could tolerate the British connection if the Irish people were taken into the partnership. It was reform they sought and here they were bold, so radical that even one hundred years later an historian could call their proposals "wild democratic schemes":[5] equal representation based on universal manhood suffrage with no test oaths, thus admitting Catholics to the franchise; no property qualification for representatives, thus opening parliament to the lower classes; annual elections, thus making the legislature responsible to public opinion; and exclusion from parliament of members of the executive and judicial branches of the government, thus ending one form of patronage by which the British cabinet, through the lord lieutenant, controlled parliament.[6]

There is a remarkable coincidence here, too telling not to be emphasized. In essence, the United Irishmen sought an end to those parts of the Irish constitution that Governor Francis Bernard had wanted incorporated into the governance of Massachusetts Bay. They were no more successful than he. Bernard obtained no reforms for Massachusetts; they obtained none for Ireland except a limitation on the pension list though not an abolition.[7] It was a minor achievement when compared to their goal of making parliament a representative body, but we must not think it an unimportant reform. Extension of the pension list had been the chief tool of corruption by which Dublin Castle kept control of the kingdom's legislature. It was, moreover, a key element of eighteenth-century British political theory, and an imperial governor lacking patronage was handicapped in his efforts to create a loyal political following. "If Punishments & Rewards are the two Hinges of Government," Bernard once complained, "this Government [Massachusetts Bay] is off its Hinges; for it can neither punish nor reward."[8] All through the eighteenth century, the Irish government could and did do both.

The only meaningful change in law—aside from the limitation placed on the pension list—was the gradual repeal of the penal code restricting the civil rights of Catholics. The United Irishmen, however, wanted all restrictions removed, and that demand, together with persecutions by the Orange lodges in the north, helped forge a political alliance between Anglican constitutional reformers and Roman Catholics.

A third sector of the population questioning British rule in Ireland were the Presbyterians, inspired in part by the American Revolution.[9] They were affected even more by the French, an event, Arthur O'Connor said, proving to Protestants that no religion "was incompatible with political freedom."[10] The French Revolution could boast of two achievements compatible with the goals of Irish reformers: the abolition of religious disqualification and the abolition of tithes.[11] "A Catholic country," Thomas Addis Emmet wrote, "had, by its conduct, contradicted the frequently repeated dogma, that Catholics were unfit for liberty; and the waning glory of the British constitution seemed to fade before the regenerated government of France." For a brief moment in time the Irish Presbyterians were convinced and many were willing to link the cause of Catholic liberty with their own.[12]

The French Revolution also produced war between France and Great Britain. The conflict frightened the Irish government into action. Attempts were made to suppress the United Irishmen, driving the organization underground and bringing into its leadership some of the more radical members whose aim was not constitutional reform alone, but an Irish republic modeled on French principles.[13]

It was John Fitzgibbon, lord chancellor of Ireland and earl of Clare, who led the government to suppress what it could not corrupt. Addressing parliament in 1789, Fitzgibbon summed up the legal policy he would adhere to all his life: "Let us agree with England in these three points—one king, one law, one religion. Let us keep these objects steadily in view, and we act like wise men."[14] He was Irish born and Irish bred but Fitzgibbon did not think like an Irishman. He did not even think British; he thought English. Never sharing the ideas of equality that stirred some of his fellow lawyers, Fitzgibbon knew precisely what his role was and how it should be played. As lord chancellor of Ireland, he was not so much a leader of government as commander of an army of occupation.[15]

It has been said of Fitzgibbon that he "was a more successful fabricator of rebels than any United Irish propagandist, for he simplified the issue and made moderation look like imbecility to the bold and like treason to the timid."[16] Sometimes he obtained new penal laws by alarming parliament with testimony carefully gathered through a secret committee chaired or directed by himself. At other times the government would refuse to explain why it needed new authority and tell the members of parliament that if they refused consent the responsibility for the consequences would rest on them.[17] Fitzgibbon almost always obtained what he asked.

The year 1796—a year when Ireland's rulers feared a French invasion—witnessed a remarkable parliamentary session. That was the year government protected the "zealous" magistrates in Ulster with an indemnity law and vested them with full discretion to draft disorderly characters into the fleet. It was also the year the writ of *habeas corpus* was suspended, the death penalty attached to certain violations of the arms-control laws, and conspiracy to murder made a felony.[18] Most notable of all, it was the year of Fitzgibbon's insurrection act.

Described as one of the most severe penal statutes ever enacted in Ireland, the insurrection act expressed the very essence of Fitzgibbon's legal theory.[19] One section permitted the lord lieutenant and council to declare any district as disturbed, granting the magistrates extraordinary powers to search for arms and arrest individuals on mere suspicion. For some lawyers these provisions represented the end of what few civil liberties remained in Ireland. The justices of the peace, complained William Sampson, "were to take the place of juries, and had the power of proclaiming counties and districts *out of the king's peace*."[20] Even more drastic was a clause making it a capital offense to "administer, or cause to be administered, or be present, aiding and assisting at the administering" of any oath "importing to bind the person taking the same, to be of any association, brotherhood, society, or confederacy formed for seditious purposes, or to disturb the public peace, or to obey the orders or rules, or commands of any committee, or other body of men, not lawfully constituted."[21]

The purpose of the "oath" section of the insurrection act as drafted and enforced by Fitzgibbon was not to root out what Thomas Hutchinson would have called sedition, but to crush political opposition. For the target of the law was the oath administered by the United Irishmen, as demonstrated by the conviction and execution of William Orr.[22] The oath,* Arthur O'Connor explained to an English whig, was so harmless Thomas Gage might not have reported its existence had it been employed by American whigs, and Gage was prone to inform London of everything that was the least suspicious.[24]

When Emmet was questioned by the Secret Committee of the House of Commons during 1798, he was asked the reasons for political discontent. He might have listed many but he was a lawyer and lawyers tend to stress legal issues. Thus he singled out for particular criticism the criminal laws of Ireland. His interrogators seemed surprised for the speaker of the house asked him how the Irish code differed from the English. Emmet replied that

---

* In the awful presence of God, I ___ ___ do voluntarily declare, That I will persevere in endeavouring to form a brotherhood of affection among Irishmen of *every* religious persuasion, and that I will also persevere in my endeavours to obtain an equal, full, and adequate representation of *all* the people of Ireland. I do further declare, that neither hopes, fears, rewards, or punishments, shall ever induce me, directly or indirectly, to inform on, or give evidence against, any member or members of this or similar societies, for any act or expression of theirs, done or made collectively or individually, in or out of this Society in pursuance of the spirit of this obligation.[23]

it punished with death the administration of illegal oaths. "That is a law," Lord Castlereagh in all seriousness pointed out, "connected with the security of the state."

"If," Emmet argued, "it is intended to keep up the ferment of the public mind, such laws may be necessary; but if it be intended to allay that ferment, they are perfectly useless."[25]

Here, in this exchange between Robert Stewart, Marquis of Londonderry and Viscount Castlereagh, and Thomas Addis Emmet, we find exposed the legal mind of eighteenth-century Ireland. Castlereagh would a few years later win fame for managing the termination of Ireland's independent parliament by unprecedented corruption, after which Emmet would be released from imprisonment and ordered into exile, eventually to become attorney general of New York. Castlereagh had once voted with the opposition but reaction against social unrest brought him into the government. He personally had supervised the arrests of the United Irish leadership—"raids" they might better be called, as they had been conducted without warrants and by military force. Security of the state alone, he tells Emmet, is justification for executing men who took oaths of religious brotherhood.

Emmet had gained renown by dramatically taking that oath in open court at the close of a trial in which he had defended a member of the United Irish society charged with swearing the same oath.[26] Laws that imposed the death penalty for pledging one to constitutional reform, he replied to Castlereagh, did not support but undermined the security of the state. Castlereagh was not listening. Fitzgibbon would not have understood.

Arthur O'Connor expressed similar thoughts when examined by the same secret committee. The United Irish had sought social harmony and representative government through peaceful means, he asserted, but the insurrection act "broke down every barrier of Liberty." The rulers of Ireland seemed bent on a policy of extermination, ignoring the violence of the Orange lodges— "whose institution was avowedly for the purpose of perpetuating religious discord and rancour"—while protecting magistrates from even civil liability when they abandoned the rule of law to crush the Catholic Defenders. These events, O'Connor claimed, "left no doubt on the mind of the [United Irish] Executive, that all the excesses and outrages were either openly or secretly the acts of the Government and Legislature of Ireland."[27]

It was then according to O'Connor, Emmet, and William James McNevin—after passage of the insurrection act and the expulsion of 4,000 Catholic peasants from the north—that the United Irishmen decided to seek the aid of republican France.[28] "We were aware it was suspected that negotiations between United Irishmen and the French, were carried on at an earlier period than that now alluded to, but we solemnly declare such suspicion was ill founded."[29]

O'Connor, Emmet, and McNevin were speaking for themselves. More radical United Irishmen such as Wolfe Tone made contact with Paris before they. That fact does not weaken their argument. For what they were saying was that they, the moderates who sought constitutional reform rather than an independent republic, were driven to a foreign alliance by the laws of Ireland and the official policy of the Irish government.

The British government also contributed to the disillusion. At a moment when hopes were high for religious emancipation, Fitzgibbon prevailed on the ministry to appoint a viceroy with instructions that further concessions to the Catholics were to be resisted no matter the cost. The day he arrived in Dublin, mobs attacked Fitzgibbon's house, soldiers were called out, and two rioters killed. The new lord lieutenant was John Jeffreys Pratt, second Earl Camden, whose family owned estates in Ireland and who, more than most of his countrymen, should have been familiar with the conditions of eighteenth-century Irish law. Yet he did not seem to realize that when he undertook to combat political opposition with criminal law he was in fact unleashing forces of indiscriminate violence—official violence to be sure, yet violence nonetheless.

It is difficult in the twentieth century to fathom the depths of eighteenth-century Irish social virulence. It may be that the British did not fully comprehend it. That was the impression of the man who had to deal with its consequences, Camden's successor as lord lieutenant, General Charles Cornwallis. Trying to explain to the British cabinet what Camden had wrought, Cornwallis wrote the ministry candid summaries of the attitudes and prejudices of the "principal persons in this country," including members of both houses of parliament. It was they, the very leaders upon whom he depended to support reconciliation, who were "averse to all acts of clemency," supporting instead the pursuit of "measures that could only terminate in the extirpation of the greater number of the inhabitants, and in the utter destruction" of Ireland. "The words Papists and Priests are for ever in their mouths, and by their unaccountable policy they would drive four-fifths of the community into irreconcilable rebellion." [30]

Cornwallis was writing his superiors in London, telling them of the legal mentality that controlled events in Ireland. If matters were left to the Anglo-Irish, he was saying, martial law would become the common law of the kingdom. Even at his own table in Dublin castle, he told a military colleague, the conversation "all tends to encourage this system of blood"; it "always turns on hanging, shooting, burning, etc., and if a priest has been put to death, the greatest joy is expressed by the whole company." [31]

Probably the best one-sentence summation of the legal mind against which Cornwallis struggled was written by another British general: "The Catholic would murder the Protestant in the name of God; the Protestant would murder the Catholic in the name of law." [32]

That law, not what Thomas Hutchinson or John Adams called "law" but Irish law, was precisely what Lord Lieutenant Camden intended to enforce. "You ask," he wrote the Duke of Portland less than a year before he would order Sir Ralph Abercromby to crush the opposition with military force, "whether his Majesty should be advised to accede to a concession which is made the excuse of rebellion. Rebellion must first be overcome. It will afterwards be to be considered how the country is to be governed."[33] Just two days earlier, in a speech to the House of Commons, a despairing Henry Grattan pleaded for the "concession" Camden and Fitzgibbon would not accept and, by foretelling the future, bared the consequences of the punitive philosophy that dominated the legal mind of British-ruled Ireland. "You argue that you can neither emancipate the Catholics nor reform the Constitution till the insurrection is put down. You cannot put it down," Grattan warned. "As coercion has advanced the United Irishmen have advanced. The measures to disarm have armed them, to make them weak and odious have made them powerful and popular. . . . You say you must subdue before you reform. Alas! you think so. But you forget that you subdue by reforming. . . . Suppose you succeed, what is your success?—a military Government."[34]

Grattan's way had been tried in America when the Stamp Act was repealed and later when other concessions were offered. It would never be tried in British-ruled Ireland, and the reason was that many of the Anglo-Irish ascendancy believed that military government would be a "success": the only answer to the Catholic problem.[35] On 11 March 1798, Camden decided to arrest the executive committee of the United Irishmen. "It must be shown," he explained, "that the Government is not afraid to act, and the capture of the heads of the conspiracy must be followed by the march of troops into the parts of the country most disturbed."[36] Interestingly, Thomas Gage had made almost the exact same point in 1775.[37] The difference was that he had been powerless to arrest anyone before his troops marched toward Lexington.

15

To Effect a Revolution[1]

THE EXECUTION
OF IMPERIAL LAW

Half a tale has been told so far and it must remain half told. When our frame of reference is the conditions of local and imperial law in eighteenth-century North America, we cannot detail the mechanics of the emergence of whig government. The "why" must await another study; it is only the "how" that is revealed by the inability of the British to seize the initiative. It is well to recall, however, that in 1774, the British tried to seize it. When Governor Thomas Gage ordered his troops to march on Concord, he did not operate under the charter that had handicapped Francis Bernard and Thomas Hutchinson. The imperial parliament had responded to the Boston Tea Party with the coercive or intolerable acts—statutes intended to bring about the reformation of whig law.

We must repeat the weary theme of imperial impotency. The acts that parliament passed in 1774 reforming the government of Massachusetts Bay were neither coercive nor intolerable. They did not seek to create a new Ireland; they sought to curb whig power. They did not succeed because they came too late. Had they been more timely they still might not have been enough. The justices of the peace were put under the governor's control and members of the council were to be appointed by London, but the Boston mob was still there and soon Gage found that his *mandamus* councillors were afraid to do their duty. A new quartering act brought the army back into town, one step London hoped would neutralize the mob. Another was appointment by the sheriff of grand and criminal traverse jurors. Futile gestures both, for the whigs closed the courts and it mattered not if the military arrested rioters or who selected juries. There was now no common-law tribunal in which to prosecute. Town meetings were curtailed, a measure that might have crippled whig power but for two facts: the coercive acts made no

150

mention of the "body" and committees of correspondence were not proscribed. Both continued to function and nonimportation was revived, perhaps enforced more efficiently than ever before. Indeed, crimes committed by whigs, such as the Boston Tea Party itself, could still be tried in Massachusetts Bay unless covered by the statute of Henry VIII. One might have expected parliament, at the very least, to have added political rioting to the list of transportable offenses, but the cabinet had not asked for so mild a departure from constitutional precedent. What it did request and receive from parliament was some protection for imperial officials, for one of the coercive statutes provided for trial, at the defendant's discretion, outside the colony. It was a valuable right made less valuable when we note it was limited to charges of capital crime committed under special circumstances. Assault, battery, and other offenses, as well as civil trespass, remained in the jurisdiction of local, provincial courts. It is not hard to imagine how much customsmen and army officers were emboldened to act in ways they previously would have avoided.

Had the whig militia not met the soldiers of Thomas Gage at Lexington and started the American Revolution, we may doubt if the decision by the imperial government to apply force would have made a substantial difference in the governance of Massachusetts Bay. Had the whigs stood aside and permitted the troops to march unmolested to Concord, they might have seized the arms and ammunition they were sent to confiscate. Even that possibility is not certain as the officers would have been advised to act with caution. Every house broken into, each civilian brushed aside could mean a potential suit for civil damages and possibly an indictment by the Middlesex county grand jury. Only if a person were killed and a capital crime charged could the defendant have moved for trial outside the colony.

It is true as previously mentioned that the whigs—angered by Chief Justice Peter Oliver's decision to receive his salary from the imperial government in London rather than the provincial assembly at Boston—had closed the courts. The people would not serve on juries and crowds stood on the steps of courthouses blocking the entrance to royal officials. Civil writs would never again be served in Massachusetts Bay on the authority of a British king. Yet we must not underestimate the ingenuity of the American whigs. They were flexible enough to devise a program that would have furnished jurors for those cases they wanted tried and at such sessions the mob would have stepped aside, permitting even Peter Oliver to take the bench.

It could be contended that the whigs would have nothing to gain by reopening the courts, even selectively, as they no longer controlled the appointment of jurors. One of the intolerable acts had taken the choice from the town meeting and vested it with the crown-appointed sheriffs. Whigs were still eligible to sit but tories might be there beside them. We may wonder if that reform would have halted whig use of the judicial process to "punish" imperial officials. Whig lawyers could still draft writs that the court could not dismiss, and defendants would have had to retain counsel at their own expense; the matter would have gone to trial, and the nuisance might have been worth the effort. While the threat may not have been serious enough to keep army officers stationed in Massachusetts Bay from doing their duty, it could be serious should that duty require the application of force giving the plaintiff the appearance of a valid cause of action. We need not conjecture that they would have avoided force; that is not the point. We may, however, suspect that officers would have avoided arbitrary, oppressive conduct of the type that, had they been in Ireland, they would have committed without a second thought. It is well to remember what they were capable of doing. Officers on both sides of the Atlantic were enlisted in the same British army and several of those serving under Thomas Gage had learned how to deal with colonials while stationed in King George's second kingdom, Ireland.

Had the troops that marched to Concord arrested whigs, their mission would have been pointless, except as a form of harassment, and again the arresting officers might have faced civil or criminal charges. With no grand juries to indict and no courts to convict, Gage could not have held them under civil law, even for a brief while. From the perspective of reestablishing imperial authority, the intolerable acts did not go far enough. A Massachusetts governor was still a long way from enjoying the discretion of an Irish viceroy. What the acts did do was give him a cooperative council, as councillors were now named by royal *mandamus*, not elected by the House of Representatives. As a result, Gage could have proclaimed martial law and with control of the council he would have been able to issue commissions of law martial for the trial of those whigs he arrested, although he might have found only army officers willing to serve. To have made such courts effective, moreover, the governor would have had to station soldiers in every part of the province. That move was impossible, and once troops left a town the whigs would have been again in command as every potential witness well knew.[2]

Had he been lord lieutenant of Ireland, we might imagine that Thomas Gage would have been a more energetic and effective defender of imperial rule. He would not have spent his time seeking legal advice and writing to London for clarifications; he would have harassed the whigs and not allowed the whigs to harass him. Should we seek the efficiency of the execution of imperial law in eighteenth-century Ireland, we could do no better than look at Ulster during 1797 when the viceroy decided to break the United Irish organization. Few regular troops were available and the government relied mainly on militia and yeomanry. The yeomanry had been created the year before, when there was fear of French invasion, and its membership was almost entirely Protestant. The United Irishmen had opposed its formation, using intimidation, abuse, seduction, and even murder to discourage recruiting. Those who enrolled came chiefly from districts that in recent years had been the scene of savage violence between Catholic Defenders and Protestant Peep-o-Day boys.[3] "Such men, with uniforms on their backs and guns in their hands, and clothed with the authority of the Government, but with scarcely a tinge of discipline and under no strict martial law, were now let loose by night on innumerable cabins."[4]

THE EXECUTION OF IMPERIAL LAW

In Belfast the government's policy met with success and was, in a sense, a test of the law that would be enforced nationwide the following year. Although martial law had not been proclaimed, "the yeomanry and militia acted almost without restraint: in the search for arms, houses were burnt down, suspected persons were flogged or tortured to make them reveal what they might know, and hundreds were sent off to the fleet."[5] The influence of the United Irishmen in local affairs was greatly weakened, thousands of guns were seized or surrendered, and the northern Presbyterians, previously a source of strength for constitutional reform and especially for republicanism in Ireland, were effectively cowed, beginning the shift to political reaction that was to shape much of Irish history even into the twentieth century.

Under both constitutional and common law much of the police action in Ulster was illegal. In eighteenth-century Ireland that fact gave little comfort to the victims and placed no restraint on the military. Some of the persons whose property had been destroyed in the search for arms did seek damages in king's bench and instituted legal proceedings against magistrates and yeomen. The government did not permit the courts to consider the cases. A new act of indemnity was passed by parliament, "which sheltered all magistrates, and other persons, employed to preserve the peace, from the consequences of every illegal act they had committed since the beginning of the year 1797, with the object of suppressing insurrection, preserving peace, or securing the safety of the State."[6] In eighteenth-century Ireland, when statutory law spoke of preserving "peace," it spoke of "public peace," the peace of the government, not the peace of the citizen.

It is important to keep a legal perspective. The situation in Ireland during the 1790s was not entirely comparable to that faced by Governor Thomas Gage in Boston during 1775. There was fear of an enemy invasion aided by internal insurrection. The alarm was often the excuse rather than the cause of suppression, but it was real and created genuine apprehension among men who had the ear of Dublin Castle. Even Wolfe Tone, the most radical of the United Irish leadership, was first arrested on suspicion he was plotting with the French. Had Samuel Adams or John Hancock ever been transported to London for trial, they would have been charged with another species of treason, less dangerous to the legal and military mind that ruled the eighteenth-century British empire than consorting with the enemy in time of war.

Still, the lawmakers of British Ireland must accept some of the blame that Arthur O'Connor and his United Irish colleagues assigned them as perpetrators of the Rising of '98. They made no attempt, as had the lawmakers of British America, to conciliate potential rebels by offering even token concessions. Shortly after the yeoman had subdued Belfast, a last effort to introduce a parliamentary reform bill was overwhelmingly defeated. Henry Grattan, chief spokesman for the constitutionalists, gave up the fight and withdrew from the House of Commons. Moderate reformers had reason for despair and extremists were again convinced that parliamentary activity was irrelevant.

Ireland drifted toward chaos as the two sides accelerated their violence.

Government terror was extended from Ulster into Munster and Leinster, where the brutal conduct of the troops was met by United Irish raids for arms and attacks on those suspected of cooperating with the authorities. Some members favored an immediate rising but the leadership felt French aid necessary to ensure success. Before it could coordinate a full-scale revolution, the lord lieutenant proclaimed martial law and ordered the arrest of the United Irish executive. Arthur O'Connor, Thomas Addis Emmet, William James McNevin, and several others were to be imprisoned for almost five years. They would never be tried and their followers were left to fight without central direction or moderate leadership.[7]

The Rising of 1798 was staged and the result was far bloodier and more violent than anything that had occurred during the American Revolution—comparable only to the civil war between tory loyalist and whig rebel that had taken place in the backcountry of Georgia and the Carolinas or on the Iroquois frontiers. To the north the commander, Henry Joy McCracken, was easily defeated. Tried at Belfast during July, he was executed the same day. To the south, especially in county Wexford, there was some momentary success, but it came mainly at the price of violence and terror. The army retaliated as if in enemy country, and it has been argued, much of the rebels' brutality can be traced to resentment against the conduct of the troops during those months. Men taken in arms were shot without trial, houses were burnt, and their inhabitants executed on the mere suspicion of having harbored fugitives. Even a member of parliament was hanged as a traitor, after a hasty court-martial and on the flimsiest of evidence.

As previously noted, the military was instructed to act without awaiting authorization from a civil magistrate, and the commander in chief, Sir Ralph Abercromby, issued general orders condemning the conduct of his own troops which, he charged, had "too unfortunately proved the army to be in a state of licentiousness which must render it formidable to everyone but the enemy."[8] The choice of the word "licentiousness" should not go unnoticed. In North America an English general, Thomas Gage, employed it repeatedly to describe the conduct of whigs. In Ireland, a Scottish general used it to describe the king's own soldiers.

We might expect Abercromby to win few friends from among the landed gentry, but that the officials of government and members of the bar would applaud his respect for the rule of law. Instead we find Lord Chancellor John Fitzgibbon calling the general a "Scotch beast" and a "perverse and sulky mule" for hoping to suppress rebellion through constitutional methods.[9] Fitzgibbon, it must be pointed out, was the highest judicial official in the kingdom, the man who should have been reminding the army of the rule of law. Thus were traditional roles reversed in eighteenth-century Ireland even more dramatically than in eighteenth-century Massachusetts Bay. In Boston a mob might swear out a warrant for the arrest of a tory against whom it had been rioting. The justice of the peace who issued the warrant might be said to abuse the judicial process, but both he and the mob adhered to the forms of law. In Ireland, the government did not always have to abuse legal process when its law officers ignored legal form.

There were Irish lawyers, but not many, who criticized the army and disagreed with Fitzgibbon that it needed a free hand. Sir Jonah Barrington, who would serve as judge of admiralty, characterized one of the court-martial executions in Wexford as "deliberate murder" and recorded that one officer simply executed men on mere suspicion.[10]

It was a period of merciless flogging, half-hanging, the pitch cap, "free quarter," looting, rape, and houseburning, sanctioned by government and almost a policy of legal vengeance. Caught between two rival terrors, the citizens of Ireland were unprotected; even a lawyer could be trapped by events. One was the barrister William Sampson whose house had been the first searched during one of Castlereagh's raids on Belfast.[11] Later arrested, he claimed that the only crime he had committed was to serve as defense council for United Irishmen.[12] Years later, addressing American audiences, Sampson described scenes of brutality that defy belief, but as a member of the bar he knew the conditions of law then existing in Ireland and when he speaks of the judicial process he has much to tell.[13] On one circuit held at Carrickfergus, he defended Joseph Cuthbert and several others who had been imprisoned for a year. He won an acquittal. Immediately the prosecutor produced a warrant under the Suspension of *Habeas Corpus* Act and the men were recommitted to custody. At the same circuit, Sampson relates, a colonel in the regular army was convicted of an unusually brutal crime of vengeance. Found guilty, he took the king's pardon from his pocket and was released.[14] It was the administration of imperial law that persuaded Sampson, though never a rebel, to sympathize with the opponents of British rule. "For my part, my interest, my connections and my hopes, lay decidedly with the court party rather than the people," he wrote after being released from prison on condition he leave Ireland forever. "But in the course of my profession as an advocate, I have been a witness of systematic outrage, such as I once thought had forever disappeared with the past ages of barbarity."[15]

It may be argued whether the actions of the government, the houseburnings, imprisonments, and executions, halted or precipitated the Rising of '98. Writing from prison, O'Connor, Emmet, and McNevin charged that the troops excited the people to rebellion; Emmet particularly insisted that the arrest of moderate leaders opposed to insurrection opened the way for a more radical, desperate element to take command.[16] One would expect the government to deny these charges, to assert that it tried to avoid rather than accelerate the bloodshed; not so in British-ruled Ireland. As Wolfe Tone had said from the dock, it was a matter of winning and once it had won the government could boast of what it pleased.[17] In its final report, the Secret Committee of the House of Lords that had questioned O'Connor, Emmet, and McNevin suggested that, unlike the American Revolution, the Irish Rising of '98 was caused as much by the enforcement of imperial law as by the people's opposition to that law. "From the vigorous and summary expedients resorted to by Government," it stated with approval, "and the consequent exertions of the military, the leaders found themselves reduced to the alternative of the immediate insurrection, or of being deprived of the means on which they relied for effecting their purpose, and to this cause is exclusively to be attributed that premature and desperate effort, the rashness of which has so evidently facilitated its suppression."[18]

The amount of blood that flowed in '98 seems appalling even in our age of total war. Rebellion may not have been crushed but potential rebels were annihilated. The cost in bitter hatred and a divided nation was not the measure taken by Dublin Castle or Lord Chancellor John Fitzgibbon. From their perspective and from the perspective of its executors in 1797 and 1798, it can be said that British imperial law in eighteenth-century Ireland, so different from that same law in contemporary North America, did not fail. For almost a century and a half after the farmers of Massachusetts fired on the soldiers of Thomas Gage, the king's writ would run in Ireland with a strength that would have astonished Chief Justice Thomas Hutchinson and brought satisfaction to Lord Chancellor John Fitzgibbon. Well into the twentieth century the law that had been unable to silence the *Boston Gazette* for even one edition would still be suppressing newspapers in Ireland. The law that scarcely touched the lives of Americans except to make them angry, could fine and imprison youths for singing the republican *Soldiers' Song* or *Who Fears to Speak of Easter Week*. The law that failed to put one Massachusetts whig into the criminal dock would continue to order the execution of Irish rebels, often by court-martial and sometimes in secret session.[19] The law that had been helpless to deal with the Boston Tea Party would continue into the 1970s to intern Irishmen without trial and on mere suspicion.

If British imperial law as executed in Ireland was more efficient and lasting than in North America, it exacted a heavy price in Irish history—a tradition of political violence and deliberate assassination. The British legal legacy to North America was exemplified by the whigs of Boston, who sought to establish the legitimacy of their actions while throwing East India Company tea into the harbor. The British legal legacy to Ireland is exemplified in the death of Lord Kilwarden, chief justice of the king's bench—dragged from his coach in the streets of Dublin and hacked to death by rebels bearing pikes.

British rule in North America was based on law and it slipped away through law. British rule in Ireland was achieved by force and maintained by force. The Rising of '98 proved how effective imperial law could be. To combat it, discontented Irish would have to resort to counterforce.

After the Rising of '98 was crushed, the tenantry of Ireland indulged in outbreaks of agrarian discontent more violent and widespread than ever before. The terror was so complete that common-law courts were rendered almost powerless. An act of February 1799 established virtual martial law and reinforcements of British troops were brought in. The Houghers, Whiteboys, and Defenders of the eighteenth-century were followed in the nineteenth century by such groups as the Ribbonmen and the Threshers, organized for and committed to violence. Some responded to local rural grievances; others fought against such symbols of imperial law as the tithe proctors of the established church. Crime rose to such heights that at times it was necessary to clear the jails with special commissions. Early in 1822 no less than thirty-five persons were sentenced to death by one judge sitting under a special commission at Cork. A common cause of homicide was that the victim had given evidence in a court of law or had taken land of which someone had been dispossessed.[20] It was a tradition of violence directed against law, and force could not end it, only legal reform could. In Ireland constitutional reform could be accomplished only with force.

The United Irishmen had urged reform through constitutional methods, but their heirs would not be the Daniel O'Connells and the homerulers who sought peaceful change. Rather their successors are found in such organizations as the Young Irelands, the Fenians, and the Irish Republican Brotherhood, all of whom, having lost faith in the constitution, relied on physical force. Catholic emancipation did not come until 1828 due to British fears of violence. More violence forced the abolition of the hated tithes, though not until 1838, and it was not until 1864, as the result of further violence, that the church of Ireland was disestablished.

The drama of 1798 was replayed almost act for act during the second decade of the twentieth century. Parallels, to be sure, are not exact for there was less mass bloodshed as the rebels did not try to put an army in the field as they had during the eighteenth century, relying instead on isolated acts of violence. After the failure of the Easter Rising of 1916, the Irish rebellion became a war of trenchcoated gunmen and official reprisals.

The British reacted much as they had in 1798. They arrested the leadership and with the same result as before. With the heads of Sinn Fein in jail the way was open for the more radical Irish Republican Brotherhood. It was British law, according to one arrested Sinn Fein officer, that made the advocates of terror "masters of the scene."[21] Again the British resorted to mass detention, mostly without trial and often outside of Ireland. The chief result was to alienate more of the population and to give rebel leaders within the prisons a chance to indoctrinate men who previously had not belonged to any political cause.

Finally the British, as in 1798, turned to reprisals and official terror. As the Protestant yeoman had been used before, now there was the Protestant constabulary. Forcible entries and looting occurred again and suspected Sinn Feiners were taken from their homes and summarily shot. One difference was that instead of burning houses, the twentieth-century British army blew them up.[22]

The extent to which the history of 1798 was repeated in 1919 is truly remarkable. Not the fighting, of course, for without a rebel field army there were no repeats of the battles of New Ross or Vinegar Hill, and hence no mass executions. But the law seemed hardly altered in any respect. The British legal mentality had not changed its view of Ireland through the generations of Daniel O'Connell, Charles Stewart Parnell, and John Redmond. There had been a major constitutional reform, however, and it made all the difference.

The average Irish citizen now could vote and Catholics could stand for parliament. A political movement with a small following in 1915 won the election of 1917, thanks in part to the executions of 1916. The reprisals of the Black and Tans ensured an even greater victory in the next general election. Irish members of parliament, chosen to sit at Westminster, sat instead in Dublin, and Ireland had a duly elected assembly to enact statutes and speak for the nation. At the same time the people turned their backs on the imperial courts, using instead Republican tribunals, making them in fact the judiciary of Ireland.[23] Except for the degree of violence, so often resulting in homicide, the situation in Ireland just before the British recognized the Free State could be compared to Massachusetts during 1775. There was now a local government and a local law which could and did take over many of the functions of imperial government and imperial law.

It has been said that the British in twentieth-century Ireland overreacted. That instead of honoring the leaders of the abortive Easter Rising with court-martial and by shooting them, they should have handed them over to magistrate courts and ridiculed the entire affair.[24] Had they done so the British would have been out of character, ignoring their own history and their legal heritage. Yet, it is claimed, by adhering to that history and that law, they executed harmless dreamers and turned a nation that would have been contented with home rule into a land of rebels. Then they went on, hanged the young Kevin Barrys, and in the process made Ireland free.

Perhaps the rulers of twentieth-century Ireland by emulating the rulers of eighteenth-century Ireland did make Irish independence inevitable. We cannot be certain and the argument may be doubted. Had the British been lenient they would have been acting more like the rulers of eighteenth-century North America than rulers of Ireland—like men such as Thomas Gage and the earl of Dartmouth who lost an even greater empire. When Samuel Adams was not arrested following the Boston Tea Party, he did not contemplate the mildness of British law and think of reconciliation with so temperate a mother country. Instead, he and his fellow whigs, free from prosecution and without fear of military reprisal, continued to stress constitutional grievances, spoke publicly of tyranny, and organized the movement that closed the imperial courts.

Had Lord French not ordered executions and mass arrests, he might not have antagonized the average citizens of Ireland and the rebellion might have been less effective as more of the population might have cooperated with the authorities or voted against the candidates of Sinn Fein. But such conduct would not have changed the constitutional issue for Arthur Griffith any more than it had for John Adams. Michael Collins if not forced into hiding might have fought a war more like that fought by George Washington, and the Irish Republican Army could have relied less on violence and terror. Yet it is difficult to argue that a lenient legal policy would have stopped a nationalistic movement created by opposition to imperial rule. More than the criminal law would have had to be reformed.

In the execution of imperial law the contrast between Ireland and the

American colonies was not so much in the use that was made of force as the use that was made of law. That the law could be enforced in Ireland was not so significant as the fact that imperial officials who did not respect that law were shielded from the consequences. In Massachusetts Bay they were not always shielded even when they obeyed the law.

16

Enforced by Mobs[1]

THE RULE OF LAW

It may be fractious to hint that mobs of eighteenth-century Massachusetts Bay adhered to law more than did the British rulers of eighteenth-century Ireland. Americans have long believed they are a most lawless people. Much questionable scholarship of recent years has tried to convince them they are right. As a task it is not difficult. There is a self-flagellatory urge in the national character that asks for little proof. One need only total up past mobs, vigilante movements, and lynchings to close the case. Comparisons to other lands are seldom ventured. Some questions are never asked as the obvious need not be deeply probed. It would be too paradoxical to inquire if the rule of violence may sometimes be the rule of law.

It is not enough to recognize that law—constitutional law—and disagreements about law were a prime cause of the American Revolution. It must also be acknowledged that law helps explain not only why but how the Revolution was fought. Rebellions are attacks on constituted authority and the power that the government can command determines the strategy of the insurgents and the course of battle. When authority is weak or so confined by legal restrictions that it cannot call upon effective force to defend established order, there is less likelihood of massive bloodshed as demonstrated by the history of military coups in many Latin American republics south of Mexico.

In eighteenth-century North America and eighteenth-century Ireland, Great Britain had sufficient military strength to meet the challenge of rebellion with deadly force. The army was present in both realms but the laws that controlled the army in each were not the same and in that fact lies much of the explanation why one was a revolution fought by the rules of warfare and the other a rising washed in blood. Indicative of the American Revolution are the facts that the whigs had openly been drilling a militia, and shortly after

Lexington Thomas Gage found himself besieged in Boston by an organized army soon to be commanded by a non-New Englander appointed by the Continental Congress meeting in public session. Indicative of the Irish risings are the covert nature of their military organizations and the fact that during the first four months of 1921 seventy-three bodies were found dead by Irish roadsides with the notice "A warning to spies."[2] The American Revolution was a struggle of marching armies, of uniformed officers known to their opponents by rank and name, and of whig civilian governments operating openly in every province. Ireland won her independence in a war of dark street corners and ambushes on lonely country lanes. From the imperial point of view, the American Revolution was a terrorless rebellion. The casualties suffered by the British were soldiers killed and wounded in conventional or guerrilla warfare. There were no Phoenix Park assassinations, no "bloody Sundays" to call for military retaliation or house-to-house searches.

Historians of the American Revolution have ignored the role played by the conditions of law. As a result they have missed the dénouement that spun the tale. Those who may doubt that law was a shaping force in the course of human events, should ask why, when compared to the Irish risings, the American Revolution from the time of the Stamp Act crisis to the confrontation at Lexington lacked incidents of bloodshed either open or clandestine.

The American whigs were not oppressed; they had few social and religious grievances. Their quarrel was with the imperial interpretation of the constitution. So too was the quarrel of those Protestant gentry who organized the United Irishmen. They sought constitutional reform by constitutional methods. Only when reform proved impossible did they turn to armed rebellion, hoping to emulate the Americans by driving out the British with a regular military command. Arrested by an arbitrary law unknown in Massachusetts Bay, they watched from prison while suppression brought forth a different type of revolution led by more desperate men with deeper, less legalistic grievances.[3]

In eighteenth-century Ireland the struggle was between the governed and the governors, and for those rebels who stormed the town of Wexford and turned the Rising of '98 into a religious crusade, the landlords and the local magistrates were the "governors," not the men who ruled the kingdom from Dublin Castle. In Massachusetts Bay the struggle was less between the governed and the governors than between different levels of government. The role played by juries sums up the difference. Where Irish juries were terrorized by violence and murder, becoming afraid to do their duty, in Boston the whigs employed juries to impose on imperial officers a milder, legalistic form of coercion making them less zealous to do their duty.

Considering the differences of law in the two realms of George III, the stress on legalism by the Massachusetts whigs is no more surprising than the disrespect for law in contemporary Ireland. Law was, more often than not, on the whigs' side. It was seldom on the side of the average Irishman.

Three factors of law contributed to the downfall of British rule in eighteenth-century North America: the conditions of imperial law, the conditions of local law, and the matter of who controlled the law. By their control of the council, the magistrates, and the grand and traverse juries, the Massachusetts whigs were assured that the agents of British imperialism would not impose arbitrary measures of the type so freely resorted to by their counterparts in Ireland. When challenging the constitutionality of parliamentary legislation—the Stamp Act or the Townshend duties for example—the Americans had less need to act outside the substantive criminal or civil law, to be "lawless" to the degree of the Irish Invincibles or the Irish Republican Army. Control of the legislature, of the executive council, and of the town meetings, put the goal of opposition through legal methods almost within their grasp.

We must not demand precise rules or definitive principles. In the fluid rivalry of two competing governments what is "legal" may be as often a subjective as an objective judgment. Whether one is willing to argue that American whigs—when they rioted in the streets or harried customs officials in the civil courts—did in fact act "lawfully" depends to a large extent upon an individual's point of view. That is our problem, especially when we think of the whig crowd and try to see it from the whig rather than the tory perspective. The challenge may be too demanding for we are all latent tories.

Consider the possibility that there are often two sides to lawlessness. A tory conscious of how the Massachusetts whigs departed from traditional principles of English common law by employing the civil traverse jury and the writ system to impose a criminal-law type sanction upon customs officials would have said that they abused the judicial process. Yet that same tory might not have thought it an abuse when the commissioners of the customs departed from similar principles of English common law and attempted to use the admiralty jurisdiction to impose a criminal-law type sanction upon John Hancock. The tory who saw a violation of the constitution when whig juries ignored admiralty judgments and rendered common-law verdicts despite being instructed that the admiralty decree had settled all legal questions, probably did not recognize a comparable violation of the constitution in that section of the Sugar Act freeing customs officers from common-law damage suits whenever an admiralty court in a nonjury *ex parte* hearing ruled that they had acted with "probable cause." [4] If Hutchinson were to say that the whigs were guilty of "manipulation" when they packed the grand juries of Suffolk county, they could have made the same charge about his conduct when releasing Corbet in order to avoid ruling on the legality of naval press gangs in the colonies or his earlier decision in the same case when he held that while civil law governed adjective matters criminal definitions were determined by common law. That decision was consistent only in the fact that both its halves aided the prosecution. Should Hutchinson concede that whigs acted within the law when their grand jurors refused to indict the rioters who destroyed his house, yet assert they acted without principle, the complaint could with equal fairness be made about him, for Hutchinson kept imperial officials informed about secret grand jury proceedings and when men such as

Gage or Bernard were indicted he saw to it that the law did not take its normal course.[5]

The judicial process was such in eighteenth-century British North America that it could be used by the political process, and each side of the controversy was willing to take whatever advantages fell its way. Most dropped on the whig side, but the whigs should not be accused of unlawful manipulations merely because the tories thought them unlawful. The whigs, for their part, believed that the British were altering an immutable constitution and Hutchinson's "manipulations" were part of their story.

A more serious charge, as it troubled Americans who accepted implicitly the whig tale of constitutional abuse yet retained a conservative's respect for the rule of law, was the assertion that much of whig violence was lawless. We have seen whigs reject this contention yet none has articulated a satisfactory argument for the legality of their use of force. Implicit in their legal theory— in John Adams's distinction between legitimate and illegitimate mobs and his praise of the Boston Tea Party—was the concept that what is "unlawful" under imperial law is not always "lawless."[6] "Lawlessness" in the whig sense implied that the act complained of—such as a riot—was not only in violation of constituted law but was performed either for an irrational purpose or for personal gain or had a negative or antisocial aim. "Lawful" or "semilawful" in the whig sense was an act contrary to statutory or common law, but when tory or imperial law was broken and the purpose was to defend whig constitutional principles the act was not necessarily "lawless." Admittedly words are being put into mouths that might not have employed them. The whigs thought more of "legitimate" force than of "semilegal," but in a discussion of attitudes about law the semantic difference is not important.

It is fair to say that Governor Francis Bernard was one high tory who never understood what whigs were up to. That rebels might be governed by a legal theory was beyond his imagination. Yet even Bernard grasped the whig distinction between the lawless rioters who sacked Hutchinson's house and the semilawful rioters who forced Andrew Oliver to resign as stamp agent.[7] It was this legal theory—a theory that apparently had no limits as it led directly to mob rule—that persuaded other Americans to recoil from the whig program. It was possible to agree with whig constitutional arguments yet, convinced that whig law would eventually become more arbitrary than parliamentary law, to end as a supporter of the imperial government.

Joseph Galloway, political ally of Benjamin Franklin and champion of rule by the elected colonial assemblies, stated the issue most concisely. He was at Annapolis, Maryland, the day the *Peggy Stewart* docked carrying East India Company tea and saw a mob bring such pressure upon her owners that they were forced to burn her with all the tea aboard. "I think Sir," he wrote a friend, "I went to Annapolis yesterday to see my Liberty destroyed."[8]

As the coffins of the "massacre" victims followed by ten to twelve thousand "mourners" went round Boston's Liberty Tree and then back during a cold March day in 1770, the Reverend Mather Byles was looking on. "They call me a brainless Tory," he remarked to a companion, "but tell me, my young friend, which is better—to be ruled by one tyrant three thousand miles away, or by three thousand tyrants not one mile away?"[9]

Theophilus Lillie—a Boston merchant who has left a minor mark on prerevolutionary legal history for the mob into whose midst Ebenezer Richardson fired buckshot had originally gathered to torment him—dared make the same point in public.[10] A month before the shooting, Lillie published in a Boston newspaper a notice taunting the whigs for constitutional hypocrisy.

> I cannot help saying, although I never entered far into the mysteries of government, having applied myself to my shop and my business, that it always seemed strange to me that People who contend so much for civil and religious Liberty should be so ready to deprive others of their natural liberty;—that Men who are guarding against being subject to Laws [to] which they never gave their consent in person or their representative, should at the same time make Laws [i.e., the nonimportation agreements], and in the most effectual manner execute them upon me and others, to which Laws I am sure I never gave my consent either in person or by my representative. . . . I own I had rather be a slave under one Master; for if I know who he is, I may, perhaps, be able to please him, than a slave to an hundred or more, who I don't know where to find, nor what they will expect from me.[11]

Finally there were surely some Americans who shared the puzzlement of Governor Thomas Gage. He professed during 1775 not to understand the recklessness with which the citizens of Massachusetts Bay seemed willing to exchange what he called "Liberty for Tyranny," obeying the decrees of "Congresses and Committees" as once they had obeyed the laws of their "antient" government. "No People," Gage wrote, "were ever governed more absolutely than those of the American Provinces are now, and no reason can be given for the People's Submission, but that it is a Tyranny they have erected themselves, as they believe, to avoid greater Evils."[12]

We should be grateful to Thomas Gage and his prodigious correspondence. He has loomed large in prerevolutionary military history. If the legal history of the prerevolutionary era is ever written he may loom even larger. Only Thomas Hutchinson reported the constitutional scene more perceptively from the imperial side than this military man. Here we see Gage once again putting his finger on the precise point in debate: what was the greater evil?

It was not a desire for local rule or American nationalism that persuaded lawminded whigs such as John Adams to suppress fear of the crowd's ultimate potential and cling to their whig principles. Rather it was the constitutional theory then current that power corrupted rulers no matter how well intentioned.[13] If government were not restrained, tyranny was unavoidable and liberty doomed. In the end the dilemma could be resolved only by individual convictions as to what was the greater danger, which alternative more dreadful and which presented the larger menace. Josiah Quincy, Jr., summed up the answer for those Americans who understood Galloway's alarm but could not share his ultimate conclusion. "It is much easier," Quincy explained, "to restrain liberty from running into licentiousness than power from swelling into tyranny and oppression."[14] Such were the "greater Evils" to which Gage referred. The mob on the streets and the self-appointed congresses presented a threat to liberty, but it was a lesser threat than posed by an unrepresentative parliament claiming supreme legislative power.

The argument has been too often misunderstood. To Americans of the whig persuasion local control was the issue, true enough. But retention of local control was, for them, the means to an end, it was not the end itself.

For tories and apostate whigs, Quincy's assurance was unproven theory and their belief that the whigs were constitutional hypocrites became an inescapable conviction. During the decade before the battle of Lexington, the slogan of the American whigs had been "No representation, no taxation."[15] After the Declaration of Independence another slogan gained acceptance. It appeared most prominently in John Adams's draft of the first Massachusetts constitution, placing the executive, legislative, and judicial powers in separate departments "to the end that it might be a government of laws, and not of men."[16] In time the idea gained currency that this clause expressed the spirit of the Revolution: that since 1765 the whigs had been struggling for a government, whether within or without the British empire, ruled by law and not by men. Surely on reading this clause tories such as Theophilus Lillie and Thomas Gage were amazed.[17]

When the conditions of law in prerevolutionary America are taken into account, it becomes apparent that one of the weakest features of British rule was that it was based on a government of laws and not of men. It was the conditions of law, not defiance of arbitrary rulers that permitted whigs to create a government that, without secrecy or surprise, took over Massachusetts in 1775. It was protection of law more than defiance of law that permitted whigs to organize and drill a standing army ready to take the field that same year. It was the conditions of law in the form of the grand jury that permitted newspapers to publish sedition and in the form of both magistrates and jurors that permitted mobs to move unmolested, harassing British officials and crippling the enforcement of imperial statutes.

Ironically it is the role of the crowd that most sharply contrasts government by imperial law with government by whig men. Even when the mob was on the streets tarring and feathering "a friend of government," the principle of governance by law not men tied the hands of royal officials. The army, so ruthlessly efficient in contemporary Ireland, was often present and possessed the physical force to intervene on the imperial side. But to have done so would have raised constitutional issues and the army stood aloof while the whigs took over not only the back alleys but the main streets and the wharves of America's seaports.

The British navy might have prevented the Boston Tea Party or at least arrested some of its participants, but there were procedural steps to be executed before it could constitutionally act and when they were not the navy remained immobilized, knowing that nonlawyers would criticize it or Hutchinson or the army for permitting the destruction of the tea—yet, at the same time knowing that the law gave it no role to play and grudgingly, yet obediently, it adhered to the law. The whigs not only appreciated that imperial government in North America was a government of law and not of men, they counted on it remaining so.

The proof may be overstated but not by very much. One reason why Boston whigs staged the Tea Party in an open manner and at the daylight hour was because they knew neither the navy in the harbor nor the army at the Castle would move against them. They knew, in other words, that the only men who could stop them were men of law serving a government of law. That was the irony of the whig slogan to Americans such as Joseph Galloway. In Annapolis when he saw another mob doing the same work, Galloway could well believe that he was witnessing the end of government by law and the beginning of government by arbitrary men.

The tories and the imperial officials may have been fearful of whig violence but the same cannot be said for the reluctant Americans, the would-be whigs who hesitated going all the way. The prerevolutionary American mob was not known for viciousness, at least when compared to mobs in other places and of other times.[18] What troubled them more than the threat of violence was the threat of arbitrary government. Crowd action in America, Howard Mumford Jones has pointed out, "seemed to be a form of direct political action, an exercise of the will of the people in the name of popular sovereignty, the assertion of fundamental law or social principle ('this is a white man's country'), or an expression of impatience with legislative or executive delay."[19]

We may agree that whigs of the prerevolutionary era sincerely believed that a crowd taking public action into its own hands might be acting as a lawful force. We may also note that the theory of the extralegality of the mob would continue to enjoy wide support in America—even among lawyers—during the nineteenth century.[20] Yet it would not do to imply that acceptance was universal or that even the faithful did not shrink. The less than faithful were repelled and the hostile were alarmed by displays of naked power unleashed on Boston's streets. It may be too, as Jones has claimed, that the mob as a manifestation of legitimate self-help was "in a sense definitely non-European."[21] For those Americans who equated Europe with stability and took comfort in the shelter of an empire ruled by Europe's most stable government, whig legal theory offered a future far more arbitrary than the current British constitution. Parliament might be unrepresentative and hence, to that degree, it was in a constitutional sense arbitrary, but it was still a deliberative body and liberty in its hands was less subject to whim and fancy than with any substitute the whigs appeared likely to establish.

Not only hesitant or timid Americans but also committed whigs recoiled from the ultimate conclusion that seemed to lie behind whig law. John Joachim Zubly, anti-Stamp Act pamphleteer and proponent of religious tolerance, was a leading whig, serving as Georgia's delegate to the Second Continental Congress until he went over to the imperial side, concluding that, "A Republican Government is little better than Government of Devils."[22] James Allen of Pennsylvania was another apostate. A lawyer, he had been a convinced whig only to turn back at the prospect of mob law. "I love the Cause of liberty," he wrote in his diary during March 1776, "but cannot heartily join the prosecution of measures totally foreign to the original plan of Resistance. The madness of the multitude is but one degree better than submission to the Tea-Act."[23]

Such may well be the true, immeasurable cost of whig legal theory—the erstwhile whigs who, unable to distinguish the Continental Congress from the mob in the street returned to the imperial fold, swelled the ranks of the loyalists, and helped provide the Revolution with its moments of ugly civil war. The doubts, the hesitancy, the eventual hostility of the converted loyalist may have been the highest price that the whigs paid for making the mob and mob violence an instrument of law. It was not that the introduction of violence destroyed the possibility of accommodation and made revolution inevitable.[24] Quite the contrary, the very nature of the British empire made some violence necessary. It was, after all, a government with no legitimate channels through which constitutional grievances could be appealed and with no forum for obtaining redress except parliament itself: the very institution against which the whigs were contending. The prerevolutionary mob and the force it brought to bear on the controversy were the best means available to demonstrate to Great Britain the depths of colonial opposition, the one way—as Arthur O'Connor and Thomas Addis Emmet were to learn too late—to bring about accommodation and change. The demise of the Stamp Act is a case in point. Although the effectiveness of the nonimportation movement at a time of business recession in the mother country was the immediate cause of its repeal, the colonists could present the constitutional argument in no other forum except the streets: by shocking London with a display of violence.

"The role of violence and the threat of violence in the American Revolution is curiously complicated," Bernard Bailyn writes. "For in that upheaval, unlike the French Revolution in which thousands were killed, directly or indirectly, as a result of mob action, there was 'a singular self-restraint . . . the participants invariably stopped short of inflicting death.'"[25] The theme of "self-restraint" has often been stressed of the prerevolutionary American mob and in turn supports the further theme that the mob was an apparatus of whig law. It was not vengeful or bloodthirsty for it had a legal purpose and performed a legal task.

The fact that the prerevolutionary crowd in Boston and other colonial seaports never turned to the butchery that reddened the lanes of Wexford in 1798 does not mean there was no terror. A mob is a mob to its victim and, as Hiller B. Zobel has emphasized, its essential impression is its unpredictability.[26] He whom a Boston mob threatened knew he had to obey and unlike the historian could take no comfort in the fact that his life would have been in greater danger had he been seized by a mob in Paris or in New Ross.

There was terror connected with many of the crowds of Revolutionary America.[27] We have the testimony of enough tories to be certain they were alarmed. The stamp agents of 1765 feared for their lives; John Mein claimed the mob would have killed him had he answered the warrant Samuel Adams obtained for his arrest; individual revenue officials were occasionally threatened with death by the mobs that seized them; and during the riot resulting from the seizure of John Hancock's sloop *Liberty*, Thomas Hutchinson was concerned for the safety of the commissioners of the customs.[28] "I confess I have not been without some apprehensions for myself," he added.[29] Even tories who held no public office expressed fear. "It is the business of the evening," one woman wrote from Boston during 1770, "to see the firearmes loaded, and lights properly placed in the store and house."[30]

We need not be surprised that timid tories such as Governor Francis Bernard thought themselves in personal danger. Their alarm is not evidence that the peril was imminent. It took little more than a rumor to send Bernard scurrying to the safety of the Castle. But we should be impressed by John Adams's concern for Chief Justice Peter Oliver—"I shuddered at the expectation that the mob might put on him a coat of tar and feathers, if not put him to death"—and by Josiah Quincy's belief that had Thomas Hutchinson's daughter not persuaded him to flee the night his house was sacked he would have been killed.[31] The next day while Hutchinson was transporting his children to their country home, his daughters became so terrified by "two or three small parties of the ruffians" along the road, they "said they should never be safe, and I was forced to shelter them that night at the Castle."[32] Nine years later one of the girls was still uneasy. "You may now know how to pity me," she wrote to her sister-in-law, "who have been running from a mob ever since the year sixty-five."[33] The sister-in-law was able to understand as her husband was then in hiding with the other consignees of the East India Company tea. "Neither of my sons have dared to appear in Boston since the latter part of November," Governor Hutchinson wrote that March, "to the total neglect and ruin of their business."[34] That same month Lieutenant Governor Andrew Oliver died and one of the Hutchinson's sons wanted to pay his respects. "My friends have been trying to sound the powers that rule at present, but do not think it safe for me to attend the funeral."[35] In fact, Chief Justice Oliver did not dare attend and Andrew was his brother.[36]

Granting there was fear—true, reasonable fear—one must return to Bailyn's point that the prerevolutionary mob in Boston, unlike some others, "invariably stopped short of inflicting death."[37] If the highest judicial officer in British-ruled Massachusetts Bay was unable to attend his brother's funeral, apprehending violence, it should be noted that the highest judicial officer in British-ruled Ireland was in danger even at his own funeral. When the lord chancellor, John Fitzgibbon, was buried, a Dublin mob attacked his coffin intending to defile his corpse.[38] Moreover, as Bailyn notes, the American prerevolutionary mob showed "a singular self-restraint."[39] Whether one sees that mob as manipulated from above by a few leading politicians such as Samuel Adams or led by its own inherent organization from below, the rioters of Boston and elsewhere were remarkably orderly in at least one rspect— their actions usually expressed a clear purpose, the execution of whig law.

"Again and again," Jesse Lemisch argues, "when the mob's leaders lost control, the mob went on to attack the logical political enemy, not to plunder." [40] If the looting of Thomas Hutchinson's house was an exception, it was an early exception not to be repeated for over ten years, and surely Thomas Hutchinson, who would have enforced the Stamp Act even though he did not favor it, was a "logical political enemy."

It is remarkable just how politically and logically the mobs selected their victims. Usually they were minor figures: the underlings of the customs service low enough down in the public service to be easily intimidated. There was also, true enough, violence reserved for influential persons, violence in the form of personal terror such as that directed against the stamp agents and violence against valuable property as during the Boston Tea Party. But in most cases it was a controlled, selective violence and, more important, an open violence. Hence it was different from the surreptitious violence of the Irish Republican Army and if its victims, such as Hutchinson's daughters, were genuinely frightened, their fright was not as longlasting or even of the same degree as the fright of the families of eighteenth-century magistrates and landowners in the west of Ireland who lived in expectation that any night their houses might be burned and they themselves killed.

Had the Boston mob of prerevolutionary days wanted blood, Captain Thomas Preston would have been a logical victim following the Boston Massacre. Once lodged in jail, he could easily have been seized by a small crowd. Yet thoughts that he might be lynched were all in the minds of tories and his fellow army officers, not in the contemplation of whigs, low or high. His death would not have served the purpose of whig law any more than would the death of Ebenezer Richardson housed in the same jail. To W. E. H. Lecky, the fact that Preston was left untouched by the Boston mob was impressive, even remarkable. He was, apparently, the one historian to have studied the eighteenth-century crowd in Ireland as well as in Great Britain and North America and it is, therefore, not without meaning that he was struck by the respect for law and the absence of any efforts at extralegal vengeance following the Boston Massacre.

> It is very remarkable that after [John] Adams had accepted the task of defending the incriminated soldiers, he was elected by the people of Boston as their representative in the Assembly, and the public opinion of the province appears to have fully acquiesced in the verdict. In truth, although no people have indulged more largely than the Americans in violent, reckless and unscrupulous language, no people have at every period of their history been more signally free from the thirst for blood, which in moments of great political excitement has been often shown both in England and France. . . . In the long period of anarchy, riot, and excitement which preceded the American revolution, there was scarcely any bloodshed and no political assassination, and the essential humanity of American public opinion which was shown so conspicuously during the trial of the soldiers at Boston, was afterwards displayed on a far wider field and in still more trying circumstances during the fierce passions of

the Revolutionary war, and still more remarkably in the triumph of the North in the War of Secession.[41]

Commenting upon this statement by Lecky, Arthur M. Schlesinger concluded, "This forbearance doubtless made it easier for the more law-abiding Whigs to condone the outbreaks but it afforded cold comfort to the victims, who never knew when a mob, fortified perhaps with alcoholic as well as patriotic spirits, might overstep the bounds."[42] While Schlesinger is a student of prerevolutionary American mobs and has much to say about their role, we must recognize that his frame of reference is somewhat narrow. He sees their function entirely in terms of applying political pressure, not of whig or imperial law. Ignoring the legal dimensions, he missed the fuller explanation for the forbearance of the mob and does not consider why "law-abiding" whigs were able to condone the "outbreaks" without risking indiscriminate violence or imperial suppression.

When the prerevolutionary era is viewed from the perspective of law and of legal institutions, the conclusion is not that American mobs showed restraint due to some inherent characteristic or that law-abiding citizens could afford to support them because of this restraint. Indeed, it may even be asked whether the "practiced crowd" of Boston was characterized by unusual forbearance when compared to mobs in other places.[43] It is true that some eighteenth-century English rioters went on rampages of violence, but on the whole, recent scholarship has shown, the property they destroyed was often as carefully selected as that destroyed by political mobs in colonial America.[44] Even in revolutionary France, where between thirty-five and forty thousand persons lost their lives, the mob was not after blood.[45] "There were notably few fatalities among the rioters' victims," Gordon S. Wood writes of contemporary Europe. "In the week-long Gordon Riots not a single person was killed by the mobs. And, in fact, 'the French Revolution in Paris, for all the destructive violence that attended it, was not particularly marked by murderous violence on the part of crowds.'"[46] If the prerevolutionary American mob showed forbearance, and it did, it was a forbearance in kind not of degree that distinguished it from mobs in eighteenth-century Europe.

One explanation why Boston rioters were disciplined was because they were part of a political movement that had other, more legal means to accomplish tasks that might otherwise have evolved upon the mob. From the point of view of those other means, the whig mob took to the streets, applying pressure on selected royal officials, primarily to supplement whig law—acting as an auxiliary enforcement for whig-dominated legal institutions such as the jury and the justices of the peace. Schlesinger's "law-abiding" whigs could condone such "outbreaks" not because of any unusual or inherent forbearance practiced by American mobs but because they were, in fact, whig mobs striking at symbols of imperial authority which were restrained by law from striking back. As they were whig mobs, other whigs who did not themselves take to the streets had good reason to expect that the crowd's activities would not lead to indiscriminate rioting or produce bloodshed.

The "law-abiding" whigs—the Hancocks, the Adamses, the Cushings—

expected the mob to act with restraint because they understood both whig law and imperial law. The tory victims of whig mobs, who did not recognize the legitimacy or even the existence of whig law, were incapable of appreciating that whig law might place restraints on whig action. The respect shown for property by the Tea Party mob impressed them less than it impressed whigs. The whigs accepted the principles of whig legal theory and were, therefore, more inclined to trust mob forbearance as they had a theoretical explanation for that forbearance. Moreover, it is not difficult to conclude that they may have been justified. How better do we account for the restraint that has impressed so many historians from Lecky to Bailyn except by admitting that the mob was aware of its public function: that it was defending constitutional principles and its members did not think of themselves as engaged in an unlawful enterprise?

More important, the "law-abiding" whigs could accept the mob as an apparatus of whig law because they anticipated that there would be no bloodshed and no brutal retaliation. Their anticipation was based not so much on the forbearance of the mob enforcing whig law as on the forbearance of royal officials enforcing imperial law. On this point the law of British-ruled North America contrasts sharply not only with the law of British-ruled Ireland but with the law of Great Britain itself. Recent scholarship has documented the remarkable but undeniable fact that during the eighteenth century in Europe, bloodshed and death occurred not when political mobs took to the streets, but when they were confronted by armed authority. As George Rude, the leading historian of "the crowd in history," has proven, it was the rioters who suffered the casualties.[47]

"Law-abiding" whigs may not have known that during political riots in the eighteenth century it was the government rather than the mob that was conspicuous for violence toward life and limb. But they did know that the British army in North America was restrained by law, that it was not employed to suppress colonial riots, and thus had good reason to believe their mobs could act with restraint. It was not merely that they would not be confronted by authority; more significantly they would not be fired upon. As a result, they would suffer no casualties and would not be driven by the sight of blood either to turn on the king's troops or go off on a rampage indiscriminately destroying property or even life. It is worth repeating that, except for those few occasions when off-duty soldiers formed one disorganized mob fighting as a crowd against a mob of whigs,[48] no lives were lost in politically motivated demonstrations as a result of a standing army being stationed in the colonies. The one exception was the Boston Massacre, and then the soldiers fired to protect their lives, not to suppress a riot.

The same is true for the courts of law. In contemporary England juries convicted rioters and judges sentenced them to death. In Massachusetts they could not even be indicted. Thus the rioters in Boston, safe from imperial law, could act openly and in daylight. Not fearing military suppression or judicial punishment, they went about their business at an unhurried, methodical pace, less likely to be panicked into excessive action or to forget their purpose for being on the streets. It was these two conditions of law—the impotency of corrective authority and freedom from prosecution—that explain the "forbearance" of the prerevolutionary American mob to the extent that it differed from the mobs of eighteenth-century Europe.

Ireland was, of course, another story. The British army there cannot be compared to the British army in England or Scotland and certainly cannot be compared to the British army in North America. In London, for example, it acted under some legal restraints as it needed orders from a civilian-magistrate before it could fire upon crowds. Yet once it did receive authority to act it could exact a fearful toll—the Lord George Gordon riots of 1780 resulted in 285 killed by the government and 25 more hanged, and it was punishing a mob that did not take one human life. In Ireland the military was under no legal restraint. The army as well as the magistrates could and did seize men on the word of anonymous informers, sending them by scores to serve in the fleet.[49] It could and did break into houses, terrorize citizens, and execute suspects without trial. When military officers violated the law, they could expect parliament to protect them with an act of indemnity or the lord lieutenant to protect them with the king's pardon. On one occasion a band of regular troops aided by Black and Tans invaded a crowd of 8,000 sports fans ostensibly to search for weapons. Before they left, twelve people had been killed and sixty wounded. The event did not occur in Wexford during the Rising of '98. It occurred at Croke Park, Dublin, and the date was November 1920.[50] An Irish mob by necessity had to be more dangerous and more indiscriminate than did an eighteenth-century political mob in North America.

When we seek to understand the relative lack of bloodshed in prerevolutionary America it is necessary to consider not merely the forbearance of whig mobs but the forbearance of imperial law. It is suppression, not a thirst for blood, that produces the clandestine violence of many revolutionaries. The Americans did not have to react as did the Irish, and the lives of Samuel Adams, future governor of Massachusetts, and William Orr, Irish martyr, illustrate the difference. In Boston Adams could openly address an illegal body meeting, perhaps even speak of treason, and did not suffer arrest.[51] Until rebellion was proclaimed, he would not have to go into hiding. In Ireland William Orr administered an oath pledging the oath taker to religious brotherhood and constitutional reform. For that act he was arrested, indicted, tried, condemned, and executed.

It was law that made the difference, not the restraint or timidity of British authorities.[52] In Ireland those same officials showed little restraint and no timidity. The independence movement of the Dublin of 1919 had need of an Irish Republican Army. The independence movement in the Boston of 1775 did not. By the very nature of British law in the two realms, the shadow of the Irish gunman was bound to be more deadly than the substance of the American whig.

And still there is the question whether it was law that made the difference. In both eighteenth-century Boston and eighteenth-century Dublin basically the same law ran—English law, English definitions, and English procedures enforced by officials of the British crown. What was different was not the substance of law but the tradition of law and the degree of local control over the institutions of law. The Massachusetts whigs may not have appreciated the irony, but they summed up the difference when they called for a government of laws and not of men. In Ireland the law was governed by men. In North America men were governed by law. It is difficult to imagine Thomas Hutchinson even contemplating the repressive statutes that flowed from the pen of John Fitzgibbon. Both were native sons of British colonies and the history of their respective lands dictated that they not only played different roles but that they assumed different attitudes toward the mutability of law. The difference, then, may not be in the substance of the law but how much those who govern respect the rule of law.

Notes

1
The American Comparison

1. "Another Inconvenience, and a great one too in these Provinces, is a Want of Power and Vigour in the executive Part of Government; you see the Laws trampled upon in the very Face of Government, in the most open and shameful manner, without any Shew of Opposition from Government or Magistrates." Gage to Barrington, 7 October 1769.

2. C.L. Sulzberger's column, *New York Times*, 12 July 1972, p. 41, col. 1.

3. Letter from General Thomas Gage to Lieutenant Colonel William Dalrymple, 28 April 1770, *Gage Papers* (MS. Clements Library, University of Michigan); Letter from Lieutenant Colonel William Dalrymple to General Thomas Gage, 5 May 1770, *Gage Papers* (MS. Clements Library, University of Michigan).

4. It was a civil-law not a common-law court and decided cases without a jury. What London sought to avoid was the colonial jury even more than colonial-appointed judges. In many colonies judges were appointed by London.

5. T.D. Sullivan, A.M. Sullivan, & D.B. Sullivan, *Speeches from the Dock: or, Protests of Irish Patriotism* 44, 49–50 (1882).

6. Ibid., 53.

7. Ibid., 137.

8. 7 W.E.H. Lecky, *A History of England in the Eighteenth Century* 352n1 (1891).

9. Contemporaries also misunderstood the significance of law. When Irish and American were compared, British commentators noticed the loyalty of the Irish parliament in contrast to the independence of American assemblies without considering that the Irish parliament was, as will be discussed in the next two chapters, controlled by British interests. See, e.g., "William Pym," *London Evening Post*, 20 August 1765, printed in *Boston Evening-Post*, 25 November 1765, p. 1, col. 1.

2

The Locus of Law

1. "In short, my Lord, this Government is now brought to this State, that if the Chiefs of the Faction are not punished or at least so far censured as to be disqualified from holding Offices; if the Appointment of the Council is not put into the Hands of the King; if the Governor & Principal Crown Officers are not provided with adequate Salaries, independent of the People, it signifies little who is Governor." Bernard to Barrington, 18 March 1769.

2. Letter from Governor Thomas Hutchinson to former Governor Francis Bernard, 24 May 1771, quoted in James K. Hosmer, *The Life of Thomas Hutchinson, Royal Governor of the Province of Massachusetts* 206 (1896).

3. Barbara Graymont, *The Iroquois in the American Revolution* 68 (1972). "In all the late *American* Disturbances, and in every Attempt against the Authority of the *British* Government, the People of *Massachusetts Bay* have taken the lead. . . . And in every fresh Mode of Resistance against the Laws, they have first set the Example. . . ." Israel Mauduit, *A Short View of the History of the Colony of Massachusetts Bay* 5 (1774).

4. Jack P. Greene, "An Uneasy Connection: An Analysis of the Preconditions of the American Revolution," in *Essays on the American Revolution* 35–43 (Stephen G. Kurtz & James H. Hutson, editors, 1973).

5. Frank MacDermot, *Theobald Wolfe Tone: A Biographical Study* 39–40 (1939); J.C. Beckett, *The Making of Modern Ireland 1603–1923* 163 (1966).

6. MacDermot, supra n. 5, at 43.

7. R.B. McDowell, *The Irish Administration 1801–1914* 52 (1964).

8. Thomas Hutchinson, *The History of the Province of Massachusetts Bay from 1749 to 1774* 353 (1828); letter from Governor Francis Bernard to Lord Barrington, 18 March 1769, in *The Barrington-Bernard Correspondence* 198 (Edward Channing & Archibald Cary Coolidge, editors, 1970).

9. Letter from Governor Francis Bernard to the Earl of Halifax, 31 August 1765, rpt. in Merrill Jensen (editor), 9 *English Historical Documents: American Colonial Documents to 1776* 679 (1955).

10. Answer of Governor Francis Bernard to the Petition of the House of Representatives to the King (1769), rpt. in 1 *The Writings of Samuel Adams* 365–66 (Harry Alonzo Cushing, editor, 1904).

11. 1 *The Diary and Letters of His Excellency Thomas Hutchinson, Esq.* 73–74 (Peter Orlando Hutchinson, editor, 1883). Francis G. Walett, "The Massachusetts Council, 1766–1774: The Transformation of a Conservative Institution," 6 *Will. & Mary Q.* 609 (1949).

12. Supra n. 8, at 198.

13. *Memoire, or, Detailed Statement of the Origin and Progress of the Irish Union Delivered to the Irish Government by Messrs. [Thomas Addis] Emmett [sic], [Arthur] O'Connor, and [William James] McNevin; Together with the Examinations of the Gentlemen Before the Secret Committees of the Houses of Lords and Commons, in the Summer of 1798* 45 (1802).

14. Beckett, supra n. 5, at 278n1; H.M. Hyde, *The Rise of Castlereagh* 73 (1933).

15. Supra n. 13, at 55–56.

16. Beckett, supra n. 5, at 209; See also 4 W.E.H. Lecky, *A History of England in the Eighteenth Century* 475–78, 559 (1891); 2 James Anthony Froude, *The English in Ireland in the Eighteenth Century* 404 (1881); Hyde, supra n. 14, at 72.

NOTES

17. Hyde, supra n. 14, at 73. For a powerful indictment of this corruption by an eighteenth-century Irish lawyer, see "Speech of 15 May 1795," in Thomas Davis, *The Speeches of John Philpot Curran* 237–39 (1861). See also Wolfe Tone's condemnation in Charles Phillips, *Curran and His Contemporaries* 235 (5th ed., 1857).

18. Letter from the Earl of Buckinghamshire to the Earl of Hillsborough, 19 November 1780, quoted in Froude, supra n. 16, at 269–70.

19. Hutchinson, supra n. 8, at 164.

20. Letter from General Thomas Gage to Secretary of State H.S. Conway, 12 October 1765, in 1 *The Correspondence of General Thomas Gage with the Secretaries of State 1763–1775* 69–70 (Clarence Edwin Carter, editor, 1931).

21. See, e.g., 3 James Anthony Froude, *The English in Ireland in the Eighteenth Century* 62 (1881); H. Trevor Colbourn, "Thomas Jefferson's Use of the Past," 15 *Will. & Mary Q.* 56, 63–69 (1958). For John Adams see H. Trevor Colbourn, *The Lamp of Experience: Whig History and the Intellectual Origins of the American Revolution* 63–69 (1965); also, at 25–36, 50–53; Carl B. Cone, *The English Jacobins: Reformers in Late Eighteenth Century England* 4 (1968).

22. See, e.g., Lecky, supra n. 16, at 465–70; 7 W.E.H. Lecky, *A History of England in the Eighteenth Century* 95 (1891).

23. Lecky, supra n. 16, at 468, 528–30.

24. Lecky, supra n. 16, at 379, 395–97, 555; Hyde, supra n. 14, at 74.

25. Arthur O'Connor's testimony before the Secret Committee of the House of Commons, 16 August 1798, rpt. in supra n. 13, at 61. See also William Sampson, *Memoirs of William Sampson* 30 (1807). For O'Connor's career see D.J. O'Donoghue, "Arthur O'Connor," 41 *Dic. Nat. Bio.* 394 (1895).

26. E.O. Sommerville & Martin Ross, *An Incorruptible Irishman: Being an Account of Chief Justice Charles Kendal Bushe, and of his Wife, Nancy Crampton, and Their Times, 1767–1843* 76 (1932).

27. Froude, supra n. 16, at 196.

28. See Rowland Berthoff & John M. Murrin, "Feudalism, Communalism, and the Yeoman Freeholder," in *Essays on the American Revolution* 263–86 (Stephen G. Kurtz and James H. Hutson, editors, 1973; Jackson Turner Main, "The Results of the American Revolution Reconsidered," 31 *The Historian* 539, 543, 553 (1969).

29. Froude, supra n. 21, at 468.

30. See R.J. Griffith's statement, quoted in Hyde, supra n. 14, at 72.

31. Quoted in 1 Thomas Addis Emmet, *Memoir of Thomas Addis and Robert Emmet with Their Ancestors and Immediate Family* 71 (1915).

32. MacDermot, supra n. 5, at 77.

33. Charles Howard McIlwain, *The American Revolution: A Constitutional Interpretation* 187–89 (1923); Eric Robin, "The American Revolution in its Political and Military Aspects" (1955), rpt. in Edmund S. Morgan (editor), *The American Revolution: Two Centuries of Interpretation* 140, 141–43 (1965); see, generally, Jackson Turner Main, *The Social Structure of Revolutionary America* (1965). See also Edmund S. Morgan, "Conflict and Consensus in the American Revolution," in *Essays on the American Revolution* 289 ff. (Stephen G. Kurtz and James H. Hutson, editors, 1973).

34. W. Alison Phillips, *The Revolution in Ireland 1906–1923* 20–21 (1923).

35. James A. Henretta, "Economic Development and Social Structure in Colonial Boston," 22 *Will & Mary Q.* 85 (1965).

36. Main, supra n. 33, at 68.

37. Quoted in Hyde, supra n. 14, at 71.

38. See argument, Gordon S. Wood, "Rhetoric and Reality in the American Revolu-

tion," 23 *Will. & Mary Q.* 3, 27–30 (1966); Michael Zuckerman, "The Social Context of Democracy in Massachusetts," 25 *Will. & Mary Q.* 523, 535 (1968).

39. Letter from Samuel Adams to Stephen Sayre, 12 January 1771, in 2 *The Writings of Samuel Adams* 134–35 (Harry Alonzo Cushing, editor, 1906).

40. John Chester Miller, *Origins of the American Revolution* 292 (1943); extract of a Letter from Dublin, 16 May 1773, *Boston Evening-Post*, 1 November 1773, p. 1, col. 2; *Boston Evening-Post*, 26 July 1773, p. 2, col. 3; Froude, supra n. 16, at 129.

41. Some of Bernard's letters urging a program of reform to strengthen British rule over American governments did get into the hands of the whigs and were used to warn the colonists that a "junto" was plotting to destroy liberty. See John Adams, "Novanglus #2," reprinted in 4 *The Works of John Adams* 25–28 (Charles Francis Adams, editor, 1851).

42. Letter from Governor Francis Bernard to Lord Barrington, 23 November 1765, in *Correspondence*, supra n. 8, at 98–100.

3

The Conditions of Law

1. "The Lawyers are the Source from Whence the Clamors have flowed in every Province. In this Province Nothing Publick is transacted without them, and it is to be wished that even the Bench was free from Blame." Gage to Conway, 21 December 1765.

2. Chief Justice Thomas Hutchinson's Charge to the Grand Jury, August Term, *Quincy Reports* 302–3 (1768).

3. See comment, Hiller B. Zobel, *The Boston Massacre* 177 (1970).

4. Supra n. 2, at 303.

5. J. C. Beckett, *The Making of Modern Ireland 1603–1923* 162 (1966). Ireland experienced a change after the American Revolution and appointments began to come from the Irish Bar, although many appointees were Englishmen practicing in Ireland. R.B. McDowell, *The Irish Administration 1801–1914* 107 (1964). For the example of South Carolina, see Robert M. Calhoon & Robert M. Weir, "The Scandalous History of Sir Egerton Leigh," 26 *Will. & Mary Q.* 37 (1969). For a court-related sinecure, the provost marshalships, see Richard Maxwell Brown, *The South Carolina Regulators* 68–73 (1963).

6. See, generally, John J. Waters & John A. Schutz, "Patterns of Massachusetts Colonial Politics: The Writs of Assistance and the Rivalry between the Otis and Hutchinson Families," 24 *Will. & Mary Q.* 543, 559–62 (1967); John J. Waters, Jr., *The Otis Family in Provincial and Revolutionary Massachusetts* (1968).

7. Oliver M. Dickinson, "Opinion of Attorney General Jonathan Sewall of Massachusetts in the Case of the *Lydia*," 4 *Will. & Mary Q.* 499, 500 (1947); Mary Beth Norton, "A Recently Discovered Thomas Hutchinson Letter," 82 *Proc. Mass. Hist. Soc.* 105–6 (1970). "Now my L[or]d, to give £600 sterling of the public money to a person that never sat as a judge—that has never held a court—that never had a case offer'd to his judgment; yea, that never was in the province where his court is stationed, excepting a few days, and this for no other end than to *qualify* himself by taking the oaths the law directs to: I say, to give so large a sum for *no service*, and to a small attorney, with the title of *judge*, now practicing in our common law courts, will not look well in the eye of the public." "An Independent Spectator to the Earl of Hillsborough," 21 March 1770, *Boston Evening-Post*, 9 April 1770, p. 2, col. 1. Actually, Sewall had made that one trip to Halifax at a time when the political situation in Boston made his absence expedient.

Supra n. 3, at 131; "Journal of the Times," 29 June 1769, pp. 112–13, in *Boston Under Military Rule 1768–1769 as Revealed in a Journal of the Times* (Oliver M. Dickerson, compiler, 1970).

8. Joseph R. Frese, "Some Observations on the American Board of Customs Commissioner," 81 *Proc. Mass. Hist. Soc.* 3, 4n5 (1969); Catherine Fennelly, "William Franklin of New Jersey," 6 *Will. & Mary Q.* 371–73 (1949); letter from Governor Thomas Hutchinson to Attorney General Jonathan Sewall, 16 September 1771, rpt. in Norton, supra n. 7, at 108.

9. Norton, supra n. 7, at 106. When Sewall died at Saint John, New Brunswick, during 1796, he was also drawing, as an exiled loyalist, a pension of £150 a year. E. Alfred Jones, *The Loyalists of Massachusetts: Their Memorials, Petitions and Claims* 259 (1930).

10. Gerard W. Gawalt, "Sources of Anti-Lawyer Sentiment in Massachusetts, 1740–1840," 14 *Am. J. Legal Hist.* 283, 285 (1970); John Adams, "Preface" in 4 *The Works of John Adams* 6 (Charles Francis Adams, editor, 1851); for the best brief discussion of the legal issues involved in the writs of assistance case see 1 *Pamphlets of the American Revolution 1750–1776* 100–103 (Bernard Bailyn, editor, 1965); Richard B. Morris, "Edmund Trowbridge," 18 *Dic. Am. Bio.* 653 (1936).

11. William E. Nelson, *The Americanization of the Common Law During the Revolutionary Era: A Study of Legal Change in Massachusetts, 1760–1830* 138 (unpublished doctoral dissertation, Harvard University, 1971).

12. 2 F. Elrington Ball, *The Judges in Ireland, 1221–1921* 183 (1927).

13. Quoted in 1 Thomas Addis Emmet, *Memoir of Thomas Addis and Robert Emmet with Their Ancestors and Immediate Family* 19 (1915).

14. Arthur O'Connor, *State of Ireland* 3 (1798).

15. Supra n. 11, at 138–39.

16. Frank MacDermot, *Theobald Wolfe Tone: A Biographical Study* 74–75 (1939). Formal law was unlikely to come to the aid of the abused. Even an aged priest, showered by "blows from his lordship's horsewhip" for being unable to grant a request beyond his power, had difficulty retaining counsel to file an action of trespass. Thomas Davis, *The Speeches of the Right Honorable John Philpot Curran* xvii (1861).

17. William Sampson, *Memoirs of William Sampson* 330 (1807).

18. Quoted in supra n. 13, at iv.

19. MacDermot, supra n. 16, at 99.

20. 4 W.E.H. Lecky, *A History of England in the Eighteenth Century* 489 (1891).

21. *Ireland From the Flight of the Earls to Grattan's Parliament: A Documentary Record* 144 (James Carty, editor, 1949).

22. But see the contrary argument, in which feudalism assumes more of an economic rather than a legal definition. Rowland Berthoff & John M. Murrin, "Feudalism, Communalism, and the Yeoman Freeholder," in *Essays on the American Revolution* 256 (Stephen G. Kurtz and James H. Hutson, editors, 1973).

23. MacDermot, supra n. 16, at 75.

24. Anon., *Forensic Eloquence: Sketches of Trials in Ireland for High Treason, Etc. Including the Speeches of Mr. Curran at Length to Which are Prefixed, A Brief Sketch of the History of Ireland, and a Biographical Account of Mr. Curran: With an Elegant Engraved Likeness of that Orator* 335 (1805).

25. Supra n. 11, at 7.

26. Quoted in supra n. 13, at iv. (De Vere lived from 1788 to 1846.)

27. Jesse Lemisch, "Jack Tar in the Streets: Merchant Seamen in the Politics of Revolutionary America," 25 *Will. & Mary Q.* 371 (1968).

28. Supra n. 11, at 139.

29. Supra n. 14, at 27. This Irish indictment of the common law would be carried to the United States by William Sampson, who became the first important post-Jeffersonian voice to urge abolition of common law in America. See William Sampson, *An Anniversary Discourse, Delivered before the Historical Society of New-York, on Saturday, December 6, 1823: Showing the Origin, Progress, Antiquities, Curiosities, and the Nature of the Common Law* (1824); Irving Browne, "William Sampson," 8 *Green Bag* 313 (1896).

4
The Civil Traverse Jury

1. "Democracy is too prevalent in America, and claims the greatest Attention to prevent it's Encrease, and fatal Effects." Gage to Barrington, 13 April 1772.

2. Carl Ubbelohde, *The Vice-Admiralty Courts and the American Revolution* 165–67 (1960).

3. Ibid., 167–68.

4. Letter from William Palfrey to John Wilkes, October 1770, George M. Elsey, "John Wilkes and William Palfrey," 34 *Pub. Col. Soc. Mass.* 411, 423 (1941).

5. Hiller B. Zobel, *The Boston Massacre* 169 (1970).

6. Chief Justice Thomas Hutchinson's Charge to the Suffolk County Grand Jury, March term, *Quincy Reports* 306, 312–13 (1769).

7. See post Ch. 6, text to n. 11.

8. 1 *Legal Papers of John Adams* 214 (L. Kinvin Wroth & Hiller B. Zobel, editors, 1965). For *Bushell's Case* see 124 *Eng. Rep.* 1006 (Common Pleas, 1677).

9. 2 *Diary and Autobiography of John Adams* 4–5 (L.H. Butterfield, editor, 1961). It is interesting to consider that a few years earlier, Adams had written that law required training and professional study: "A man whose Youth and Spirits and Strength, have been spent in Husbandry, Merchandize, Politicks, nay in Science or Literature will never master so immense and involved a science." Supra n. 5, at 9. Thomas Hutchinson, who believed juries should follow the instructions of judges, wrote, on the other hand: "I never presumed to call myself a Lawyer. The most I could pretend to was when I heard the Law laid on both sides to judge which was right." Supra n. 5, at 10. Of course, each man's attitude toward the independence of the jury was shaped by current politics. John Adams, in his diary, made clear that he thought of the jury as part of the whig struggle against arbitrary government: "As the Constitution requires, that, the popular Branch of the Legislature, should have an absolute Check so as to put a peremptory Negative upon every Act of the Government, it requires that the common People should have as compleat a Controul, as decisive a Negative, in every Judgment of a Court of Judicature. No Wonder then that the same restless Ambition, of aspiring Minds, which is endeavouring to lessen or destroy the Power of the People in Legislation, should attempt to lessen or destroy it, in the Execution of Lawes. The Rights of Juries and of Elections, were never attacked singly in all the English History. The same Passions which have disliked one have detested the other, and both have always been exploded, mutilated or undermined together." 2 *Diary*, cited supra this note, at 3.

10. William E. Nelson, *The Americanization of the Common Law: The Impact of Legal Change on Massachusetts Society, 1760–1830* 28 (1975).

11. Ibid., 26.

12. Supra n. 5, at 223. In one case, however, John Adams was not permitted to argue

law, though it may be significant that the trial at bar concerned slander, and Adams was stopped from saying that the words in question were not actionable. See *Quincy Reports* 564 (1865); 1 *Legal Papers*, supra n. 8, at 142, 149.

13. For a definition and discussion of "compounding," see supra n. 5, at 15.

14. Letter from Governor Francis Bernard to the Lords of Trade, 6 August 1761, quoted in Appendix II, *Quincy Reports* 553–54n2 (1865).

15. Letter from Governor Francis Bernard to former Governor Thomas Pownall, 28 August 1761, quoted in Appendix II, *Quincy Reports* 555n2 (1865).

16. Supra n. 14, at 555n2.

17. Ibid.

18. The inferior court of common pleas was staffed by four judges, any three of whom were a quorum.

19. Supra n. 15, at 555–56n2.

20. Letter from Governor Bernard to the Lords of Trade, 2 August 1761, quoted in Appendix II, *Quincy Reports* 556n4 (1865).

21. Quoting Hutchinson's *History*. Ibid., 557n4.

22. 1 *Legal Papers*, supra n. 8, at 215.

23. *Angier* v *Jackson*, *Quincy Reports* 84 (1763); see John Adams's "Note," in 1 *Legal Papers*, supra n. 8, at 218.

24. Supra n. 10, at 26–27.

25. *Erving* v *Cradock*, *Quincy Reports* 553, 556 (1761).

26. Thomas Hutchinson, *The History of the Province of Massachusetts Bay, From 1749 to 1774* 161 (1828).

27. At least whigs appear to have been surprised—as well as outraged—to learn some years later that Governor Bernard had ordered the register of admiralty to use the king's share from another seizure to pay Cradock's defense attorney. Letter from Governor Francis Bernard & Thomas Lechmere to William Story, 19 October 1761, printed in *Boston Evening-Post*, 11 June 1770, p. 1, col. 2; Letter from PROBUS to the Editor, 21 August 1770, *Boston Evening-Post*, 27 August 1770, p. 2, col. 1.

28. Hiller B. Zobel, "Law Under Pressure: Boston 1769–1771," in *Law and Authority in Colonial America* 187, 197 (George Athan Billias, editor, 1965). In fact the verdict was even higher for it included the costs of court in addition to damages. *Boston Evening-Post*, 29 July 1771, p. 3, col. 2.

29. Robinson confessed starting the brawl and being responsible for all the insults, wounds, and injuries. "He the said John Robinson, Esq.; was greatly at Fault, is very sorry for his Conduct and Behaviour that Night towards the said James Otis, and asks the Pardon of the said James Otis." Statement of John Robinson filed with the Superior Court, Suffolk County, printed in *Boston Evening-Post*, 14 September 1772, p. 2, col. 1.

30. As this was private litigation it is doubtful whether Robinson's damages would have been paid by the revenue service. The possibility, however, may offer an explanation why the matter was not pressed. Advised by his lawyers that he had a cause of action for libel against Robinson and perhaps other customs commissioners in 1769, Otis had decided not to sue. If he won, he explained, the verdict would be meaningless as it would not serve to "reform" the defendants. "Should I recover ever so high damages at law," he said, "I know of nothing to restrain them from paying them out of the public Chest, which money, extorted as it is, I desire not to touch." *The Boston Gazette*, 11 September 1769, p. 2, col. 3.

31. Zobel, supra n. 28, at 197. The whigs and their British friends cited the settlement to demonstrate the "Generosity" of whig law. Letter from Samuel Adams to

Arthur Lee, 9 April 1773, rpt. in 3 *The Writings of Samuel Adams* 24 (Harry Alonzo Cushing, editor, 1907). See also post n. 33.

32. Supra n. 20, at 556–57n4.

33. The method of selecting juries in Massachusetts was altered that year by one of the so-called Intolerable Acts. When introduced the acts touched off a debate in parliament over the quality of whig law. Colonel Isaac Barre argued: "When a Commissioner of the Customs, aided by a number of ruffians, assaulted the celebrated Mr. *Otis* in the midst of the town of *Boston,* and with the most barbarous violence, almost murdered him, did the mob, which is said to rule that town, take vengeance on the perpetrators of this inhuman outrage against a person who is supposed to be their demagogue? No Sir, the law tried them; the law gave heavy damages against them; which the irreparably injured Mr. *Otis* generously forgave upon an acknowledgement of the offense. Can you expect any more instances of such magnanimity under the principle of the Bill now proposed?" Speech of Colonel Isaac Barre, 15 April 1774, rpt. in 1 *American Archives*: Archives: Fourth Series 114 (Peter Force, editor, 1837).

34. For example, consider the customs laws as explained by Alfred S. Martin: "A strict observation of the laws was almost impossible. Despite instructions and rate books, few men were qualified to understand all the ramifications of the acts. Who was to judge the subtle flavors of the wines imported, or to know accurately the hundreds of different classes of cloths and other goods brought in? The written guides given to local officials were veritable miracles of elaboration, but special exceptions and provisions changed from day to day and the legal niceties involved were exasperating and bewildering. . . .

"The laws were not only involved and forever changing but the statutes if literally interpreted occasionally operated to defeat their original purpose. Under the regulations made in 5 George II, c. 22 the exportation of hats from one colony to another was forbidden under severe penalty. [John] Swift [collector at Philadelphia] was of the opinion that he would 'as soon eat fire as sign a cocket for Hatts,' yet what was he to do when a consignment came directly from Manchester to Philadelphia for merchants in New Jersey or Delaware? A shipment of hats came from Bermuda with a certificate from the collector and comptroller there that they were legally imported. Should the shipment be seized? Both Swift and the commissioners were of the opinion that such action would be contrary to the purpose of the act which was designed to promote the English hat industry. Further, were goods subject to duty if they had been shipped before the imposition of a duty but not landed until after it was in effect? When the Crown attorney general and the Board of Customs disagreed on all these points, what was the collector to do? To enforce the law according to its letter left him open to civil action by outraged merchants; non-enforcement might lead to dismissal by the Board of Trade." Alfred S. Martin, "The King's Customs: Philadelphia, 1763–1774," 5 *Will. & Mary Q.* 201, 203–4 (1948).

35. Edmund S. Morgan & Helen M. Morgan, *The Stamp Act Crisis: Prologue to Revolution* 177 (paperback ed. 1970).

36. Ibid., 178.

37. "Auchmuty alone seems to have had the courage to advise flatly that the clearances be issued without stamps." Ibid., 181; 136.

38. The prevailing theory was that certification that stamps were unavailable would be a good plea in bar of seizure. Thus John Hancock wrote his London correspondents: "Our Custom house is now open as usual & clearance taken without stamps. That I apprehend there will be no risque on your side. . . . Should there be any Difficulty in

London as to Marshalls [John Marshall was the ship's captain] clearance, You will please to represent the circumstances that no stamps could be obtained and we cannot obtain a more Regular Clearance. In which case I think I am to be justified, & am not liable to a seizure. . . . The Custom houses to the Southward are open & vessells clear as usual, the officers certifying that no stamps are to be had." Letter from John Hancock to Bernards & Harrison, 21 December 1765, Abram English Brown, *John Hancock: His Book* 99 (1898).

London officials, anticipating repeal of the Stamp Act, agreed with Hancock and no vessels were seized. An exception to the general rule was the attorney general of North Carolina who seized two vessels, holding that merchants were not protected by the mere fact stamps were unavailable. "They should have tender'd the King's Duties to the Officers of the Customs, and demanded proper Clearances, &c. and on being refused, they should have made the like Tender to a Notary Public, and offer'd a Protest.—Had these Matters been complied with, so as to be duly prov'd on a Trial, I should think the [vice-admiralty] Judge would decree, that the Vessels and Cargoes were not forfeited." Opinion of Attorney General Robert Jones of North Carolina, *The Massachusetts Gazette*, 27 March 1766, p. 4, col. 1.

39. As the potential defendant, by refusing to issue clearance without stamps, had, in common-law definitions, done nothing, he could not be sued in trespass. It is an old maxim of English common law that "not doing is no trespass" unless there is a duty to act: a duty imposed by law, such as the duty on an innkeeper to protect the property of guests. An innkeeper could be sued in trespass by a guest whose goods were stolen from the defendant's inn even though the defendant proved he did nothing to aid the thief. "Not doing" is no defense for the innkeeper as the law imposed on him a duty to act. Unless seeking consequential damages, the plaintiff in that action will sue in trespass as he need prove only the loss of his goods. If he sued in case the burden would be on him to prove that the innkeeper-defendant had been guilty of deceit or carelessness or negligence.

40. See discussion. Supra n. 10, at 17. "There was, in short, little that one acting on behalf of government could do without rendering himself liable to an action at law in the event that he wronged another." Ibid., at 18. A similar doctrine prevailed in England. "If an officer of the public is guilty of neglect of duty, or a palpable branch of it, of non-feasance or of mis-feasance . . . the party aggrieved shall have an action *on the case*, for damages to be assessed by a jury." 3 William Blackstone, *Commentaries on the Laws of England* 163 (1768).

41. At a time when the "common sort" could live comfortably on £40 a year, the comptroller had a salary of £70 and the collector of £100. Moreover, there was money to be made on fees. During 1768–69 (a winter of nonimportation agreements) the substitute collector at Salem took in fees of £443 sterling during six months. The post had a salary of £40. Joseph R. Frese, "Some Observations on the American Board of Customs Commissioners," 81 *Proc. Mass. Hist. Socy.*, 3, 4–5 (1969). See also supra n. 5, at 66.

42. Chief Justice Thomas Hutchinson's Charge to the Suffolk County Grand Jury, *Quincy Reports* 309–10 (1769). See also James K. Hosmer, *The Life of Thomas Hutchinson, Royal Governor of the Province of Massachusetts Bay* 138 (1896).

43. Note, however, that the plaintiff could sue in trepass the captain of the naval vessel.

44. While parliament did little to protect military officers and civil officials from whig law suits, it did try to shield customsmen from harassment by local law. The Sugar Act of 1764 provided that should an action be brought against a revenue agent for seizing goods in the line of duty, the presiding judge could certify "probable cause" and even though the jury returned a verdict against the defendant, the plaintiff "shall not

be intitled to above two pence damages, nor to any costs of suit; nor shall the defendant in such prosecutions be fined above one shilling" (4 George III, cap. 15, sec. 46 [1764], 26 *Statutes at Large*, at 51). The language was surely as unambiguous as any drafted by an eighteenth-century parliament. It failed in its purpose, however, for the plaintiff's lawyer could keep out of the record the facts that the action had, as the statute required, been brought "on account of the seizing of any . . . ship or goods" (Ibid.) Again, the plaintiff would allege an ordinary trespass, say nothing about the customs seizure, and deny any defense put forth. To certify "probable cause" the judge would have to go outside the record, which would have made the certification of doubtful legality. John Laurens of South Carolina collected a judgment of £1,400 local money despite the Sugar Act. (Thomas C. Barrow, *Trade and Empire: The British Customs Service in Colonial America 1660–1775* 234 [1967]), and in Rhode Island Lieutenant Dudingston of the revenue sloop *Gaspee* had three judgments returned against him in 1772 (Edward Channing, "The American Board of Commissioners of the Customs," 43 *Mass. Hist Soc. Proc.* 477, 486–87 [1910]). We should not be surprised that the "two pence" proviso of the Sugar Act failed in its purpose. At the time of Erving's suit against Cradock there had been on the statutes books for almost 100 years an act of parliament permitting defendants who faced either a civil or criminal charge stemming from enforcement of the imperial revenue laws to cite the appropriate law as a defense and plead the general issue. The presiding judge was then enjoined "to acquit and indemnify them and every of them of and from all such units, indictments, information or prosecutions, for or concerning any matter or thing acted or done in the due necessary performance and execution of their respective trusts and imployments therein" (13 & 14 Charles II, cap. II, sec. 16 [1662], 8 *Statutes at Large*, at 88). The proviso was intended to give immunity to an official such as Cradock. Because of the dynamics of pleading, Cradock could not bring the proviso to the attention of the court and his statutory immunity was worthless.

45. Perhaps more annoying than harassment suits was the fact revenue officials had no chance of suing successfully for damages if they were the injured party in a fracas. "The officers," a commissioner of the American customs complained, "had no probability of obtaining redress for any injuries they received, by a process at Law, before a Jury of the People who held the very Laws under which the officers acted, to be Unconstitutional" (Henry Hulton, *Some Account of the Proceedings of the People in New England from the Establishment of a Board of Customs in America, to the Breaking out of the Rebellion in 1775* 57 [MS, Princeton University]). For the appraisal of this problem by a Massachusetts tory lawyer, see Daniel Leonard, "Massachusettensis #10," rpt. in *The American Colonial Crisis: The Daniel Leonard-John Adams Letters to the Press 1774–1775* 60–61 (Bernard Mason, editor, 1972). See also Hutchinson's comment, text to n. 31 supra.

5

The Uses of the Grand Jury

1. "The method of appointing our Grand Juries lies open to management. Whoever pleases, nominates them at our town-meetings; by this means one who has suppos'd to be a principal in the Riots of the 10th of June last was upon that Jury whose business it was to inquire into them." Letter of Judge Peter Oliver, 13 February 1769.

2. Partisan considerations even affect judicial attitudes toward members of the bar. William Henry Curran, *The Life of the Right Honorable John Philpot Curran* 142–44

(1820). Counsel would tell jurors that the court would explain the law. Thomas Davis, *The Speeches of the Right Honorable John Philpot Curran* 143 (1861). In criminal cases, however, we often see defense attorneys defining the penal statutes. See, e.g., Curran, supra this note, at 235–39. The power was not as broad as today. Damages, for example, could not be set aside for excess. *Speeches*, supra this note, at 387.

3. Quartering Act of 24 March 1765, rpt. in Henry Steele Commager, *Documents of American History* 62–63 (1934). Letter from General Thomas Gage to the Earl of Hillsborough, 31 October 1768, in 1 *The Correspondence of General Thomas Gage with the Secretaries of State 1763–1775* 202 (Clarence Edwin Carter, editor, 1931). See argument in Message from the House of Representatives to Governor Francis Bernard, 15 July 1769, *Boston Evening-Post*, 17 July 1769, p. 2, col. 2; rpt. in 1 *The Writings of Samuel Adams* 371–76 (Harry Alonzo Cushing, editor, 1904). If the plaintiff's scruples did not permit the denial, he could sue in trespass, although he would run a risk. The court might hold that the requisition was lawful despite the fact that the assembly had passed no enabling statute—that is, it was legal under the mutiny act alone—and dismiss the action. The plaintiff, to avoid dismissal, would have to deny that the trespass had been committed for purposes of requisition.

4. Letter from Lieutenant Governor Thomas Hutchinson to General Thomas Gage, 22 June 1770, rpt. in Randolph G. Adams, "New Light on the Boston Massacre," 47 *Proc. Am. Antiquarian Soc.* 259, 312 (1937); Letter from General Thomas Gage to the Earl of Hillsborough, 7 July 1770, in *Correspondence*, supra n. 3, at 263–64; Letter from James Murray to Lieutenant Colonel William Dalrymple, 27 July 1770, rpt. Adams, supra this note, at 324.

5. See, e.g., Letter from Lieutenant Colonel William Dalrymple to General Thomas Gage, 27 March 1770, rpt. in Adams, supra n. 4, at 295; Letter from same to same, 2 April 1770, rpt. in ibid., 299–300. Letter from same to same, 12 August 1770, *Gage Papers* (MS, Clements Library). Letter from same to same, 26 August 1770, rpt. in Adams, supra n. 4, at 324. For a discussion of the law requiring Dalrymple to have a magistrate present, see John Phillip Reid, "In a Constitutional Void: The Enforcement of Imperial Law, the Role of the British Army, and the Coming of the American Revolution," 22 *Wayne Law Review* 1, 9–30 (1975). Letter from James Murray to Lieutenant Colonel William Dalrymple, 27 August 1770, rpt. in *Letters of James Murray Loyalist* 167 (Nina Moore Tiffany, editor, 1901). Dalrymple had told Murray "that the spirit of the law seemed to be that the troops are only to be called out when the actual appearance of Tumults vindicate the measure, and not upon every surmise of future intentions." Letter from Lieutenant Colonel William Dalrymple to General Thomas Gage, 27 August 1770, *Gage Papers* (MS, Clements Library). The significant point is not that Dalrymple correctly stated the law, but that had he been stationed in Ireland he would not have given the law such consideration—had he bothered with law at all.

6. See, e.g., the case of Captain Ponsonby Molesworth. John Richard Alden, *General Gage in America* 172 (1948); Hiller B. Zobel, *The Boston Massacre* 139–40 (1970). Admittedly Molesworth was guilty of breach of the peace as he ordered his men to use bayonets in retaliation for threats and physical blows rendered without weapons. See Letter from Lieutenant Colonel William Dalrymple to General Thomas Gage, 30 November 1769, quoted in Zobel, 143. But in Ireland the offense would have been pardoned.

7. The lawfulness of his actions must be taken as established by his acquittal.

8. Testimony of Doctor John Jeffries, quoted in 3 *Legal Papers of John Adams* 214

(L. Kinvin Wroth & Hiller B. Zobel, editors, 1965). See also *The Boston Gazette*, 31 December 1770, p. 3, col. 1.

9. Edgar Holt, *Protest in Arms: The Irish Troubles 1916–1923* 58–59 (1961).

10. O.A. Sherrard, *A Life of John Wilkes* 186 (1930); but see R. W. Postgate, *That Devil Wilkes* 134 (1929). 2 Percy Fitzgerald, *The Life and Times of John Wilkes, M.P.* 8–9 (1888); Horace Bleackley, *Life of John Wilkes* 199 (1917); George Rude, *Wilkes and Liberty: A Social Study of 1763 to 1774* 54–55 (1962); Postgate, supra this note, at 146; Fitzgerald, supra this note, at 10.

11. Sherrard, supra n. 10, at 187. Such, of course, is an historian's answer, and not the reason Barrington's legal advisors had in mind when they approved the "letter."

12. 1 Bernard Bailyn (editor), *Pamphlets of the American Revolution 1750–1776* 72 (1965).

13. The prime examples are custom officials indicted for murder following the Boston Massacre.

14. See, e.g., Letter from General Thomas Gage to Secretary at War Welbore Ellis, 15 May 1765, in 2 *The Correspondence of General Thomas Gage with the Secretaries of State, and with the War Office and the Treasury 1763–1775* 288 (Clarence Edwin Carter, editor, 1933); Letter from General Thomas Gage to the Earl of Shelburne, 23 December 1766, in *Correspondence*, supra n. 3, at 117. The army had to respond in kind. When Albany heard troops were being transferred from Crown Point to town the corporation "determin'd to pull down the new Barracks immediately." The commanding officer stopped the destruction "by ordering part of the garrison into them until the troops arriv'd." Letter from Colonel John Bradstreet to General Gage, 23 November 1765, *Gage Papers* (MS, Clements Library).

15. Letter from Lieutenant Governor Thomas Hutchinson to General Thomas Gage, 1 April 1770, rpt. in Adams, supra n. 4, at 298. See also, for the comments of a tory chief justice, *Peter Oliver's Origin & Progress of the American Rebellion: A Tory View* 91 (Douglass Adair & John A. Schutz, editors, 1961).

16. 4 William Blackstone, *Commentaries on the Laws of England* 151 (1769).

17. Chief Justice Thomas Hutchinson's Charge to the Suffolk Grand Jury, March term, *Quincy Reports* 309 (1769).

18. Charles Phillips, *Curran and his Contemporaries* 37 (3d ed. 1857).

19. But noted for private libel. 1 Sir Jonah Barrington, *Personal Sketches of His Own Times* 219 (3d ed., 1871); 2 James Anthony Froude, *The English in Ireland in the Eighteenth Century* 401 (1881); Frank MacDermot, *Theobald Wolfe Tone: A Biographical Study* 118 (1939).

20. Anon., *Forensic Eloquence: Sketches of Trials in Ireland For High Treason, Etc. Including the Speeches of Mr. Curran at Length to Which are Prefixed, A Brief Sketch of the History of Ireland, and a Biographical Account of Mr. Curran: With an Elegant Engraved Likeness of that Orator* 136, 44, 134, 166 (1805).

21. Arthur O'Connor, "Mr. O'Connor's Address to the Irish Nation," rpt. in ibid., 167.

22. 7 W.E.H. Lecky, *A History of England in the Eighteenth Century* 351 (1891).

23. 2 Elrington Ball, *The Judges in Ireland, 1221–1921* 183 (1927).

24. R.B. McDowell, *The Irish Administration 1801–1914* 135 (1964); J.C. Beckett, *The Making of Modern Ireland 1603–1923* 178 (1966). See Curran's argument that one jury was selected by an agent employed by local landowners. Curran, supra n. 2, at 170 n. 4 W.E.H. Lecky, *A History of England in the Eighteenth Century* 377 (1891); Letter from Lord Lieutenant Townshend to Home Secretary Rochford, 18 March 1772, quoted in Froude, supra n. 19, at 115–16. "The better type of landowner on the commission was

more often than not an absentee and the worse type were ill fitted to exercise judicial functions." F.H. Newark, *Notes on Irish Legal History* 21 (2d ed., pamphlet, 1964). 6 W.E.H. Lecky, *A History of England in the Eighteenth Century* 539–40 (1891). Supra n. 22, at 181, 192.

25. 3 James Anthony Froude, *The English in Ireland in the Eighteenth Century* 484 (1881).

26. MacDermot, supra n. 19, at 228.

27. Arthur O'Connor, *State of Ireland* 158–59n (1798). W.J. Fitzpatrick, "Roger O'Connor," 41 *Dic. Nat. Bio.* 407–9 (1895).

28. D.J. O'Donoghue, "Arthur O'Connor," 41 *Dic. Nat. Bio.* 394 (1895). Joseph Gurney, *The Trial of James O'Coigly, Arthur O'Connor, John Binns, John Allen, and Jeremiah Leary for High Treason* (1798); supra n. 25, at 324, 327.

29. For the view of an Irish judge, see Barrington, supra n. 19, at 154. See also the case of Wolfe Tone's brother, Macdermot, supra n. 19, at 289. Curran moved for *habeas corpus* at king's bench. It was issued but historians are not certain if the army refused to accept it. The outcome was not altered. Tone, despairing at the order that he be hanged as a traitor rather than shot as a soldier, committed suicide. T.D. Sullivan, A.M. Sullivan, & D.B. Sullivan, *Speeches From the Dock: Or, Protests of Irish Patriotism* 25 (1882); supra n. 25, at 495; Curran, supra n. 2, at 272–74.

30. 2 *Legal Papers of John Adams* 174 (L. Kinvin Wroth & Hiller B. Zobel, editors, 1965); Hiller B. Zobel, *The Boston Massacre* 72 (1970); Oliver M. Dickerson, "Opinion of Attorney General Jonathan Sewall of Massachusetts in the Case of the *Lydia*," 4 *Will. & Mary Q.* 499, 503–4 (1947).

31. The Boston vice-admiralty court, for example, ruled that "landing" was not essential to constitute importation. Bringing prohibited goods into port, showing a fraudulent intent, though without landing or breaking bulk, was sufficient to work a forfeiture of ship and cargo. *Bishop* v. *Brig Freemason, Quincy Reports* 387 (1763).

32. 2 *Legal Papers*, supra n. 30, at 186.

33. 2 *Legal Papers*, supra n. 30, at 183. For the interlocutory decrees, see Appendix I, *Quincy Reports* 461–62 (1865).

34. Ibid., 183–84, 184.

35. *Massachusetts Spy*, 14 November 1771, p. 1, col. 2–3.

36. "It is said that the Piece . . . (from its Nature and Tendency) is the most daring Production ever published in America." *Boston Evening-Post*, 18 November 1771, p. 2, col 3. Articles of this nature, it was contended, could tear the country apart. *Boston Evening-Post*, 3 February 1772, p. 2, col. 1.

37. Bernard Bailyn, *The Ordeal of Thomas Hutchinson* 198 (1974). The charge that the refusal to return a true bill was a violation of the jurors' oaths was publicly repeated in a newspaper Hutchinson had established. *The* (Boston) *Censor*, 7 March 1772, p. 62. The grand jury disagreed: "The Grand Jury look upon it that in the exercise of the Powers they are vested with, by the Laws of the Land, they are accountable to no Man, however great; but only to God and their own Conscience." Statement of the Suffolk County Grand Jury, 31 August 1773, printed in *Boston Evening-Post*, 13 September 1773, p. 3, col. 1.

38. Bailyn, supra n. 37, at 119. John Adams was to claim: "That the high whigs took *care* to get themselves chosen of the grand juries, I do not believe. Nine-tenths of the people were high whigs; and therefore it was not easy to get a grand jury without nine whigs in ten, in it." *Novanglus #5*, 4 *The Works of John Adams* 73 (Charles Francis Adams, editor, 1851).

39. The realization seems to have made the tories even shriller than the whigs in

accusing the other side of slander. *The* (Boston) *Censor*, 7 March 1772, p. 61; *Boston Evening-Post*, 11 May 1772, p. 1, col. 1; *Boston Evening-Post*, 18 May 1772, p. 1, col. 1; *Boston Evening-Post*, 2 March 1792, p. 2, col. 1. Some writers went to the governor's defense, others said Hutchinson was as much to blame for "throwing Dirt instead of Reason" as were his opponents. *Boston Evening-Post*, 6 April 1772, p. 1, col. 1.

40. Article by "X.Y.," *Boston Evening-Post*, 17 August 1772, p. 3, col. 2.

41. Letter from Governor Thomas Hutchinson to Lord Hillsborough, 1 October 1772, in 5 *Documents of the American Revolution 1770–1783* 200 (K.G. Davies, editor, 1974).

42. The technique of writers directing their words to the king was then becoming somewhat common as the newspapers grew bolder. See, e.g., *Boston Evening-Post*, 17 February 1772, p. 1, col. 1; *Boston Evening-Post*, 28 October 1771, p. 1, col. 2.

43. Arthur M. Schlesinger, *Prelude to Independence: The Newspaper War on Britain 1764–1776* 147–48 (1958).

44. Rumors that Hutchinson planned some action circulated around Boston. Commenting on the *Spy* article a whig argued that "if the bare imputation of treason, usurpation and tyranny to the governors of the state be so distructive to the public tranquility with what terrors may we not be filled from the open and most obstinate endeavors for their absolute establishment?" "Pomponius Atticus," *Boston Evening-Post*, 28 September 1772, p. 2, col. 2. This theme was one the *Spy* had been implying since it had been founded two years before. See, e.g., the report of the trial of Woodfall before Lord Mansfield. *The Massachusetts Spy*, 8 September 1770, p. 1, col. 1–2.

45. Schlesinger, supra n. 43, at 146.

46. In fact, the most insulting comments found in Boston newspapers directed against the king were lifted from the London press. See, e.g., *The Massachusetts Spy*, 21 August 1770, p. 1, col. 1–2.

47. Especially the Massachusetts government act (14 Geo. III, cap. 45 (1774), 30 *Statutes at Large*, at 381) which will be discussed below.

48. Schlesinger, supra n. 43, at 148.

6

The Criminal Traverse Jury

1. "The Judges, particularly Judge Oliver, have gained great Reputation, by their Candour and Firmness; and declared they would do Justice impartially in Defiance of the Threats thrown out against them." Gage to Barrington, 12 November 1770.

2. *Boston Evening-Post*, 18 March 1771, p. 2, col. 1.

3. *Boston Evening-Post*, 14 January 1771, p. 1, col. 3.

4. *The Boston Gazette and Country Journal*, 5 March 1770, p. 2, col. 1. Shortly before the crowd attacked Richardson, a newspaper referred to him as "the famous Informer." *Boston Evening-Post*, 26 February 1770, p. 3, col. 1. See also Letter from William Palfrey to John Wilkes, 5 March 1770, in George M. Elsey, "John Wilkes and William Palfrey," 34 *Pub. Col. Soc. Mass.* 411, 416, (1941); Declaration of Benjamin Goodwin, 20 October 1766, printed in George G. Wolkins, "Daniel Malcom and Writs of Assistance," 58 *Mass. Hist. Soc. Proc.* 5, 46 (1924); Letter from the Inhabitants of Boston to Dennis de Berdt, 22 October 1766, in *A Report of the Records Commissioners of the City of Boston Town Records, 1768 to 1769* 194 (Report #16, 1886). The commissioners of the American customs published a notice denying that Richardson was employed by the revenue service. *The Boston Chronicle*, 5 March 1770, p. 76, col. 3. But Thomas

Hutchinson described Richardson as a landwaiter or minor customs officer "and, before that, an informer against illicit traders." Thomas Hutchinson, *The History of the Province of Massachusetts Bay From 1749 to 1774* 269 (1828). See the very harsh appraisal of Richardson written years later by John Adams. Letter from John Adams to J. Morse, 20 January 1816, printed in 10 *The Works of John Adams* 210 (Charles Francis Adams, editor, 1856).

5. Letter from Acting Governor Thomas Hutchinson to General Thomas Gage, 25 February 1770, quoted in 2 *Legal Papers of John Adams* 399 (L. Kinvin Wroth & Hiller B. Zobel, editors, 1965). The man referred to by Hutchinson was William Molieneux, a violent whig. For his role in the affair, see Hiller B. Zobel, *The Boston Massacre* 176 (1970).

6. *Peter Oliver's Origin & Progress of the American Rebellion: A Tory View* 85 (Douglass Adair & John A. Schutz, editors, 1961).

7. Anonymous narrative in Francis Bernard Papers, rpt. in 2 *Legal Papers*, supra n. 5, at 401–2.

8. 2 *Legal Papers*, supra n. 5, at 401. Judge Oliver exaggerated when he explained that, had they not agreed, Richardson "would have been murdered by the Rabble; & the Judges . . . been exposed to Assassination." Supra n. 6, at 86.

9. Letter from Acting Governor Thomas Hutchinson to Lord ———, 21 April 1770, quoted in 2 *Legal Papers*, supra n. 5, at 404–5.

10. Supra n. 6, at 86.

11. Ibid., 86–87.

12. This and the following quote from contemporary diaries, quoted in 2 *Legal Papers*, supra n. 5, at 406.

13. Letter from Acting Governor Thomas Hutchinson to the Earl of Hillsborough, 15 May 1771, quoted in ibid., 408; Letter from Acting Governor Thomas Hutchinson to Former Governor Thomas Pownall, 15 May 1771, quoted in ibid., 408–9.

14. They might suspend sentence but could do little else. See Hutchinson, supra n. 4, at 287n. But see also his statement that all offenses except treason could be pardoned. Ibid., 160. It is possible Hutchinson did not possess this power because he was only acting governor or the power may have been vested in a governor or lieutenant governor by his instructions (which, as yet, Hutchinson had not received).

15. Thomas Davis, *The Speeches of the Right Honorable John Philpot Curran* 279 (1861).

16. *Speeches of the Right Honourable John Philpot Curran, Master of the Rolls in Ireland, in the Late Very Interesting State Trials* 197–98 (4th ed., 1815).

17. William Henry Curran, *The Life of the Right Honourable John Philpot Curran* 169–70 (1820).

18. 1 Sir Jonah Barrington, *Personal Sketches of His Own Times* 91 (3d ed., 1871). This case was not concerned with politics. Had it been, the officer might have obtained an act of amnesty from parliament.

19. Anon., *Forensic Eloquence: Sketches of Trials in Ireland for High Treason, Etc. Including the Speeches of Mr. Curran at Length to Which are Prefixed, A Brief Sketch of the History of Ireland, And a Biographical Account of Mr. Curran: With an Elegant Engraved Likeness of that Orator* 12 (1806).

20. 7 W.E.H. Lecky, *A History of England in the Eighteenth Century* 352 (1891).

21. See motions by Curran in other cases, supra n. 15, at 182; supra n. 17, at 171; supra n. 16, at 119–216. One difference was that in Ireland the jury was expected to take its law from the court. Supra n. 19, at 256, 268.

22. Supra n. 20, at 354.

23. Ibid., 359–60. Informers furnish another contrast between Ireland and North America. In Massachusetts, grand jurors made the names of informers public despite pleas by judges. In Ireland informers were an accepted part of many prosecutions. See summary, Henry S. Eeles, *Lord Chancellor Camden and his Family* 221–24 (1934). Even defense attorneys are known to have been in the pay of Dublin castle. Frank MacDermot, *Theobald Wolfe Tone: A Biographical Study* 151 (1939); Leon O'Broin, *The Unfortunate Mr. Robert Emmet* 149, 164 (1958).

24. Charles Phillips, *Curran and His Contemporaries* 181 (3d ed., 1857).

25. Supra n. 6, at 87.

26. 2 *Legal Papers*, supra n. 5, at 411. For a typical reaction in the press, see *The Massachusetts Spy*, 21 March 1771, p. 1, col. 3.

27. Clarence S. Brigham, *Paul Revere's Engravings* 66 (rev. ed., 1969). The doggerel named each judge. "Old Lines thrown out by, 'twas then we were in hopes,/ That you would soon be hung with *new made* Ropes." "Old Lines" referred to Judge Benjamin Lynde, the oldest member of the court. "New made Ropes" did not imply lynching Richardson, but meant Nathaniel Ropes, recently appointed to the bench. In Dublin Paul Revere would have gone to jail.

28. Hiller B. Zobel, "'Law Under Pressure' Boston 1769–1771," in *Law and Authority in Colonial America* 187, 198–205 (George Athan Billias, editor, 1965).

29. 2 *Legal Papers*, supra n. 5, at 339–40. For the trial see *The Boston Gazette and Country Journal*, 9 August 1773, p. 1, col. 2–3.

30. *The Massachusetts Spy*, 17 December 1772, p. 2, col. 1–2. John Adams, one of his defense attorneys, was convinced of his innocence.

31. See Hutchinson's comments. 3 Thomas Hutchinson, *The History of the Colony and Province of Massachusetts-Bay* 300–302 (Lawrence Shaw Mayo, editor, 1936). See also 2 *Legal Papers*, supra n. 5, at 340.

32. James K. Hosmer, *The Life of Thomas Hutchinson, Royal Governor of the Province of Massachusetts Bay* 138 (1896).

33. Arthur M. Schlesinger, *Prelude to Independence: The Newspaper War on Britain 1764–1776* 108 (1958). Zobel, supra n. 5, at 158–59.

7
The Legitimacy of Whig Law

1. "After all, unless Laws are supported, and enforced, it's needless to make any: Repealing some Laws, and altering others because the Americans will not obey them, is a sure Way to engage the Americans to disobey every Law that is inconvenient to them, and to regard the Legislature in a Light, I shall not venture to name." Gage to Barrington, 7 October 1769.

2. 1 William Backstone, *Commentaries on the Laws of England* 38 (1765).

3. John Adams, "Diary," in 2 *The Works of John Adams* 254 (Charles Francis Adams, editor, 1850).

4. John Adams, "A Dissertation on the Canon and Feudal Law," rpt. in 3 *The Works of John Adams* 456 (Charles Francis Adams, editor, 1851).

5. 1 George Otto Trevelyan, *The American Revolution* 73 (1921).

6. Letter from Edmund Pendleton to James Madison, Sr., 15 February 1766, rpt. in 19 *Proc. Mass. Hist. Soc.* 109–11 (1905). Also rpt. in part in 1 David John Mays, *Edmund Pendleton 1721–1803: A Biography* 170–71 (1952).

7. Richard Maxwell Brown, *The South Carolina Regulators* 1 (1963).

8. Carl Ubbelohde, *The Vice-Admiralty Courts and the American Revolution* 159–61 (1960). Failure of the advocate general could be especially serious when no common-law prosecutor was available to assume his duties. One of the commissioners of the American customs complained that in many colonies the attorney general was not an official of the crown but "was Attorney for the interest of the Province, and not for the Crown." Even when appointed by authority from London he might give revenue agents little assistance, "especially if he had no Salary from the Crown." [Henry Hulton], *Some Account of the Proceedings of the People in New England from the Establishment of a Board of Customs in America, to the Breaking out of the Rebellion in 1775* 58 (MS, Princeton University).

9. Letter from William Bollan to the Duke of Newcastle, 12 April 1766, rpt. in 59 *Proc. Mass. Hist Soc.* 418 (1926).

10. See *Scolly* v. *Dunn, Quincy Reports* 74 (1763); 2 *Legal Papers of John Adams* 68 (L. Kinvin Wroth & Hiller B. Zobel, editors, 1965).

11. As could imperial law officers. For a ruling upholding the validity of colonial common-law prohibitions staying the imperial vice-admiralty process, see Opinion of Attorney General [of England] Richard West, 20 June 1720, George Chalmers, *Opinions of Eminent Lawyers on Various Points of English Jurisprudence Chiefly Concerning the Colonies* 510–21 (1858).

12. For a London lawyer's defense of colonial common-law prohibitions against vice admiralty, see Jer[emiah] Dummer, *A Defence of the New-England Charters* 29–33 (1721).

13. "A legal culture," according to Paul Bohannan, "is that which is subscribed to (whether they know anything about it or not, and whether they act within it or 'agree' with it or not) by the people of a society." In "The Differing Realms of the Law," in *The Ethnography of Law* 33, 38 (Laura Nader, editor, 67 *American Anthropologist* "Special Publication," 1965).

14. Pauline Maier, "Popular Uprising and Civil Authority in Eighteenth-Century America," 27 *Will. & Mary Q.* 3, 10 (1970).

15. Letter from Governor Thomas Hutchinson to John H. Hutchinson, 14 February 1772, quoted in James K. Hosmer, *Samuel Adams* 132 (1899).

16. "Protest of the House of Representatives Against Convening and Holding the [General] Court out of Boston, June 19, 1771," in *Speeches of the Governors of Massachusetts, from 1765 to 1775; and the Answers of the House of Representatives to the Same* 304 (1818).

17. Thomas Hutchinson, *The History of the Province of Massachusetts Bay From 1749 to 1774* 343 (1828).

18. Chief Justice Thomas Hutchinson's Charge to the Grand Jury, March Term, *Quincy Reports* 306, 307–8 (1769).

19. Entry of 7 February 1771, rpt. in 2 *Diary and Autobiography of John Adams* 3–5 (L.H. Butterfield, editor, 1961). See also supra, Ch. 4, n. 8, 9.

20. It might be thought that in a government such as Virginia, where the governor was not subject to the council's veto as in Massachusetts and where the people did not assemble in town meetings, London could keep localism from becoming a powerful force. Such was not the case, however, and localism in Massachusetts therefore cannot be attributed entirely to the peculiarities of that colony's charter. As in Massachusetts, the key to law enforcement in prerevolutionary Virginia was the justice of the peace. Commissions were granted by the governor, and in theory he should have been able to appoint king's men to that office and make their tenure subject to his will. In fact the opposite was true, and long before Lord Dunmore arrived in Williamsburg the gover-

nors had lost almost all power of appointment to the justices themselves, for reasons explained by Charles S. Sydnor: "Through the vigor and effectiveness of their opposition to the governor, the Virginia justices established the point that for all practical purposes they could hold office for life. The personnel of the courts therefore changed but slowly; many a man served for twenty or thirty years. Out of the 1600 persons who served at one time or another as justices during the last score of years before the American Revolution, some 1200 of them were still on the bench when the last lists were made in this period.

"The justices also established the practice of having the governor make additions to the court only on the recommendation of those who were already on the court. . . .

"The governor was not bound by the law to accept the court's nomination, but because the court ordinarily consisted of the leading men of the county, men whose support he would wish to retain, he was usually disposed to follow their advice. If he did not, the previous members of the court might refuse to continue in office and thus virtually bring local government to a standstill. So it was in Spotsylvania County on June 5, 1744, when 'Wm Johnston Gent, being asked whether he would accept & swear to the Commission of the Peace; now Produced, Answered, That he would not Accept and Swear to the Sd: Commission because Anthony Strother, William Hunter and William Lyne are put in the Commission without a Recommendation from the Court.' Six other of the gentlemen justices followed the course taken by William Johnston, one of them observing that he refused 'by reason he believes Doctor Wm Lyne has begged himself into the Comm: being not Recommended by [t]he Court, which he takes to be slighting the Court.'

"By such means as this the legal power of the governor to choose and commission justices was reduced to such an extent that he did little more than give formal approval to the wishes of the courts." *American Revolutionaries in the Making: Political Practices in Washington's Virginia* 76–77 (1965 ed.).

21. Letter from the Earl of Dunmore to the Earl of Dartmouth, 24 December 1774, reprinted in 1 *American Archives: Fourth Series* 1062 (Peter Force, editor, 1833).

22. For an elaboration of the evidence, see John Phillip Reid, "In a Defensive Rage: the Uses of the Mob, the Justification in Law, and the Coming of the American Revolution," 49 *N.Y.U. Law Rev.* 1043, 1086–91 (1974).

23. Richard W. Van Alstyne, *Empire and Independence: The International History of the American Revolution* 60 (1965); Charles Howard McIlwain, *The American Revolution: A Constitutional Interpretation* 117–19 (1923). For the significance of the doctrine of sovereignty during the prerevolutionary era, see 1 Bernard Bailyn, *Pamphlets of the American Revolution, 1750–1776* 115–38 (1965).

24. For the "good law," see Fritz Kern, *Kingship and Law in the Middle Ages* 91, 181, (S.B. Chrimes, trans., 1970).

8
The Import of Local Control

1. "If it is asked why the Governor does not turn all the Justices of the Peace out of Commission, and put others in who will do their Duty? It is Answered, that the Governor can neither appoint Justices or turn them out, but by Consent of Council; and that the Council opposes everything proposed by the Governor for the Service of Government, that is unpopular." Gage to Hillsborough, 31 October 1768.

2. Letter from Lieutenant Governor Thomas Hutchinson to former Governor

NOTES

Thomas Pownall, 8 March, 1766, rpt. in *Prologue to Revolution: Sources and Documents on the Stamp Act Crisis, 1764–1766* 124 (Edmund S. Morgan, editor, 1959).

3. "Rescue" was the crime of freeing a person legally held by the authorities. 4 William Blackstone, *Commentaries on the Laws of England* 131 (1769); 1 *The Law Practice of Alexander Hamilton* 88 (Julius Goebel Jr., editor, 1964). Bernard and others used the word also to describe the seizure from government officials of contraband goods held as potential evidence.

4. Letter from Governor Francis Bernard to the Lords of Trade, 18 August 1766, quoted in *Quincy Reports* 446n (1865).

5. Letter from Governor Francis Bernard to the Lords of Trade, 3 April 1766, quoted in Benjamin Woods Labaree, *The Boston Tea Party* 54–55 (paperback ed., 1968).

6. Supra n. 2, at 124.

7. Appendix I, *Quincy Reports* 463 (1865).

8. Letter of 15 August 1765, in Malcolm Freiberg (editor), "An Unknown Stamp Act Letter," 78 *Proc. Mass. Hist. Soc.* 138, 140, 141 (1966); *The Massachusetts Gazette and the Boston News-Letter*, 22 August 1765, p. 2, col. 2.

9. Freiberg, supra n. 8, at 141.

10. Letter from Lieutenant Governor Thomas Hutchinson to Richard Jackson, 30 August 1765, rpt. in James K. Hosmer, *The Life of Thomas Hutchinson Royal Governor of the Province of Massachusetts Bay* 91–92 (1896).

11. Josiah Quincy, "Destruction of the House of the Chief Justice," *Quincy Reports* 169–70 (1865); Diary entry for 15 August 1765, in 1 *Diary and Autobiography of John Adams* 259–60 (L.H. Butterfield, editor, 1961).

12. That is treason resulting from an usurpation of the king's function—when the purpose of the mob's action was public rather than private. Examples from colonial history include driving smallpox carriers from towns, attacking Indians on the frontier, or tearing down whorehouses in seaports.

13. The proclamation: "Our sovereign lord the king chargeth and commandeth all persons being assembled, immediately to disperse themselves, and peaceably to depart to their habitations, or to their lawful business; upon the pains contained in the act of this province made in the twenty-fourth year of his majesty King George the Second, for preventing and suppressing of riots, routs and unlawful assemblies. God save the king." Act of 14 February 1750/51, "Chapter 17," *Province Laws—1750–51* (3d Sess.).

14. For current English common law, see 4 William Blackstone, *Commentaries on the Laws of England* 146–47 (1769). See also William Seagle, "Riots," 13 *Ency. Soc. Science* 388, 389 (1934).

15. Chief Justice Thomas Hutchinson's Charge to the Suffolk County Grand Jury, March Term, *Quincy Reports* 113 (1765).

16. One aspect apparently not understood by Bostonians was that members of a mob could be charged with murder should a death result from mob activities. In 1765 Hutchinson took pains to explain the law "for the benefit of all present, as they are a pretty large Concourse of People." Not only did a defendant face hanging, but would "have to [prove] how he came to be there," and anyone proven to have encouraged or assisted the riot "for aught I see must have been convicted; for there are no Accessories in Murder; all are Principals." Ibid., 114.

17. An Act Enabling Sheriffs, Constables &c, to Require Aid and Assistance in the Execution of their Respective Offices Referring to Criminals (1698), in 1 *Acts and Resolves* 354 (1869).

18. Declaration of Sheriff Stephen Greenleaf, 1 October 1766, printed in George G.

Wolkins, "Daniel Malcom and Writs of Assistance," 58 *Mass. Hist. Soc. Proc.* 5, 38 (1924). Everyone knew the informer was Ebenezer Richardson.

19. Chief Justice Thomas Hutchinson's Charge to the Suffolk County Grand Jury, March Term, *Quincy Reports* 116 (1765).

20. Diary entry for 30 December 1765, in 2 *The Works of John Adams* 169–70 (Charles Francis Adams, editor, 1850).

21. The sheriff had told the crowd that the name of the informer was never revealed. Such, to be true, was customary law, for the practice was that informers' identities were kept secret and they did not accompany revenue men on raids. Statutory law was not so clear. The act of parliament authorizing Writs of Assistance (the writ involved in this situation) provided that if the information upon which a search was conducted "prove to be false," then "the party injured shall recover his full damages and costs against the informer, by action of trespass to be therefore brought against such informer." 12 Charles II, cap. 19, sec. 4 (1660), 7 *Statutes at Large*, at 460. The right granted by this statute was a nullity if the identity of the potential defendant remained unknown.

22. 1 *The Diary and Letters of his Excellency Thomas Hutchinson, Esq.* 71 (Peter Orlando Hutchinson, editor, 1883).

23. 3 Thomas Hutchinson, *The History of the Colony and Province of Massachusetts-Bay* 91 (Laurence Shaw Mayo, editor, 1936).

24. Letter from Governor Francis Bernard to Board of Trade, 12 October 1765, quoted in 1 *American Archives: Fourth Series* 14 (Peter Force, editor, 1837).

25. John C. Miller, *Origins of the American Revolution* 286–87 (1943).

26. Hiller B. Zobel, *The Boston Massacre* 230 (1970).

27. *Boston Evening-Post*, 23 December 1765, p. 1, col. 2. If a magistrate, Chief Justice Hutchinson instructed the Suffolk County Grand Jury, "in order to support any one particular Party or depress another, shall venture, under Colour of his Office, to administer an Oath to any one, he is guilty of a very high Offence against the Laws and deserves a very severe Punishment." Chief Justice Thomas Hutchinson's Charge to the Suffolk County Grand Jury, March Term, *Quincy Reports* 306, 311 (1769).

28. See, e.g., supra n. 26, at 132–44.

29. John Phillip Reid, "A Lawyer Acquitted: John Adams and the Boston Massacre Trials," 18 *Am. J. Legal Hist.* 189, 198–207 (1974).

30. William Sampson, *Memoirs of William Sampson* 30 (1807).

31. 7 W.E.H. Lecky, *A History of England in the Eighteenth Century* 53 (1891).

32. Frank MacDermot, *Theobald Wolfe Tone: A Biographical Study* 154 (1939).

33. T.D. Sullivan, A.M. Sullivan, & D.B. Sullivan, *Speeches From the Dock: Or, Protests of Irish Patriotism* 55 (1882).

34. Supra note 22, at 179n.

35. Letter from Governor Francis Bernard to the Earl of Halifax, 31 August 1765, rpt. in Merrill Jensen (editor), 9 *English Historical Documents: American Colonial Documents to 1776* 675–80 (1955).

36. Thus nine years later another governor of Massachusetts Bay would write: "The Officers of the Militia have in most Places been forced to resign their Commissions, And the Men choose their Officers, who are frequently made and unmade." Letter from Governor Thomas Gage to the Earl of Dartmouth, 30 October 1774, in 1 *The Correspondence*, supra n. 41, at 383.

37. Pauline Maier, "Popular Uprising and Civil Authority in Eighteenth-Century America," 27 *Will. & Mary Q.* 19 (1970); Edmund S. Morgan & Helen M. Morgan, *The Stamp Act Crisis: Prologue to Revolution* 164 (paperback ed., 1963).

38. *The Boston Chronicle*, 13 June 1768, p. 247, col. 2.

39. Minutes of the Commissioners of the American Customs, 11 June 1768, *Boston Evening-Post*, 18 September 1769, p. 1, col. 2. The assertion proved to be true. Letter from Governor Francis Bernard to the Earl of Hillsborough, 14 June 1768, *Letters to the Ministry from Governor Bernard, General Gage, and Commodore Hood* 32 (1769).

40. Letter from the Commissioners of the American Customs to the Lords of Trade, 16 June 1768, *Boston Evening-Post*, 18 September 1769, p. 1, col. 1.

41. Chief Justice Thomas Hutchinson's Charge to the Suffolk County Grand Jury, August Term, *Quincy Reports* 177–79 (1765). Reference to "crimes which come within your own Knowledge" was sarcasm on Hutchinson's part. He knew some grand jurors had intimate knowledge of the facts. Leaving little to chance, town meetings made certain that some members of every grand-jury panel were being asked to indict themselves. Following the *Liberty* riot, Boston selected as a juror the man everyone, including Governor Bernard, knew had been "the Head of the Mob." Supra n. 25, at 287–88; supra n. 26, at 77. Later, Hutchinson himself made no effort to bring those responsible for the Boston Tea Party to trial before a local court. The grand jurors returned for Boston, he explained to the Earl of Dartmouth, "were among the principal promoters of the meetings which occasioned the destruction of the tea, and were undoubtedly selected to prevent any prosecutions." Supra n. 22, at 114.

42. See excuse given by merchants of Boston why they could not use civil litigation to oppose pressure by the mob forcing them not to import British goods. Hiller B. Zobel, "Law Under Pressure: Boston 1769–1771," in *Law and Authority in Colonial America* 187, 195 (George Athan Billias, editor, 1965). Victims of Boston's famous tar and feather operation also knew better than to sue. *Peter Oliver's Origin & Progress of the American Rebellion: A Tory View* 94 (Douglas Adair & John A. Schutz, editors, 1961); but see 1 *Legal Papers of John Adams* 39n33 (L. Kinvin Wroth & Hiller B. Zobel, editors, 1965).

43. But see Zobel, supra n. 26, at 56.

9
The Execution of Whig Law

1. "Your Lordship sees the Seeds of Anarchy and Licentiousness, are thick Sown through the Colonies, I hope they will not ripen in our Days." Gage to Barrington, 6 August 1771.

2. Generally speaking, pain was not the object of whig "punishment," humiliation was. Victims of tar and feathers were publicly exhibited, sometimes dragged all over town in a cart, and held up to ridicule, not physically tortured. This sanction was especially effective in small communities, such as Boston, when applied against men from the lower economic and educated classes than those of more independent status. See discussion in John Phillip Reid, "In a Defensive Rage: the Uses of the Mob, the Justification in Law, and the Coming of the American Revolution," 49 *N.Y.U. Law Rev.* 1043, 1070–85 (1974).

3. Carl Ubbelohde, *The Vice-Admiralty Courts and the American Revolution* 118 (1960). Similarly, Boston merchants, when asked by Hutchinson to resist nonimportation programs, refused; until parliament "made provision for the punishment of the confederacies, all would be ineffectual." Letter from Acting Governor Thomas Hutchinson to the Earl of Hillsborough, 27 April 1770, quoted in Report of Lords' Committee, 20 April 1774, rpt. in 1 *American Archives: Fourth Series* 26 (Peter Force, editor, 1837).

NOTES

Thomas Gage became almost ridiculous when the best he could suggest to merchants who suffered mob terror was to prosecute the rioters in England—if and when the rioters set foot in Great Britain. John Richard Alden, *General Gage in America* 171 (1948).

4. See, e.g., Virginia Resolutions, 16 May 1769, rpt. in Merrill Jensen (editor), 9 *English Historical Documents: American Colonial Documents to 1776* 722 (1955); South Carolina Resolutions, 19 August 1769, ibid., 723; Resolutions of the Town of Ipswich, 17 December 1772, *Boston Evening-Post*, 18 January 1773, p. 1, col. 3; Resolves of the Town of Charles Town [South Carolina], 8 July 1774, *Boston Evening-Post*, 25 July 1774, p. 2, col. 1. While the act was limited to treason it should be pointed out that the definition of treason was broad enough to include the actions of many whigs who were only rioters and did not participate in plots or conspiracies. See Justice Thomas Hutchinson's Charge to the Suffolk County Grand Jury, August Term, *Quincy Reports* 221 (1766).

5. Letter from General Thomas Gage to Lord Barrington, 6 January 1773, in 2 *The Correspondence of General Thomas Gage with the Secretaries of State, and with the War Office and the Treasury 1763–1776* 632 (Clarence Edwin Carter, editor, 1933). Massachusetts' Chief Justice Oliver agreed with Gage. *Peter Oliver's Origin & Progress of the American Rebellion: A Tory View* 99 (Douglas Adair & John A. Schutz, editors, 1961).

6. Edward Channing, "The American Board of Commissioners of the Customs," 43 *Mass. Hist. Soc. Proc.* 477, 486–87 (1910). The American board had to pay the commander's judgments. Supra n. 4, at 253.

7. Letter from the Earl of Hillsborough to Governor Francis Bernard, 12 October 1768, quoted in Hiller B. Zobel, *The Boston Massacre* 77 (1971). See also Letter from General Thomas Gage to Secretary of State H.S. Conway, 16 January 1766, in 1 *The Correspondence of General Thomas Gage with the Secretaries of State 1763–1775* 82 (Clarence Edwin Carter, editor, 1931).

8. An example is the case of the New York "lawless Ruffians" outlined post Ch. 10, text to n. 3, 4.

9. Jesse Lemisch, "The American Revolution Seen From the Bottom Up," in *Towards a New Past: Dissenting Essays in American History* 21 (Barton J. Bernstein, editor, 1968).

10. 1 *Pamphlets of the American Revolution, 1750–1776* 581–82 (Bernard Bailyn, editor, 1965).

11. Pauline Maier, "Popular Uprising and Civil Authority in Eighteenth-Century America," 27 *Will. & Mary Q.* 3, 24 (1970). See generally the discussion at pp. 18–27. Gordon S. Wood, "A Note on Mobs in the American Revolution," 23 *Will. & Mary Q.* 635, 641 (1966).

12. Maier, supra n. 11, at 4.

13. George Rude, *The Crowd in History* 66 (1964). See also the detailed proof in George Rude, *Wilkes and Liberty: A Social Study of 1763 to 1774* 13–14 (1962).

14. "Suppose a press gang should come on shore in this town, and assault any sailor, or householder in King street, in order to . . . impress him without any warrant, as a seaman in his majesty's service, how far do you suppose the inhabitants would think themselves warranted by law to interpose against that lawless press gang! I agree that such press gang would be [an unlawful assembly]. If they were to impress an inhabitant, and carry him off for a sailor, would not the inhabitants think themselves warranted by law to interpose in behalf of their fellow citizen?" Frederic Kidder, *History of the Boston Massacre March 5, 1770. Consisting of the Narrative of the Town,*

the Trial of the Soldiers, and a Historical Introduction 242–43 (1870). There seems to have been a belief among the common people, in at least some parts if not all of the colonies, that a citizen had the right to resist a peace officer making an arrest, that one could oppose authority with force and did not have to submit to arrest. See, e.g., Douglas Greenberg, "The Effectiveness of Law Enforcement in Eighteenth-century New York," 19 *Am. J. Legal Hist.* 173, 176–77, 187 (1975).

15. Thus violence in defense of "a fundamental principle of the constitution" was justified "because there was no tribunal in the constitution, from whence redress could have been obtained." John Adams, *Novanglus* #6, in 4 *The Works of John Adams* 88 (Charles Francis Adams, editor, 1851). For an outline of the whig belief that there was a constitutional self-defense justification for the use of force when basic rights were being threatened, see supra n. 2, at 1050–52.

16. Answer of the House of Representatives to Lieutenant Governor Thomas Hutchinson, 24 April 1770, rpt. in Thomas Hutchinson, *The History of the Province of Massachusetts Bay, From 1749 to 1774* 503 (1828). See also Message of the House of Representatives to Governor Francis Bernard, 13 June 1769, rpt. in 1 *The Writings of Samuel Adams* 345 (Harry Alonzo Cushing, editor, 1904).

17. See discussion, Maier, supra n. 11, at 22–24.

18. Ibid., 15, 8.

19. Letter from Governor Francis Bernard to the Earl of Halifax, 31 August 1765, rpt. in Jensen (editor), supra n. 4, at 675–80. Also, Peter Oliver referred to the attack on Hutchinson's house as part of "the Reign of Anarchy in Boston!" In the next sentence he says that "it was in vain to struggle against the *Law of Otis.*" *Peter Oliver's Origin*, supra n. 5, at 53. Also see John Adams's distinction between "popular" and "private" mobs in *Familiar Letters of John Adams and his Wife Abigail Adams During the Revolution* 19–20 (1875).

20. Maier, supra n. 11, at 26–27.

21. Letter from Lieutenant Governor Thomas Hutchinson to Former Governor Thomas Pownall, 8 March 1766, rpt. in *Prologue to Revolution: Sources and Documents on the Stamp Act Crisis* 126 (Edmund S. Morgan, editor, 1969). See also Hutchinson's account of a confrontation with the magistrates of Boston who told him that a mob acting illegally against an innocent person might with justification use the same violence against a militant tory. Hutchinson, supra n. 16, at 260–61.

22. Letter from Lieutenant Governor Thomas Hutchinson . . . supra n. 16, at 125.

23. Letter from Governor Thomas Hutchinson to Former Governor Francis Bernard, 24 May 1771, rpt. in James K. Hosmer, *The Life of Thomas Hutchinson, Royal Governor of the Province of Massachusetts Bay* 206–7 (1896).

24. Instructions of the Town of Boston to James Otis et al., 17 June 1768, in *A Report of the Record Commission of the City of Boston Containing the Boston Town Records, 1758 to 1769* 259 (Report 16, 1886); *The Boston Chronicle*, 20 June 1768, p. 254, col. 1–3. *Romney* had been sent to Boston to press men. Letter from Commodore Samuel Hood to George Grenville, 14 September 1768, in 2 Mrs. Napier Higgins, *The Bernards of Abington and Nether Winchenden: A Family History* 117 (1903). At least one man, a young black apprentice, had been pressed and Boston's selectmen had protested. *The Boston Gazette and Country Journal*, 20 June 1768, p. 1, col. 3; Entry for 13 June 1768, "Diary of John Rowe," 10 *Proc. Mass. Hist. Soc.* 11, 67 (1895). Thus the rioters who tried to rescue *Liberty* included many sailors. *Boston Evening-Post*, 20 June 1768, p. 2, col. 1.

25. Message from the Council to Governor Francis Bernard, 29 July 1768, *The Boston Chronicle*, 17 October 1768, p. 394, col. 2. See also adoption of the argument in

"An Appeal to the World," 18 October 1769, rpt. in 1 *The Writings*, supra n. 16, at 409–10.

26. "This Conduct provoked the People who had collected on the Shore." *Boston Evening-Post*, 20 June 1768, p. 2, col. 1.

27. The riot "was occasioned by the unprecedented & [un]lawful manner of seizing the Vessel." Report of the Committee appointed to vindicate the town of Boston . . . , 18 October 1769, in *A Report*, supra n. 24, at 308. See also Resolution of the Council, 30 June 1768, in *Speeches of the Governor of Massachusetts, from 1765 to 1775; and the Answers of the House of Representatives to the Same* 157 (1818).

28. Answer of the Council to Governor Francis Bernard, 26 September 1768, in *Letters to the Right Honourable The Earl of Hillsborough, From Governor Bernard, General Gage, and the Honourable His Majesty's Council for the Province of Massachusetts-Bay* 131 (1768); Address of the Council to General Thomas Gage, 27 October 1768, in ibid., 131–32.

"However culpable the said disorderly Persons were, the Officers who seized, or those by whose Orders such unusual and violent Measures were pursued in seizing and taking away the said Vessel, were not faultless: It being highly probable that no such Disorders would have been committed, if the Vessel had not been with an armed Force, & with many Circumstances of Insult & Threats, carried away from the Wharf." Proceedings of the Council, 29 June 1768, *Boston Evening-Post* (Supplement), 10 October 1768, p. 1, col. 3. See also Answer of the Council to Governor Bernard, 29 June 1768, *The Boston Gazette and Country Journal*, 10 October 1768, p. 2, col. 2.

29. Letter from Thomas Cushing [for the Massachusetts Convention] to Dennys de Berdt, 27 September 1678 [sic], *The Boston Chronicle*, 17 October 1768, p. 396, col. 2. For other instances of whigs making the general argument see Answer of the Council to the Speech of Governor Thomas Hutchinson of January 6. 25 January 1773, rpt. in supra n. 23, at 370–71; Answer of the House of Representatives to the Speech of the Governor, of Sixth January. 26 January 1773, rpt. in ibid., 380.

30. Hutchinson, supra n. 16, at 191.

31. *The Boston Chronicle*, 20 June 1768, p. 253, col. 1.

32. Ibid.

33. The "town meeting" was said by a whig newspaper to consist "of a larger Number than was ever known on any Occasion." *Boston Evening-Post*, 20 June 1768, p. 2, col. 2.

34. Letter from Samuel Adams to Arthur Lee, 31 December 1773, rpt. in 3 *The Writings of Samuel Adams* 74 (Harry Alonzo Cushing, editor, 1907).

35. Petition of the Town of Boston to Governor Francis Bernard, 14 June 1768, *The Boston Gazette and Country Journal*, 20 June 1768, p. 2, col. 1; *The Boston Chronicle*, 20 June 1768, p. 253, col. 1–2.

36. Hutchinson, supra n. 16, at 192–93. James Otis was the spokesman for the committee.

37. Answer of Governor Francis Bernard to the Boston Town Meeting, 15 June 1768, *The Boston Gazette and Country Journal*, 20 June 1768, p. 2, col. 2; *The Boston Chronicle*, 20 June 1768, p. 253, col. 3; Bernard said that impressment "is practiced in Great Britain, and all other [of] his Majesty's dominions, and therefore I cannot dispute it in this part of them. But I shall use my utmost endeavors to get it regulated so as to avoid all the inconveniences to this town which you are apprehensive of." *The Boston Gazette and Country Journal*, 20 June 1768, p. 2, col. 1–2.

38. The constitutional theory was that towns were not competent bodies to address the governor directly. The captain of *Romney* pledged not to impress men married in the

province or employed in the trade along shore or in the neighboring colonies. Also a man recently pressed would be released. Ibid., 3, col. 1; *The Boston Chronicle*, 20 June 1768, p. 253, col. 3.

10
The Legal Mind of the American Whig

1. "No common Means will reduce them now to a legal Obedience and Subordination; you have tried the temper of the Council and of the Magistrates, and you have found upon trial, that every Part of the Civil Government is of the same Leaven with the People." Gage to Barrington, 6 July 1770.

2. See, e.g., descriptions in Letter from General Thomas Gage to Lord Barrington, 22 July 1769, in 2 *The Correspondence of General Thomas Gage with the Secretaries of State, and with the War Office and the Treasury 1763–1775* 518 (Clarence Edwin Carter, editor, 1933); Letter from same to same, 7 October 1769, in ibid., 526–27.

3. Such was the complaint of William Henry Drayton. *The South Carolina Gazette*, 3 August 1769, p. 1, col. 2. See the whiggish answer of Christopher Gadsen in *The South Carolina Gazette*, 28 September 1769, p. 2, col. 1.

4. Arthur M. Schlesinger, *The Colonial Merchants and the American Revolution* 190 (1918).

5. Letter from George Washington to Robert Cary, 25 July 1769, in 2 *The Writings of George Washington* 270n1 (Worthington Chauncey Ford, editor, 1889).

6. Letter from the Committee of Correspondence of Boston to other Committees of Correspondence, 17 December 1773, rpt. in 3 *The Writings of Samuel Adams* 72 (Harry Alonzo Cushing, editor, 1907).

7. "During the whole of this transaction, neither the Governor, Magistrates (who are appointed by the Governor) Owners or Revenue Officers of this Place, ever called for my assistance; if they had, I could easily have prevented the execution of this Plan." Letter from Admiral Montague to the Lords of the Admiralty, 17 December 1773, *Boston Evening-Post*, p. 2, col. 1.

8. See Proceedings of the Massachusetts Council, 29 November 1773, rpt. in Francis S. Drake, *Tea Leaves: Being a Collection of Letters and Documents Relating to the Shipment of Tea to the American Colonies in the Year 1773, by the East India Tea Company* 319 (1884); Francis G. Walett, "The Massachusetts Council, 1767–1774," 6 *Will. & Mary Q.* 605, 614–15 (1949). The question whether Hutchinson needed consent of the council is open to dispute. The whigs maintained an armed guard on one of the tea ships and technically the members of that guard could have been proclaimed rebels. The governor, to have employed troops to quell them, would not have needed the aid of a magistrate or consent of the council (as he did when proceeding against civilian rioters). The definition of rebellion might not be precise and could have given him hesitation, but the decision of proclaiming a state of rebellion was vested in him by the charter. He did not have to obtain the advice and consent of the council.

9. "An Impartial Observer," *Boston Evening-Post*, 20 December 1773, p. 2, col. 3.

10. *Boston Evening-Post*, 16 May 1774, p. 2, col. 1.

11. *Dartmouth* had by law first to make entry at the customshouse before being granted a pass. Entry at the customshouse was what the whigs could not allow as the tax on tea would then have been paid, the precedent established, and their constitutional argument rendered that much weaker. John Phillip Reid, "The Ordeal by Law of Thomas Hutchinson," 49 *N.Y.U. Law Rev.* 593, 608–12 (1974).

NOTES

12. The "Body" was the name adopted by the whigs when first assembled to vote on and enforce the nonimportation association. It served to distinguish such gatherings from regular town meetings and, during the tea crisis, was found convenient as it allowed non-Bostonians to attend and vote.

13. Statement of the Boston Body Meeting, 16 December 1773, *Boston Evening-Post*, 20 December 1773, p. 2, col. 2.

14. At midnight, there would have been a constructive entry at the customshouse, as a result of which the tax would have been paid.

15. Anon., "Proceeding of Ye Body Respecting the Tea," (L.F.S. Upton, editor), 22 *Will. & Mary Q.* 287, 298 (1965).

16. Supra n. 9, at 2, col. 3.

17. Letter from John Andrews to William Barrell, 18 December 1773, in Winthrop Sargent (editor), "Letters of John Andrews, Esq., of Boston," 8 [1st series] *Proc. Mass. Hist. Soc.* 316, 325–26 (1866).

18. *Boston Evening-Post*, 2 May 1774, p. 2, col. 2.

19. "A Bostonian," *Boston Evening-Post*, 27 June 1774, p. 4, col. 1.

20. Letter from Samuel Adams to Arthur Lee, 31 December 1773, in supra n. 6, at 76. See also Merrill Jensen (editor), 9 *English Historical Documents: American Colonial Documents to 1776* 771 (1955).

21. Letter from the Committee of Correspondence of Boston to the Committee of Plymouth, 17 December 1773, rpt. in supra n. 6, at 72.

22. Dedham Resolves, 5 January 1774, *Boston Evening-Post*, 28 February 1774, p. 4, col. 1.

23. Supra n. 15, at 298. "A watch . . . was stationed to prevent embezzlement, and not a single ounce of Tea was suffered to be purloined by the populace: One or two persons being detected in endeavouring to pocket a small quantity were stripped of acquisitions and very roughly handled." Supra n. 9, at 2, col. 3.

24. Supra n. 17, at 326.

25. *The Massachusetts Gazette and the Boston Weekly News-Letter*, 23 December 1773, p. 1, col. 3.

26. Letter from Samuel Adams, supra n. 20, at 76.

27. Thomas Hutchinson, *The History of the Province of Massachusetts Bay, From 1749 to 1774* 438 (1828).

28. Letter from Governor Thomas Hutchinson to the Earl of Dartmouth, 17 December 1773, rpt. in Richard Frothingham, "Paper Delivered on the One Hundredth Anniversary of the Destruction of the Tea in Boston Harbor," 13 [1st series] *Proc. Mass. Hist. Soc.* 173 (1874).

29. Supra n. 27, at 439.

30. Walett, supra n. 8, at 615–16.

31. Supra n. 27, at 439.

32. Letter from Governor Thomas Hutchinson to Israel Mauduit, December 1773, rpt. in Frothingham, supra n. 28, at 171.

33. Letter from Governor Thomas Hutchinson to former Governor Francis Bernard, 1 January 1744, rpt. in Frothingham, supra n. 28, at 174.

34. Letter from Samuel Adams, supra n. 20, at 75–76. See also Letter from Samuel Adams to Arthur Lee, 25 January 1774, in supra n. 6, at 79.

35. Letter from Samuel Adams to —— ——, 28 December 1773, quoted in Frothingham, supra n. 28, at 178.

36. Walett, supra n. 8, at 616.

37. *London Chronicle*, 22 March 1774, rpt. Frothingham, supra n. 28, at 178–79.

38. *London Gazetteer*, 7 April 1774, rpt. in 1 *American Archives: Fourth Series* 242, 244 (Peter Force, editor, 1837).

39. Entry for 17 December 1773, in 2 *The Works of John Adams* 324 (Charles Francis Adams, editor, 1850).

40. For Adams's public defense of the Tea Party see Adams, *Novanglus #6*, 4 *The Works of John Adams* 79–91 (Charles Francis Adams, editor, 1851), esp. p. 90: "All men will agree that such steps ought not to be taken but in cases of absolute necessity, and that such necessity must be very clear. But most people in America now think the destruction of the Boston tea was absolutely necessary, and therefore right and just."

11
The Conditions of Imperial Law

1. "It is necessary too that Great Britain should not only assert, but also support that Supremacy which she claims over the Members of the Empire, or she will soon only be supreme in Words, and we shall become a vast Empire composed of many Parts, disjointed and independent of each other, without any Head." Gage to Barrington, 13 April 1772.

2. *The Boston Gazette and Country Journal*, 1 May 1769, p. 1, col. 1–2. For Commodore Hood's orders see Hiller B. Zobel, *The Boston Massacre* 113–14 (1970).

3. 2 *Legal Papers of John Adams* 316 (L. Kinvin Wroth & Hiller B. Zobel, editors, 1965). See also testimony of the naval midshipman. Ibid., 301.

4. Ibid., 277; 3 Thomas Hutchinson, *The History of the Colony and Province of Massachusetts-Bay* 167n (Lawrence Shaw Mayo, editor, 1936); Zobel, supra n. 2, at 119; supra n. 3, at 277.

5. Adams later recalled that he carried the defense alone as the once splendid mind of James Otis had almost slipped beyond the pale of sanity. "His unhappy distemper was then in one of its unlucid intervals, and I could hardly persuade him to converse with me a few minutes on the subject; and he constantly and finally refused to appear publicly in the cause." Letter from John Adams to William Tudor, 30 December 1816, 2 *The Works of John Adams* 224n (Charles Francis Adams, editor, 1850). But a contemporary reported that Otis took the lead and was active in the defense, making motions and arguments. Letter from Colonel Jones Robertson to General Thomas Gage, 24 May 1769, *Gage Papers* (MS, Clements Library).

6. Supra n. 3, at 275–78; Zobel, supra n. 2, at 122–29; 1 *The Diary and Letters of his Excellency Thomas Hutchinson, Esq.* 74–75 (Peter Orlando Hutchinson, editor, 1883); Hutchinson, supra n. 4, at 167. Bernard, who as governor was president of the court, was so confused he first indicated a grand jury and then a traverse jury would have to be called, though he also thought the defendants might have to be sent to Great Britain for trial by an English jury, an event they would have found as threatening as trial before the American commissioners without a jury. It was Hutchinson who persuaded the court to proceed at civil law without a jury. For Hutchinson's account of this, his most impressive legal triumph over John Adams, see Hutchinson, supra n. 4, at 167.

7. Hutchinson's argument was technical and not too convincing. The eagerness of the court to avoid trial by a jury of Suffolk county whigs was of course an overriding factor independent of the merits of his interpretation of what were, on the surface, two conflicting statutes, but among those he had to persuade were two competent lawyers, Admiralty Judge Robert Auchmuty and Advocate General Jonathan Sewall. Still, we may wonder if they were persuaded by law. Hutchinson told them that London expected

them to uphold the imperial position: that they "would have been liable to a severe censure if they had proceeded to trial by jury, as it would have had no foundation or law to support it." 1 *The Diary*, supra n. 6, at 75.

8. There was, for example, the question of what law, common or civil, controlled the adjective and substantive law. The procedure made little difference, as both common and civil law allowed the same evidence to be introduced and the burden of proof was not a sophisticated factor at that time. Substantive law was vital, however. Under common law the defendants, if found not guilty of murder, still would have to satisfy the court that the homicide was justifiable or they could be convicted of manslaughter. Civil law did not know manslaughter, only murder. Thus if Lieutenant Panton's attempt to impress them had been illegal, they stood a better chance at acquittal with civil law, as even Irish seamen had a right to defend themselves against unlawful imprisonment and the intent necessary to commit murder would be extremely difficult to prove. Common law allowed the court to weigh the further question whether they were justified in using a deadly weapon. If not, they could be found guilty of manslaughter. Even that possibility raised a further issue for which no one had an answer. Defendants convicted of manslaughter could, at common law, plead benefit of clergy, be branded on the thumb, and then be set free. Pleading clergy was a peculiarity of common law, unknown to civil law. Could it be invoked in admiralty for a conviction of common-law manslaughter? Supra n. 3, at 278–79; Zobel, supra n. 2, at 124.

9. Letter from the Earl of Hillsborough to Governor Francis Bernard, 30 July 1768, cited in Zobel, supra n. 2, at 86.

10. 6 Anne, cap. 37, sec. 9 (1707), 11 *Statutes at Large*, at 438. It is a commentary upon the availability of legal precedents in the colonies that at least twice English law officers had ruled that this statute had expired. Opinion of Attorney General Edward Northey, 10 February 1715/16, and Opinion of Attorney General Dudley Ryder and Solicitor General John Strange, 17 July 1740, George Chalmers, *Opinions of Eminent Lawyers* 232 (1858). Had Hutchinson known of these opinions it is quite likely the court would not have found the defendants not guilty.

11. "Nay, I think that Impresses may be allowed to be legal, and yet Corbit might have a Right to resist. . . . The Custom may be admitted to extend so far [as to provide the naval officer with a privilege against civil suit], and yet it will not follow, that the Seaman has not a Right to resist, and keep himself out of the officer's Power." Supra n. 3, at 322.

12. Letter from John Adams to J. Morse, 20 January 1816, 10 *The Works of John Adams* 208 (Charles Francis Adams, editor, 1856).

13. Letter from John Adams, supra n. 5, at 226n.

14. Hutchinson, supra n. 4, at 167n. For Adams's explanation that Hutchinson and his colleagues "dreaded" publication of the statute of Anne see Letter from John Adams, supra n. 5, at 226n; supra n. 12, at 209.

15. Hiller B. Zobel, "Law under Pressure: Boston 1769–1771," in *Law and Authority in Colonial America* 192 (George Athan Billias, editor, 1965).

16. See testimony of William Peacock and James Silley, supra n. 3, at 301 & 309.

17. 4 William Blackstone, *Commentaries on the Laws of England* 191–94 (1769).

18. See explanation given to the Boston Massacre jury, Judge Edmund Trowbridge's Charge to the Jury (Soldiers' case), 5 December 1770, in 3 *Legal Papers of John Adams* 286–87 (L. Kinvin Wroth & Hiller B. Zobel, editors, 1965).

19. Zobel, supra n. 14, at 192.

20. Letter from Governor Francis Bernard to Lord Barrington, 4 March 1768, in *The Barrington-Bernard Correspondence* 148 (Edward Channing & Archibald Cary

NOTES

Coolidge, editors, 1912). See also Letter from Governor Francis Bernard to the Earl of Hillsborough, 19 March 1768, rpt. in Merrill Jensen (editor), 9 *English Historical Documents: American Colonial Documents to 1776* 738 (1955). The advice of the council was of some consequence as the governor could not request troops without its consent and the policy of London had been not to send soldiers to a colony unless the governor requested them. Letter from Lord Barrington to Governor Francis Bernard, 13 December 1766, in *The . . . Correspondence*, at 119.

21. Letter from Governor Francis Bernard to General Thomas Gage, 27 August 1765, ibid., 227–28; Letter from Governor Francis Bernard to Lord Barrington, 20 July 1768, ibid., 167–68.

22. John Richard Alden, *General Gage in America* 163 (1948).

23. Because the Mutiny Act was reenacted at each session of parliament it is not printed in *Statutes at Large*. For the full text see *Boston Evening-Post*, 10 October 1768, p. 4, col. 1–2. For a brief discussion see Clarence E. Carter, "The Office of Commander in Chief: A Phase of Imperial Unity on the Eve of the Revolution," in Richard E. Morris (editor), *The Era of the American Revolution* 170, 197–98 (Harper Torchbook ed., 1965).

24. Answer of the Council to Governor Francis Bernard, 26 September 1768, *The Boston Gazette and Country Journal* (Supplement), 26 September 1768, p. 1, col. 1–2; *Boston Evening-Post* (Supplement Extraordinary), 26 September 1768, pp. 1–2; Letter from General Thomas Gage to the Earl of Hillsborough, 10 September 1768, in 1 *The Correspondence of General Thomas Gage with the Secretaries of State 1763–1775* 195 (Clarence Edwin Carter, editor, 1931); Letter same to same, 7 September 1768, ibid., 191.

25. The Quartering Act of 15 May 1765, rpt. in Jensen, supra n. 20, at 657.

26. Letter from General Thomas Gage to the Earl of Hillsborough, 31 October 1768, in 1 *The Correspondence*, supra n. 24, at 202. See also Letter from Samuel Adams to Dennys de Berdt, 3 October 1768, rpt. in 1 *The Writings of Samuel Adams* 248 (Harry Alonzo Cushing, editor, 1904).

27. Even Thomas Hutchinson, it is claimed, thought that the council had found a legal loophole. John Shy, *Toward Lexington: The Role of the British Army in the Coming of the American Revolution* 304 (1965). Perhaps, but it seems doubtful. Legal precisian that he may have been, Hutchinson was not a strict constructionist when interpreting the king's statutes. He, too, called the council's law "absurd." Letter from Thomas Hutchinson to [Thomas Whately], 4 October 1768, in *Copy of Letters Sent to Great Britain, by his Excellency Thomas Hutchinson, the Hon. Andrew Oliver, and several other Persons, Born and Educated Among Us* 12 (1773).

28. Letter from General Thomas Gage to Secretary of State H.S. Conway, 6 May 1766, in 1 *The Correspondence*, supra n. 24, at 89–90. See also Letter from General Thomas Gage to the Earl of Hillsborough, 2 July 1771, ibid., 302.

29. Letter from General Thomas Gage to the Earl of Hillsborough, 31 October 1768, ibid., 202.

30. Letter from General Thomas Gage to Secretary of State H.S. Conway, 6 May 1766, in 1 *The Correspondence*, supra n. 24, at 89. See also Letter from General Thomas Gage to Lord Barrington, 21 February 1766, in 2 *The Correspondence of General Thomas Gage with the Secretaries of State, and with the War Office and the Treasury 1763–1779* 339 (Clarence Edwin Carter, editor, 1933); Letter from same to same, 7 October 1769, in ibid., 526.

31. Letter from Thomas Gage to the Earl of Shelburne, 3 April 1767, in 1 *The Correspondence*, supra n. 24, at 127.

32. Supra n. 29, at 202.

33. *Boston Evening-Post*, 10 October 1768, p. 4, col. 1–2. See also *The Boston Gazette and Country Journal* (Supplement), 10 October 1768, p. 1, col. 1.

34. Letter from General Thomas Gage to the Earl of Halifax, 23 January 1765, in 1 *The Correspondence*, supra n. 24, at 49.

35. Supra n. 29, at 204.

36. *The Boston Gazette and Country Journal* (Supplement), 10 October 1768, p. 1 col. 1.

37. The Quartering Act of 24 March 1765, in Henry Steele Commager, *Documents of American History* 62 (1934).

38. Zobel, supra n. 2, at 104.

39. Supra n. 29, at 204. For Bernard's account of his strategy, see Answer of Governor Francis Bernard to the Petition Of the House of Representatives to the King (1769), reprinted in 1 *The Writings*, supra n. 26, at 364.

40. The whigs did accuse Bernard of violating the Mutiny Act in this instance, although for political reasons they preferred to rely on the familiar argument that he was not authorized to act until the barracks at the castle were occupied. Petition of the House of Representatives to the King, 27 June 1769, rpt. in 1 *The Writings*, supra n. 26, at 352–53.

41. Letter from the Earl of Hillsborough to General Thomas Gage, 8 June 1768, rpt. in Jensen, supra n. 20, at 717. For a summary of Gage's orders see Zobel, supra n. 2, at 85.

42. Letter from the Earl of Hillsborough to Governor Francis Bernard, 11 July 1768, quoted in John Cary, *Joseph Warren: Physician, Politician, Patriot* 79 (1961). For a summary of the "impossibilities" thrust on Bernard by Hillsborough, see Zobel, supra n. 2, at 85–86.

43. Shy, supra n. 27, at 298.

44. Randolph G. Adams, "New Light on the Boston Massacre," 47 *Proc. Am. Antiquarian Soc.* 259 (1936). Such was the official British position. See Letter from the Earl of Shelburne to General Thomas Gage, 11 December 1766, in 2 *The Correspondence*, supra n. 30, at 48.

45. Letter from General Thomas Gage to the Earl of Hillsborough, 26 September 1768, in 1 *The Correspondence*, supra n. 24, at 196.

46. Ibid., 197. See also Letter from General Thomas Gage to Lord Barrington, 4 February 1769, in 2 *The Correspondence*, supra n. 30, at 499.

47. Letter from General Thomas Gage to Lieutenant Colonel William Dalrymple, 25 September 1769, *Gage Papers* (MS, Clements Library). The New York events to which Gage referred were the activities of the nonimportation association (which used force to seize goods imported by nonmembers) and mob attacks on two customs informers.

48. Message of House of Representatives to Governor Francis Bernard, 13 June 1769, in 1 *The Writings*, supra n. 26, at 345.

49. Letter from Governor Francis Bernard to Lord Barrington, 20 October 1768, rpt. in *The . . . Correspondence*, supra n. 20, at 179.

50. Letter from General Thomas Gage to the Earl of Hillsborough, 31 October 1768, in 1 *The Correspondence*, supra n. 24, at 205.

51. 3 Francis Newton Thorpe (editor), *The Federal and State Constitutions, Colonial Charters, and other Organic Laws of the States, Territories, and Colonies Now or Heretofore Forming the United States of America* 1884 (1909).

52. H.M. Stephens, "Sir Ralph Abercromby," 1 *Dic. Nat. Bio.* 43, 44–45 (1885).

53. Legal historians include E.O. Somerville & Martin Ross, *An Incorruptible Irishman: Being an Account of Chief Justice Charles Kendal Bushe, and of his Wife, Nancy Crampton, and their times, 1767–1843* 84 (1932). Also see Examination of T.A. Emmet before the Secret Committee of the House of Lords, 10 August 1798, rpt. in [Thomas Addis Emmet, Arthur O'Connor, & William James McNevin], *Memoire, or Detailed Statement of the Origin and Progress of the Irish Union Delivered to the Irish Government by Messrs. Emmett [sic], O'Connor, and McNevin; Together with the Examinations of the Gentlemen Before the Secret Committees of the Houses of Lords and Commons, in the Summer of 1798* 33 (1802).

54. Frank MacDermot, *Theobald Wolfe Tone: A Biographical Study* 278 (1939).

55. 7 W.E.H. Lecky, *A History of England in the Eighteenth Century* 428–30 (1891); for a pro-British summary, see 3 James Anthony Froude, *The English In Ireland in the Eighteenth Century* 341–42 (1969 rpt.).

56. Henry S. Eeles, *Lord Chancellor Camden and His Family* 217–20 (1934).

57. Lecky, supra n. 55, at 433.

58. 2 J. Roderick O'Flanagan, *The Lives of the Lord Chancellors and Keepers of the Great Seal of Ireland* 230–31 (1870); Lecky, supra n. 55, at 433–36. For the summary of a Belfast barrister who later became a famous New York lawyer, see William Sampson, *Memoirs of William Sampson* 21 (1807).

59. General Gage, however, did believe that the sheriff was empowered to apply to the military for peacekeeping assistance. Letter from General Thomas Gage to Lieutenant Colonel William Dalrymple, 19 August 1770, *Gage Papers* (MS, Clements Library).

60. Stephen Greenleaf, sheriff of Suffolk county, was an exception. He supported Hutchinson and Bernard yet remained popular with whigs. *Boston Evening-Post* (Supplement), 30 December 1765, p. 2, col. 3; George P. Anderson, "Ebenezer Mackintosh: Stamp Act Rioter and Patriot," 26 *Pub. Col. Soc. Mass.* 15, 41 (1924). Yet on every recorded occasion Greenleaf did not take it upon himself to proclaim a crowd to be rioters. Instead, he sought assistance of magistrates. See, e.g., Declaration of Stephen Greenleaf, 1 October 1766, printed in George G. Wolkins, "Daniel Malcom and Writs of Assistance," 58 *Mass. Hist. Soc. Proc.* 5, 37 (1924).

61. Speech of Thomas Pownall in the House of Commons, 22 April 1774, rpt. in 1 *American Archives: Fourth Series* 75 (Peter Force, editor, 1837). For the opinion of another former governor see Speech of George Johnstone in the House of Commons, 25 March 1774, rpt. in ibid., 55. For the reaction of Hutchinson to these assertions of gubernatorial authority see Entries of 5 July & 19 July 1774, in 1 *The Diary*, supra n. 6, at 183, 194–95.

62. For a detailed discussion, see John Phillip Reid, "In a Constitutional Void: The Enforcement of Imperial Law, the Role of the British Army, and the Coming of the American Revolution," 22 *Wayne Law Rev.* 1, 22–25 (1975).

63. Supra n. 22, at 167.

64. Letter from General Thomas Gage to the Earl of Hillsborough, 7 July 1770, in 1 *The Correspondence*, supra n. 24, at 263.

65. For a summary of how whig law harassed the British troops, "pelting" them with warrants, writs, and indictments, see Zobel, supra n. 2, at 132–44.

12
The Emergence of Whig Government

1. "Committees of Merchants . . . contrive to exercise the Government they have set up, to prohibit the Importation of British Goods, appoint Inspectors, tender Oaths to the Masters of Vessels, and enforce their Prohibitions by coercive Measures. In Times less dissolute, and licentious, it wou'd be matter of Astonishment, to hear that British Manufactures were prohibited in British Provinces, by an illegal Combination of People, who at the same Time, presume to trade under the Protection of the British Flagg in most Parts of the World; and surely wonderfull, that such an Imperium should be set up, and at length established without the least Shew of Opposition." Gage to Barrington, 2 December 1769.

2. Letter from General Thomas Gage to Lord Barrington, 2 December 1769, in 2 *The Correspondence of General Thomas Gage with the Secretaries of State, and with the War Office and the Treasury 1763–1775* 530 (Clarence Edwin Carter, editor, 1933).

3. See, e.g., Agreement of the "Merchants and Traders" of Philadelphia, *Boston Evening-Post*, 25 November 1765, p. 2, col. 2; Agreement of Annapolis, Maryland, 22 June 1769, *The Boston Chronicle*, 13 July 1769, p. 224, col. 1; Solemn League and Covenant of Berkshire County, July 1774, *Boston Evening-Post*, 25 July 1774, p. 2, col. 3.

4. Letter from General Thomas Gage to Lord Barrington, 7 October 1769, in supra n. 2, at 527. See also supra n. 1.

5. Colonies without town meetings depended on mass meetings (Philadelphia), grand-jury resolutions (Delaware), subscription (Charles Town), and provincial conventions (Maryland).

6. Thomas Hutchinson, *The History of the Province of Massachusetts Bay, From 1749 to 1774* 182 (1828).

7. *The Boston Gazette and Country Journal*, 9 October 1769, p. 1, col. 2.

8. *The Massachusetts Gazette and the Boston Weekly Newsletter*, 5 October 1769, p. 3, col. 1; *The Boston Gazette and Country Journal*, 20 November 1769, p. 3, col. 2.

9. Merchants Meeting, 17 January 1770, *The Boston Chronicle*, 1 February 1770, p. 38, col. 1–2; Hiller B. Zobel, *The Boston Massacre* 167 (1970); Bernard Bailyn, *The Ordeal of Thomas Hutchinson* 134–35 (1974).

10. Marblehead Town Meeting, 10 May 1770, *The Essex Gazette*, 15 May 1770, p. 1 col. 1; Portsmouth Town Meeting, *Boston Evening-Post*, 16 April 1770, p. 2, col. 3.

11. Letter from Acting Governor Thomas Hutchinson to the Earl of Hillsborough, 8 August 1769, quoted in Arthur M. Schlesinger, *The Colonial Merchants and the American Revolution, 1763–1776* 163 (1918).

12. *The Boston Gazette and Country Journal*, 7 May 1770, p. 3, col. 1.

13. *The Massachusetts Gazette & the Post Boy and Advertiser*, 2 January 1775, p. 1, col. 3.

14. Letter from Thomas Hutchinson to the Earl of Dartmouth, 2 December 1773, quoted in Benjamin Woods Labaree, *The Boston Tea Party* 125 (Paperback ed., 1968).

15. 14 George III, cap. 19 (1774), 30 *Statutes at Large*, at 336–41.

16. Letter from Governor Thomas Hutchinson to the Earl of Hillsborough, 19 April 1771, quoted in James K. Hosmer, *The Life of Thomas Hutchinson, Royal Governor of the Province of Massachusetts Bay* 206 (1896). It is said that "Hutchinson often complained that the legal requirements were regularly ignored." Supra n. 14, at 124.

17. Letter from Lieutenant Governor Thomas Hutchinson to John Pownall, 26

March 1770, quoted in Hosmer, supra n. 16, at 189. It has been estimated that by 1773 there were 2,500 men in Boston. Supra n. 14, at 124.

18. Statement of Provincial Secretary Andrew Oliver, 13 March 1770, *The Boston Gazette and Country Journal*, 24 September 1770, p. 2, col. 1–2.

19. For example, the Virginia Association, 18 May 1769, *Boston Evening-Post*, 12 June 1769, p. 4, col. 3.

20. Letter from Lord Dunmore to the Earl of Dartmouth, 24 December 1774, quoted in H.E. Egerton, *The Causes and Character of the American Revolution* 112 (1923). For different wording attributed to this letter see 1 *American Archives: Fourth Series* 1061–62 (Peter Force, editor, 1837).

21. Supra n. 6, at 261.

22. Supra n. 14, at 35. See also supra n. 11, at 179; Letter from Lieutenant Governor Thomas Hutchinson to the Earl of Hillsborough, 27 April 1770, paraphrased in Report of the Lords' Committee, 20 April 1774, rpt. in 1 *American Archives*, supra n. 20, at 26.

23. Thus one edition of the *Boston Gazette* published the minutes of a Connecticut town meeting that resolved to publish the names of persons who violated the agreement. Town meeting of Norwich, 29 January 1770, *The Boston Gazette and Country Journal*, 5 February 1770, p. 2, col. 1. On the following page was local Boston news including the following: "The Public is hereby informed that Israel Williams, Junr., . . . has within a few Days past purchased Goods at Wm. Jackson's Shop, Brazen Head, Boston." Ibid., 3, col. 1.

24. Merchants Meeting, 17 January 1770, *The Boston Gazette and Country Journal*, 22 January 1770, p. 3, col. 1; supra n. 6, at 266–67. For another example of the effectiveness of mass visitation, see James K. Hosmer, *Samuel Adams* 140–41 (1899).

25. 4 W.E.H. Lecky, *A History of England in the Eighteenth Century* 536 (1891). In Dublin, however, names were published and a boycott enforced, leading the viceroy to warn that the "faction" was stirring "the mob." Maurice R. O'Connell, *Irish Politics and Social Conflict in the Age of the American Revolution* 136–38 (1965).

26. All the nonimportation agreements contained such expressions. See, e.g., Last [9th] Article, Resolutions of county representatives at Annapolis, Maryland, 29 June 1769, rpt. in [*Nile's*] *Chronicles of the American Revolution* 29–30 (Alden T. Vaughan, editor, 1965).

27. Supra n. 6, at 267.

28. Particularly questions about cashiering officers for quartering troops within Boston's limits. Zobel, supra n. 9, at 170.

29. Supra n. 6, at 267–68.

30. Ibid., 268.

31. Letter from Lieutenant Governor Thomas Hutchinson to the Earl of Hillsborough, 24 January 1770, quoted in Zobel, supra n. 9, at 171.

32. *The Boston Gazette and Country Journal*, 29 January 1770, p. 1, col. 1; *Boston Evening-Post*, 29 January 1770, p. 2, col. 1; supra n. 6, at 268; supra n. 11, at 177.

33. Zobel, supra n. 9, at 170.

34. Supra n. 6, at 268.

35. Letter from Lieutenant Governor Thomas Hutchinson to the Earl of Hillsborough, 24 January 1770, quoted in Zobel, supra n. 9, at 171.

36. Letter from Lieutenant Governor Thomas Hutchinson to Governor Francis Bernard, 28 August 1770, quoted in Hosmer, supra n. 16, at 196. See also same to same, 6 October 1769, quoted in ibid., 166–67.

37. Supra n. 6, at 182.

38. For an excellent legal defense of nonimportation utilizing whig law, see "Determintus," *The Boston Gazette and Country Journal*, 8 January 1770, p. 1. col. 2.

39. Letter from Lieutenant Governor Thomas Hutchinson to the Earl of Hillsborough, 9 October 1770, quoted in Hosmer, supra n. 6, at 168. William Hawkins, *A Treatise of the Pleas of the Crown* Book 1, Ch. 19, Sec. 44, p. 54–55 (1771). Blackstone's definition of *praemunire* was even less applicable. 4 William Blackstone, *Commentaries on the Laws of England* 117 (1769).

40. Ibid., 159; Hawkins, supra n. 39, Book 1, Ch. 80, Sec. 10, at 236.

41. Hawkins, supra n. 39, Book 1, Ch. 17, Sec. 25, at 37.

42. William Henry Drayton of South Carolina formulated the best legal theory for prosecuting nonimportation associations. They were, he argued, illegal confederacies. *The South Carolina Gazette*, 16 November 1769, p. 1, col. 2. Hutchinson also suspected they might be prosecuted as confederacies. Letter from Lieutenant Governor Thomas Hutchinson to Robert Jackson, 4 October 1770, quoted in Hosmer, supra n. 16, at 166; supra n. 11, at 172.

43. *The South Carolina Gazette*, 26 October 1769, p. 1, col. 1.

44. Letter from Andrew Oliver to Thomas Whately, 12 August 1769, *Copy of Letters Sent to Great-Britain, by his Excellency Thomas Hutchinson, the Hon. Andrew Oliver, and several other Persons, Born and Educated Among Us* 35 (1773).

45. Blackstone, supra n. 39, at 123.

46. Resolution of 15 December 1768, rpt. in Report, supra n. 22, at 22.

47. The legal puzzle was recognized in London: "If the combination at Boston is not a breach of any standing law, (which I believe it is) ought it not to be immediately declared so by an act of the legislature? It is true, that private persons cannot be compelled to buy or sell against their will; but unlawful combinations, supported by public subscription and public engagements, are and ought to be subject to the heaviest penalties of the law." *London Public Advertiser*, 16 December 1767, quoted in *Boston Evening-Post*, 29 February 1768, p. 2, col. 3.

48. Massachusetts Circular Letter to Colonial Legislatures, 11 February 1768, rpt. in Merrill Jensen (editor), 9 *English Historical Documents: American Colonial Documents to 1776* 714–16 (1955); Hosmer, supra n. 16, at 139; supra n. 6, at 204.

49. Hutchinson, supra n. 6, at 204.

50. Resolutions of the Boston Town Meeting, 13 September 1768, Jensen, supra n. 48, at 719–20; for Adams's theory, see Report of the Town of Boston, 23 March 1773, rpt. in 3 *The Writings of Samuel Adams* 5–6 (Harry Alonzo Cushing, editor, 1907).

51. Richard D. Brown, "The Massachusetts Convention of Towns, 1768," 26 *Will. & Mary Q.* 94 (1969). Barely half the delegates had served in the previous session of the general court. Ibid., 95.

52. Supra n. 6, at 206.

53. See, e.g., Letter from General Thomas Gage to Lord Barrington, 26 September 1768, supra n. 2, at 488; Letter from Lord Barrington to Governor Francis Bernard, 12 February 1768, in *The Barrington-Bernard Correspondence* 184 (Edward Channing & Archibald Cary Coolidge, editors, 1912); and for Bernard calling it "treason," Catherine Drinker Bowen, *John Adams and the American Revolution* 325–27 (1950).

54. Anon., *An Impartial History of the War in America Between Great Britain and Her Colonies* 88–89 (1780). See also John C. Miller, *Sam Adams: Pioneer in Propaganda* 161 (1936).

55. Supra n. 6, at 210.

56. Letter from John Fitzgibbon to the High Sheriffs, 10 September 1784, rpt. in 2

NOTES

J. Roderick O'Flanagan, *The Lives of the Lord Chancellors and Keepers of the Great Seal of Ireland* 174–75 (1870).

57. Supra n. 6, at 206.

58. Supra n. 56, at 176–77; 2 James Anthony Froude, *The English in Ireland in the Eighteenth Century* 419n1 (1969 rpt.).

59. Supra n. 56, at 177–78; Froude, supra n. 58.

60. Discussion here and in the two following paragraphs based on Letter of 17 November 1792, in 3 Froude, *The English in Ireland in the Eighteenth Century* 58, 59, 69–70,72 (1969 rpt.).

61. Ibid., 115; Frank MacDermot, *Theobald Wolfe Tone: A Biographical Study* 123 (1939); supra n. 56, at 215 n1.

62. Supra n. 56, at 215.

63. William Henry Curran, *The Life of the Right Honourable John Philpot Curran* 156 (1820).

64. Letter from Governor Francis Bernard to —— ——, 23 December 1768, in *The . . . Correspondence*, supra n. 53, at 254.

65. Letter from Lord Barrington, supra n. 53, at 184; supra n. 64, at 254.

66. Supra n. 64, at 256–57.

67. Supra n. 6, at 206.

68. Resolves of Parliament and Address to the King, 9 February 1769, Jensen, supra n. 48, at 721–22.

69. Supra n. 6, at 218–19.

70. Supra n. 68, at 722. This was the same statute of Henry that the British would be unable to enforce in the case of the *Gaspee*. See supra Ch. 9, text from n. 3 to n. 6.

71. Letter from General Thomas Gage to Lord Barrington, 14 May 1769, supra n. 2, at 509–10.

72. Letter from Governor Francis Bernard to Lord Barrington, 18 March 1769, in *The . . . Correspondence*, supra n. 53, at 197.

73. 8 W.E.H. Lecky, *A History of England in the Eighteenth Century* 19–30 (1891).

74. Ibid., 24–30.

75. 1 *The Diary and Letters of His Excellency Thomas Hutchinson, Esq.* 207 (Peter Orlando Hutchinson, editor, 1883).

76. Supra n. 6, at 173; Hosmer, supra n. 16, at 166–67.

77. Letter from Lieutenant Governor Thomas Hutchinson to Governor Francis Bernard, 6 October 1769, quoted in Hosmer, supra n. 16, at 166–67.

78. Letter from Former Governor Thomas Hutchinson to the Earl of Dartmouth, February 1774, supra n. 75, at 115.

79. Quoted in supra n. 11, at 175. See also Hosmer, supra n. 24, at 175.

80. See Resolutions of the Massachusetts House of Representatives, 28 May 1773, supra n. 26, at 62–63.

81. Hosmer, supra n. 16, at 250; supra n. 6, at 398.

82. Letter from Lieutenant Governor Thomas Hutchinson to the Earl of Hillsborough, [10] March 1770, rpt. in *Proc. Mass. Hist. Soc.* 483, 485–86 (1863); supra n. 6, at 273–77. Hutchinson believed he did not have constitutional power to order the troops out of Boston. Frederic Kidder, *History of the Boston Massacre, March 5, 1770, Consisting of the Narrative of the Town, the Trial of the Soldiers and a Historical Introduction* 43 (1870).

83. Letter from Governor Thomas Gage to the Earl of Dartmouth, 30 October 1774, in 1 *The Correspondence of General Thomas Gage With the Secretaries of State 1763–1775* 383 (Clarence Edwin Carter, editor, 1931).

84. Letter from Governor Thomas Gage to the Earl of Dartmouth, 17 February 1775, ibid., 392.

85. Letter from Governor Thomas Gage to the Earl of Dartmouth, 25 June 1775, in ibid., 408.

13
The Irish Comparison

1. "Although the French Revolution and Jacobin principles may be the immediate cause of the events which have lately taken place in Ireland, yet the remote and ultimate cause must be derived from its true origin, the oppression of centuries." Sir Ralph Abercromby, quoted in 7 W.E.H. Lecky, *A History of England in the Eighteenth Century* 439 (1891).

2. Charles Phillips, *Curran and His Contemporaries* 80 (3d ed., 1857).

3. Ibid., 219.

4. 1 James Anthony Froude, *The English in Ireland in the Eighteenth Century* 409–10 (1881).

5. J.C. Beckett, *The Making of Modern Ireland 1603–1923* 176 (1966).

6. Supra n. 4, at 413, 415.

7. Supra n. 5, at 176.

8. Ibid., 177; 4 W.E.H. Lecky, *A History of England in the Eighteenth Century* 337 (1891).

9. The movement was savage and widespread enough to be noted in colonial newspapers. See, e.g., *Boston Evening-Post*, 31 May 1773, p. 4, col. 2. For the tithe, supra n. 5, at 177; Henry S. Eeles, *Lord Chancellor Camden and His Family* 204 (1934).

10. 4 Lecky, supra n. 8, at 353.

11. Speech of 31 January 1787, quoted in 2 James Anthony Froude, *The English in Ireland in the Eighteenth Century* 476–77 (1881).

12. Ibid., 476, 478, 483.

13. Supra n. 5, at 178.

14. Supra n. 11, at 120.

15. Ibid., 119.

16. By the next year it was reported that hardly a ship sailed from Ireland for America but was "filled with multitudes of useful artisans, their wives and children." Extract of a letter from Dublin, 16 August 1773, *Boston Evening-Post*, 1 November 1773, p. 1, col. 2. Irish immigrants were arriving in great numbers in New York. *Boston Evening-Post*, 26 July 1773, p. 2, col. 3. The migration and its potential menace were not missed by the British military. "Emigrants from Ireland have arrived also at Philadelphia, where we are informed Arms were immediately put in their hands upon their landing. There are many Irish in the Rebel Army, particularly amongst the Rifle-Men." Letter from General Thomas Gage to the Earl of Dartmouth, 20 September 1775, in 1 *The Correspondence of General Thomas Gage with the Secretaries of State 1763–1775* 415 (Clarence Edwin Carter, editor, 1931).

17. H.M. Hyde, *The Rise of Castlereagh* 72 (1933); supra n. 1, at 15.

18. Supra n. 11, at 408–9. See also E. Œ. Somerville & Martin Ross, *An Incorruptible Irishman, Being an Account of Chief Justice Charles Kendal Bushe, and his wife Nancy Crampton, and their times, 1767–1843* 67–68 (1932).

19. Supra n. 11, at 411–12.

20. Letter from the Duke of Rutland to Lord Sydney, 25 August 1784, quoted in ibid., 412.

21. 1 Thomas Addis Emmet, *Memoir of Thomas Addis and Robert Emmet with their Ancestors and Immediate Family* 100 (1915).

22. Supra n. 1, at 172.

23. Letter from Lord Lieutenant Camden to the Duke of Portland, 6 November 1795, rpt. in ibid., 172n1.

24. Quotes in this paragraph from Letter from Lord Lieutenant Camden to Chief Secretary Pelham, 30 October 1795, quoted in ibid., 173 n1, 173.

25. The Insurrection Act, 1796, rpt. in *Irish Historical Documents 1172–1922* 207–8 (Edmund Curtis & R.B. McDowell, editors, 1943). For discussion see supra n. 1, at 195; Hyde, supra n. 17, at 142.

26. Hyde, supra n. 17, at 142; supra n. 5, at 257.

27. Hyde, supra n. 17, at 142.

28. Supra n. 5, at 257.

29. After his arrest in 1798, Arthur O'Connor, one of the leaders of the United Irishmen, was questioned by a secret committee of the House of Commons. During the interrogation, Lord Castlereagh asserted that the government had nothing to do with the Orangemen or their "oath of extermination." To that statement O'Connor replied: "You, my Lord, from the station you fill, must be sensible that the Executive of any country has it in its power to collect a vast mass of information, and you must know from the secret nature, and the zeal of the Untion [i.e., United Irishmen], that its Executive must have the most minute information of every act of the Irish Government. As one of the Executive, it came to my knowledge, that considerable sums of money were expended throughout the nation in endeavouring to extend the Orange system, and that the Orange oath of extermination was administered; when these facts are coupled, not only with general impunity, which has been uniformly extended towards all the acts of this infernal association, but the marked encouragement its members have received from Government, I find it impossible to exculpate the Government from being the parent and protector of these sworn extirpators." Examination of Arthur O'Connor before the Secret Committee of the House of Commons, 16 August 1798, in *Memoire, Or, Detailed Statement of the Origin and Progress of the Irish Union Delivered to the Irish Government by Messrs. [Thomas Addis] Emmett [sic], [Arthur] O'Connor, and [William James] McNevin; Together with the Examinations of the Gentlemen Before the Secret Committees of the Houses of Lords and Commons, in the Summer of 1798* 53 (1802).

30. See e.g., Examination of William James McNevin before the Secret Committee of the House of Lords, 7 August 1798, supra n. 29, at 71. See also Letter from Lord Lieutenant Fitzwilliam to the Duke of Portland, January 1795, quoted in supra n. 1, at 53–54.

31. Supra n. 1, at 150.

32. Supra n. 4, at 441.

33. Letter from Governor Francis Bernard to Lord Barrington, 5 July 1766, in *The Barrington-Bernard Correspondence* 110 (Edward Channing & Archibald Cary Coolidge, editors, 1912).

34. Supra n. 2, at 38.

35. Examination of T.A. Emmett [sic] before the Secret Committee of the House of Lords, 10 August 1798, supra n. 29, at 33–34.

14
The Legal Mind of British-Ruled Ireland

1. "*Secret Committee of the House of Commons*: What do you think would tranquilize the people of Ireland, and induce them to give up their arms?

"*Arthur O'Connor*: That is a question which would require the best head to answer, and the best heart to execute; I am not so ignorant of human nature as to suppose, that those men who have so long engrossed the enormous emoluments of ill, and unjusly acquired power, will ever restore them to the people, however manifest it must appear to an unprejudiced mind, that the most dreadful ruin awaits the present fruitless effort which is made to retain them." From the Examination of Arthur O'Connor before the Secret Committee of the House of Commons, 16 August 1798, in *Memoire, or, Detailed Statement of the Origin and Progress of the Irish Union Delivered to the Irish Government by Messrs. [Thomas Addis] Emmett [sic], [Arthur] O'Connor, and [William James] McNevin; Together with the Examinations of the Gentlemen Before the Secret Committees of the Houses of Lords and Commons, in the Summer of 1798* 57 (1802).

2. Examination of William James McNevin before the Secret Committee of the House of Lords, 7 August 1798, supra n. 1, at 71.

3. 2 James Anthony Froude, *The English in Ireland in the Eighteenth Century* 433 (1881).

4. "The declaration, resolutions, and constitution of the societies of United Irishmen," rpt. in *Irish Historical Documents 1172–1922* 238–39 (Edmund Curtis & R.B. McDowell, editors, 1943).

5. 7 W.E.H. Lecky, *A History of England in the Eighteenth Century* 362–63 (1891).

6. Supra n. 4, at 237–38.

7. 3 James Anthony Froude, *The English in Ireland in the Eighteenth Century* 105–6 (1881).

8. Letter from Governor Francis Bernard to Lord Barrington, 20 October 1768, *The Barrington-Bernard Correspondence* 179 (Edward Channing & Archibald Cary Coolidge, editors, 1912).

9. Frank MacDermot, *Theobold Wolfe Tone: A Biographical Study* 53 (1939).

10. Arthur O'Connor, *State of Ireland* 131, 133 [1798].

11. 6 W.E.H. Lecky, *A History of England in the Eighteenth Century* 161 (1891).

12. 1 Thomas Addis Emmet, *Memoir of Thomas Addis and Robert Emmet with their Ancestors and Immediate Family* 79–80 (1915).

13. J.C. Beckett, *The Making of Modern Ireland 1603–1923* 252 (1966). But see supra n. 2, at 18.

14. Supra n. 3, at 501.

15. Supra n. 9, at 40; G.P. MacDonell, "John Fitzgibbon, Earl of Clare," 19 *Dic. Nat. Bio.* 156–57 (1889); Beckett, supra n. 13, at 235–36, 270; supra n. 3, at 258–59.

16. Supra n. 9, at 41.

17. Supra n. 7, at 91–92.

18. See supra Ch. 13, text to note 25; supra n. 9, at 226–27; H.M. Hyde, *The Rise of Castlereagh* 159 (1933).

19. Supra n. 5, at 197.

20. William Sampson, *Memoirs of William Sampson* 30 (1807).

21. The Insurrection Act of 1796, supra n. 4, at 204–8.

22. For public reaction to Orr's trial and execution, see supra n. 5, at 351–52. For

Orr's own comment on the law and a comment by a defense attorney, see supra n. 20, at 430.

23. Anon., *Forensic Eloquence: Sketches of the Trials in Ireland High Treason, Etc. Including the Speeches of Mr. Curran at Length to Which are Prefixed, a Brief Sketch of the History of Ireland, and a Biographical Account of Mr. Curran: With an Elegant Engraved Likeness of that Orator* 432 (1805).

24. See Letter from Arthur O'Connor to C.J. Fox, 24 December 1796, quoted in supra n. 5, at 225.

25. Examination of Thomas Addis Emmett [sic] before the Secret Committee of the House of Commons, 14 August 1798, supra n. 2, at 95.

26. Frederick C. Hicks, "Thomas Addis Emmet," 6 *Dic. Am. Bio.* 145, 146 (1931).

27. Examination of Arthur O'Connor before the Secret Committee of the House of Commons, 16 August 1798, supra n. 1, at 46–47.

28. 4,000 was O'Connor's figure. Ibid.

29. Ibid., 17.

30. Letter from Lord Lieutenant Charles Cornwallis to the Duke of Portland, 8 July 1798, quoted in supra n. 9, at 284.

31. Letter from Lord Cornwallis to General Ross, 24 July 1798, quoted in ibid., 285.

32. Letter of General Hutchinson, quoted in ibid., 308.

33. Letter from Lord Lieutenant Camden to the Duke of Portland, 18 May 1797, quoted in supra n. 7, at 254.

34. Speech of 16 May 1797, quoted in ibid., 259.

35. For example, thirty-two years earlier newspaper readers in America learn this fact from a writer complaining of Catholic Whiteboys of Munster and Presbyterian Oakboys of Ulster, but most of all of the discontent of Catholic tenants in the south: "This is the present state of the Southern provinces, and will never be effectively remedied, 'till a Protestant militia be set on a more extensive footing, paid as in England; and in the counties where Protestants enough are not to be had, Protestants be brought to settle and for some years be paid enough annually to maintain them out of the public treasury." *The South-Carolina Gazette*, 6 October 1766, p. 2, col. 2.

36. Letter from Lord Lieutenant Camden to the Duke of Portland, 11 March 1798, quoted in supra n. 7, at 322; Thomas Pakenham, *The Year of Liberty: The Story of the Great Irish Rebellion of 1798* 45 (1969).

37. "Your next Despatches will probably require a different Conduct, and I shall wait for them impatiently as I conclude they will require me to make Many preparations to act Offensively; for to keep quiet in the Town of Boston only, will not terminate Affairs; the Troops must March into the Country." Letter from Governor Thomas Gage to Lord Barrington, 10 February 1775, in 2 *The Correspondence of General Thomas Gage with the Secretaries of State, and with the War Office and the Treasury 1763–1775* 669 (Clarence Edwin Carter, editor, 1933).

15

The Execution of Imperial Law

1. "If our meer object had been to effect a revolution, the British Ministry, and the Irish Government were effecting one more violently and rapidly than we wished for; we clearly perceived, that the measures they adopted to prevent revolution, were the most effectual that could be devised to ensure it. When we viewed the state of the British empire, we were convinced we need not take much pains merely to make revolution."

From the Examination of Arthur O'Connor before the Secret Committee of the House of Commons, 16 August 1798, in *Memoire, or, Detailed Statement of the Origin and Progress of the Irish Union Delivered to the Irish Government by Messrs.* [*Thomas Addis*]*Emmett* [*sic*], [*Arthur*] *O'Connor, and* [*William James*]*McNevin; Together with the Examinations of the Gentlemen Before the Secret Committees of the Houses of Lords and Commons, in the Summer of 1798* 51 (1802).

2. See discussion supra Ch. 11, text between n. 50 and 51. It is true that Gage could have arrested whigs for trial in England under the statute of Henry VIII. Following John Sullivan's raid on Fort William and Mary in Portsmouth Harbor, the attorney and solicitor generals in London had been pressured to rule that "persons guilty of Treason in America may either be prosecuted there, or in this Kingdom, under the Statute of King Henry the Eighth." Letter from the Earl of Dartmouth to Governor Thomas Gage, 15 April 1775, in 2 *The Correspondence of General Thomas Gage with the Secretaries of State, and with the War Office and the Treasury 1763–1775* 196 (Clarence Edwin Carter, editor, 1933). The charge had to be treason and Gage knew it was almost impossible to gather evidence to satisfy the burden of proof required for conviction. He had attempted to do so with regard to the Tea Party and did not even obtain the name of a single participant. If he could not do so after so open and public an affair, he could not hope to get testimony concerning other whig conspiracies, many of which were secret and underground. For the same reason he would not have found law-martial courts very effective. In Ireland the evidence would have been purchased from informers if the government desired a trial. If not, it would have merely locked up Samuel Adams, John Hancock, and James Bowdoin just as it did O'Connor, Emmet, and McNevin.

3. J.C. Beckett, *The Making of Modern Ireland 1603–1923* 260 (1966); Frank MacDermot, *Theobald Wolfe Tone: A Biographical Study* 228 (1939); 7 W.E.H. Lecky, *A History of England in the Eighteenth Century* 301 (1891).

4. 7 Lecky, supra n. 3, at 302. For other details see Thomas Pakenham, *The Year of Liberty: The Story of the Great Irish Rebellion of 1798* 61–73 (1969).

5. Beckett, supra n. 3, at 260.

6. 7 Lecky, supra n. 3, at 444–45. A similar law was passed in 1796 providing: "Whereas, to preserve the public peace, magistrates and other officers have apprehended and sent suspected persons out of the kingdom, have seized arms and entered houses, and done divers acts not justifiable according to law, all suits for things done to preserve the public peace since January 1, 1795, shall be void." Quoted in 3 James Anthony Froude, *The English in Ireland in the Eighteenth Century* 172n1 (1881).

7. Beckett, supra n. 3, at 261–62.

8. 7 Lecky, supra n. 3, at 430.

9. MacDermot, supra n. 3, at 279; Thomas Pakenham, *The Year of Liberty: The Story of the Great Irish Rebellion of 1798* 55 (1969).

10. 2 Sir Jonah Barrington, *Personal Sketches of His Times* 349–50, 353, 372 (Townsend Young, editor, 3d ed., 1871).

11. H.M. Hyde, *The Rise of Castlereagh* 153 (1933).

12. William Sampson, *Memoirs of William Sampson* 345 (1807). Had Sampson been candid he could have conceded some cause for suspicion as he once presided over a Protestant meeting that petitioned for Catholic civil rights.

13. Describing Dublin in 1798, Sampson wrote: "In every quarter of the metropolis, the shrieks and groans of the tortured were to be heard, and that, through all hours of the day and night. Men were taken at random, without process or accusation, and tortured at the pleasure of the lowest dregs of the community." Ibid., 4.

14. Ibid., 433.

15. Ibid., 32–33.

16. O'Connor, Emmet, and McNevin, in supra n. 1, at 23–24; Examination of Thomas Addis Emmett [sic] before the Secret Committee of the House of Lords, 10 August 1798, in ibid., 33.

17. "In a cause like this, success is everything. Success, in the eyes of the vulgar, fixes its merits. Washington succeeded and Kosciuszko failed." Tone quoted in Charles Phillips, *Curran and His Contemporaries* 199 (3d ed., 1857).

18. Report of the Secret Committee of the House of Lords, quoted in 8 W.E.H. Lecky, *A History of England in the Eighteenth Century* 31 (1891). On pp. 32, 33 Lecky has written perhaps the best summary of the causes of the Rising of '98 as they related to the condition of law then existing in Ireland: "It was a desperate policy, and it had desperate results. If regarded purely as a military measure, it was certainly successful, but it must be added that it was largely responsible for the ferocity with which the rebellion was waged, and that it contributed enormously to the most permanent and deadly evils of Irish life. The hatred and distrust of law and Government, the inveterate proneness to seek redress by secret combination and by barbarous crimes, the savage animosities of class and creed and party, that make Irish government so difficult, were not created, but they were all immensely strengthened, by the events which I am relating. It must be added, too, that if martial law forced the rebellion into a premature explosion, and thus made it comparatively easy to deal with it, it also undoubtedly turned into desperate rebels multitudes who, if they had been left unmolested, would have been, if not loyal subjects, at least either neutral spectators or lukewarm and half-hearted rebels. . . . The worst and most dangerous men came inevitably to the front. Many crimes were committed. There was no regular and well-disciplined force like the modern constabulary sufficiently powerful to maintain the peace. Martial law was declared, and the tortures, the house burnings, and other manifold abuses that followed it soon completed the work, and drove the people in large districts to desperation and madness."

19. Edgar Holt, *Protest in Arms: The Irish Troubles 1916–1923* 69, 118–19, 139, 190, 222 (1961).

20. 2 F. Elrington Ball, *The Judges of Ireland 1221–1921* 262–64 (1927).

21. Darrell Figgis, *Recollections of the Irish War* 217–18 (n.d.)

22. Supra n. 19, at 219, 238; see also 217–21.

23. Supra n. 21, at 298–300.

24. See supra n. 19, at 118.

16

The Rule of Law

1. "Your Lordship is acquainted with the Usurpation and Tyranny establish'd here by Edicts of Town Meetings enforced by Mobs, by assuming the sole Use and Power of the Press, and influencing the Pulpits; by nominating and intimidating of Juries, and in some Instances threatening the Judges. And this Usurpation has by Time acquired a Firmness I fear is not to be annihilated at once, or by ordinary Methods. A free and impartial Course of Justice whereby Delinquents can be brought to Punishment I apprehend to be the chief Thing wanting." Gage to Dartmouth, 5 July 1774.

2. Edgar Holt, *Protest in Arms: The Irish Troubles 1916–1923* 241 (1961).

3. "Self-preservation was the motive which drove me into rebellion," one of those leaders later explained. "As to effecting a change of Government, it gave me little

trouble or thought. . . . The poor people engaged in the Irish rebellion of 1798 had very little idea of political government. Their minds were more occupied with their own sufferings or enjoyments; and many, I might say most, were compelled to join in the rebellion on pain of death." 8 W.E.H. Lecky, *A History of England in the Eighteenth Century* 33 (1891).

4. 4 George III, cap. 15, sec. 46 (1764), 26 *Statutes at Large*, at 51. This provision is discussed supra Ch. 4, n. 44. For an argument that the "probable cause" proviso was manipulated by customs men in an abusive manner, see Edmund S. Morgan, *The Birth of the Republic, 1763–98* 38 (1956).

5. Hutchinson told the commissioners of the customs they were about to be indicted for slandering the people of Boston. Thomas C. Barrow, *Trade and Empire: The British Customs Service in Colonial America 1660–1775* 237, 320n27 (1967). When Gage was indicted along with the customs men Hutchinson wrote to him: "The day after the business of the Superior Court was finished, the Clerk set out upon a journey to New Hampshire and did not return until Monday last and having orders from the Court to give no copies of the extraordinary indictments he did not lodge them with the rest. I always intended to forward a copy to you thinking it not impossible that you would chuse to forward it to the Ministry." Letter from Acting Governor Thomas Hutchinson to General Thomas Gage, 10 January 1770, *Gage Papers* (MS, Clements Library).

6. John R. Howe, Jr., *The Changing Political Thought of John Adams* 11–14 (1966).

7. See supra Ch. 9, text to n. 19. Thomas Hutchinson understood the same distinction when the magistrates of Boston told him that they had no duty to protect John Mein, the tory newspaper editor, from a whig mob as he was an enemy of the people, but that they should have dispersed a mob that had attacked a sailor mistakenly believed to be a customs informer. Thomas Hutchinson, *The History of the Province of Massachusetts Bay, From 1749 to 1774* 260–61 (1828).

8. Quoted in Benjamin Woods Labaree, *The Boston Tea Party* 168 (Paperback ed., 1968). A year later Galloway argued that whig America was "governed by the barbarian rule of frantic folly, and lawless ambition . . . freedom of speech suppressed, the liberty and secrecy of the press destroyed, the voice of truth silenced; a lawless power established throughout the Colonies, forming laws for the government of their conduct, depriving men of their natural rights, and inflicting penalties more severe than death itself, upon a disobedience to their edicts." Julian P. Boyd, *Anglo-American Union: Joseph Galloway's Plans to Preserve the British Empire, 1774–1788* 45–46 (1941).

9. Wallace Brown, *The Good Americans: The Loyalists in the American Revolution* 74 (Paperback ed., 1969).

10. Lillie refused to join the nonimportation association. The whigs fixed a sign reading "IMPORTER" pointing to his house that gathered a group of boys on a school holiday. Richardson, angered by the crowd, tore down the sign and the mob chased him into his house. See supra Ch. 6, text between notes 4 and 6.

11. Defense of Theophilus Lillie, 9 January 1770, *Boston Evening-Post*, 15 January 1770, p. 4, col. 3.

12. Letter from Governor Thomas Gage to the Earl of Dartmouth, 25 June 1775, in 1 *The Correspondence of General Thomas Gage with the Secretaries of State 1763–1775* 408 (Clarence Edwin Carter, editor, 1931).

13. See Gordon S. Wood, *The Creation of the American Republic 1776–1787* 18–45 (Norton Library ed., 1972).

14. Josiah Quincy, *Memoir of the Life of Josiah Quincy, Jr., of Massachusetts: 1744–1775* 304 (1874).

15. The words are Hutchinson's. See supra Ch. 2, text to n. 19.

16. 4 *The Works of John Adams* 230 (Charles Francis Adams, editor, 1851).

17. For a clear statement of the legal issues raised by a loyalist lawyer, see Letter from Peter Van Schaack to the New York Provincial Convention, 25 January 1777, in *The American Tory* 46–47 (Morton Borden & Penn Borden, editors, 1972).

18. Howard Mumford Jones, *O Strange New World* 290 (1964); Richard Hofstader & Michael Wallace, *American Violence: A Documentary History* 13–14 (1970).

19. Jones, supra n. 18, at 292.

20. For prerevolutionary era see discussion supra Ch. 9 and 10, and John Phillip Reid, "In a Defensive Rage: the Uses of the Mob, the Justification in Law, and the Coming of the American Revolution," 49 *N.Y.U. Law Rev.* 1043 (1974). For the nineteenth century see Richard Maxwell Brown, "Legal and Behavioral Perspectives of American Vigilantism," in 5 *Perspectives in American History* 95 (Donald Fleming & Bernard Bailyn, editors, 1971); David Grimsted, "Rioting in Its Jacksonian Setting," 77 *Am. Hist. Rev.* 361 (1972).

21. Jones, supra n. 18, at 292. Though it may have seemed so to American tories it was not non-English. See Reid, supra n. 20, at 1067–69.

22. Supra n. 13, at 95. For a discussion of this attitude, see Mary Beth Norton, "The Loyalist Critique of the Revolution," in *The Development of a Revolutionary Mentality* 127, 142 (First Library of Congress Symposium on the American Revolution, 1972).

23. Supra n. 9, at 77.

24. See argument, Hiller B. Zobel, *The Boston Massacre* 28 (1970).

25. 1 *Pamphlets of the American Revolution, 1750–1776* 581 (Bernard Bailyn, editor, 1965).

26. See discussion, supra n. 24, at 28. See also James K. Hosmer, *The Life of Thomas Hutchinson, Royal Governor of the Province of Massachusetts Bay* 307 (1896).

27. Not only in the prerevolutionary era but also after the war began. See supra n. 9, at 133–39.

28. See, e.g., letter of 8 December 1765, quoted in 1 Mays, *Edmund Pendleton* 167–68 (1952); "Their plan was to get me into the Custody of the Officer & it being then dark, to knock [me] on the head; & then their usual saying might have been repeated that it was done by Boys & Negroes, or by Nobody" (Supra n. 24, at 158–59); Letter from Lieutenant Governor Thomas Hutchinson to Thomas Whately, August 1768, in *Copy of Letters Sent to Great-Britain by His Excellency Thomas Hutchinson, The Hon. Andrew Oliver, and Several Other Persons Born and Educated Among Us* 6 (1773).

29. Letter from Lieutenant Governor Thomas Hutchinson to Thomas Whately, 4 October 1768, supra n. 28, at 10. Hutchinson attributed his nephew's death to his stubborn opposition to the nonimportation movement. It was hastened "by anxiety of mind, from the abuse he has met with and he was seized coming out of a Justice's house, to whom he had applied for a Warrant against a fellow who had attacked his House a few nights before." Letter from Governor Thomas Hutchinson to General Thomas Gage, 19 August 1770, *Gage Papers* (MS, Clements Library). Another tragedy may have been the daughter of Benjamin Hallowell, customs official at Boston. He claimed that due to the harassment of Bostonians his daughter was deprived of her reason and died at age fifteen. E. Alfred Jones, *The Loyalists of Massachusetts: Their Memorials, Petitions and Claims* 158 (1930).

30. Letter from Mrs. Barnes to Elizabeth Smith, June 1770, in *Letters of James Murray Loyalist* 178 (Nina Moore Tiffany, editor, 1901). For a series of such letters see *Letters of a Loyalist Lady: Being the Letters of Anne Hulton, sister of Henry Hulton, Commissioner of Customs at Boston, 1767–1776* (1927).

31. 2 *The Works of John Adams* 328 (Charles Francis Adams, editor, 1851); *Peter*

Oliver's Origin & Progress of the American Rebellion: A Tory View 111n21 (Douglass Adair & John A. Schutz, editors, 1961); *Quincy Reports* 168–71 (1865).

32. Letter from Chief Justice Thomas Hutchinson to Richard Jackson, 30 August 1765, quoted in Hosmer, supra n. 26, at 93.

33. Letter from Peggy Hutchinson to Polly Hutchinson, 25 January 1774, in 1 *The Diary and Letters of His Excellency Thomas Hutchinson, Esq.* 108 (Peter Orlando Hutchinson, editor, 1883).

34. Quoted in Francis S. Drake, *Tea Leaves: Being a Collection of Letters and Documents Relating to the Shipment of Tea to the American Colonies in the Year 1773, by the East India Tea Company* 325n1 (1884).

35. Letter from Thomas Hutchinson, Jr., to Elisha Hutchinson, 7 March 1774, supra n. 33, at 129–30.

36. Hosmer, supra n. 26, at 314.

37. Supra, text to n. 25.

38. 2 J. Roderick O'Flanagan, *The Lives of the Lord Chancellors and Keepers of the Great Seal of Ireland* 282–83 (1870); G.P. MacDonell, "John Fitzgibbon, Earl of Clare," 19 *Dic. Nat. Bio.* 156, 158 (1889).

39. Supra, text to n.25.

40. Jesse Lemisch, "The American Revolution Seen From the Bottom Up," in *Towards a New Past: Dissenting Essays in American History* 20 (Barton J. Bernstein, editor, 1968).

41. 3 W.E.H. Lecky, *A History of England in the Eighteenth Century* 400–401 (1891).

42. Arthur M. Schlesinger, "Political Mobs and the American Revolution, 1765–1776," 99 *Proc. Am. Philosophical Soc.* 244, 246–47 (1955).

43. Supra n. 25, at 583.

44. See, e.g., William Hutton, *The Life of William Hutton, F.A.S.S. including a Particular Account of the Riots at Birmingham in 1791* 248–71 (1817).

45. Donald Greer, *The Incidence of the Terror During the French Revolution* 37 (1935).

46. Gordon S. Wood, "A Note on Mobs in the American Revolution," 23 *Will. & Mary Q.* 635, 638 (1966).

47. "In the great English riots of the 1730's to 1840's, whether urban or rural, there were remarkably few fatal casualties among the rioters' victims. There were none at all in the Wilkite, Birmingham, Bristol, anti-Irish, 'No Popery,' and 'Swing' and other rural disturbances; not even in the armed rising at Newport in 1839. . . . No farmer, miller, magistrate, or forestaller appears to have been fatally injured in the riots of 1766. . . . This record contrasts sharply with the toll of life exacted among the rioters by the military and the law courts. Twenty-five Gordon rioters were hanged in 1780, a dozen or more food rioters in 1766, 8 London coal heavers and 2 (or maybe 3) weavers in 1769, 30 or more Luddites in 1812–13, and 9 'Swing' rioters in 1830. The military took a far heavier toll: 5 rioters were shot at Norwich in 1740; 10 were killed and 24 wounded in the West Riding turnpike riots of 1753; over 100 colliers were killed or wounded at Hexham in 1761; 8 rioters were shot dead at Kidderminster, 8 at Warwick, 2 at Frome, and 1 at Stroud in the food riots of 1766; 11 demonstrators (they were hardly rioters) were shot dead at St. George's Fields in London in 1768; 285 were killed outright or died of wounds in the Gordon Riots." George Rude, *The Crowd in History: A Study of Popular Disturbances in France and England 1730–1848* 255 (1964).

48. For example, the various riots in New York City for possession of the Liberty Pole. *The Boston Gazette and Country Journal*, 5 February 1770, p. 2, col. 3; *The Boston Chronicle*, 8 February 1770, p. 46, col. 3.

49. 3 James Anthony Froude, *The English in Ireland in the Eighteenth Century* 166–67 (1881).

50. Supra n. 2, at 229.

51. It is submitted that Adams's speech to the Boston "body" on 30 November 1773 during the Tea Party crisis would easily have been adjudged treason in Ireland and might have been in England under the statute of Henry VIII had Governor Thomas Gage been able to obtain two witnesses willing to testify. (In Ireland he would have needed only one.) L.F.S. Upton (editor), "Proceedings of Ye Body Respecting the Tea," 22 *Will. & Mary Q.* 287, 292–93 (1965).

52. See suggestion to this effect, supra n. 46, at 639–40.

Acknowledgments

This study of the conditions of law in prerevolutionary Massachusetts was begun in response to a request by G.O.W. Mueller, the Chief of the United Nations Crime Prevention and Criminal Justice Section, and Edward M. Wise of Wayne State Law School that I contribute to a volume of essays they were preparing in honor of Jerome Hall. The article written for them appeared in *Studies in Comparative Criminal Law Dedicated to Jerome Hall*, published in 1974 by Charles C. Thomas. That paper is now Chapter 4 of this book, thanks to the cooperation of Professors Mueller and Wise. As this work was written during a transcontinental trip, it could not have been completed without the generous hospitality of Joseph Ryan of Naples, Florida, and William and Jane Walsh of Woodside, California. My first insight into the important contribution made by Franklin Pierce to the historiography of the American Revolution was furnished by my sister, Susan, as we drove through the state of Sonora, Mexico. A debt of gratitude is also due Martha Ephraim, Wendy Van Bellingham, Gerald Klein, Scott Singer, and a very special one to the enthusiastic and dedicated cooperation of Christian Adams. Among professional colleagues, I wish to thank Jackson Turner Main and David Thomas Konig for their words of encouragement, and, most of all, William E. Nelson of Yale Law School for an afternoon of Revolutionary activity: discussing Massachusetts writs and touring Pennsylvania battlefields. It was Professor Nelson who, after reading the first draft of this manuscript, came to New York and spent a long day convincing me that the Irish comparison, originally employed sparingly to illustrate the conditions of Massachusetts law that might not be obvious to nonlawyers, was worthy of being treated as a secondary theme in this book. Not one to downgrade the Irish, I adopted Nelson's advice.

Sullivan House
Durham, New Hampshire
10 September 1976

JOHN PHILLIP REID

Index

INDEX